Teaching and Understanding Science

2ND EDITION

Graham Peacock & Robin Smith

Hodder & Stoughton

A MEMBER OF THE HODDER HEADLINE GROUP

Order queries: please contact Bookpoint Ltd, 39 Milton Park, Abingdon, Oxon OX14 4TD. Telephone: (44) 01235 400414, Fax: (44) 01235 400454. Lines are open from 9.00 - 6.00, Monday to Saturday, with a 24 hour message answering service.
Email address: orders@bookpoint.co.uk

British Library Cataloguing in Publication Data

Peacock, Graham
 Teaching and Understanding Science. –
 (Primary Bookshelf Series)
 I. Title II. Smith, Robin III. Series

ISBN 0 340 64763 9

First published 1992
Second edition 1995
Impression number   14 13 12 11 10 9 8 7 6 5 4
Year   2003 2002 2001 2000 1999 1998

Copyright © 1992, 1995 Graham Peacock and Robin Smith

All rights reserved. No part of this publication may be reproduced or transmitted in any form or by any means, electronic or mechanical, including photocopy, recording, or any information storage and retrieval system, without permission in writing from the publisher or under licence from the Copyright Licensing Agency Limited. Further details of such licences (for reprographic reproduction) may be obtained from the Copyright Licensing Agency Limited, of 90 Tottenham Court Road, London W1P 9HE.

Typeset by Wearset, Boldon, Tyne and Wear
Printed in Great Britain for Hodder & Stoughton Educational, a division of Hodder Headline Plc, 338 Euston Road, London NW1 3BH by Scotprint Ltd, Musselburgh, Scotland.

Contents

Introduction

AT 2 Life Processes and Living Things 5
    Key stage 1 6
    Key stage 2 27

AT 3 Materials and their Properties 50
    Key stage 1 50
    Key stage 2 62

AT 4 Physical Processes 84
    Key stage 1 84
    Key stage 2 106

Introduction

We have written this book to help teachers understand the science underlying the activities they do with their pupils. We have also included additional ideas about topics often covered in primary schools. The book is designed as a guide to the basic scientific ideas which underpin the National Curriculum science programmes of study. These are explained in straightforward terms and illustrated with simple activities for pupils. This book is a quick reference guide to the wide range of science that primary schools now cover. It will be particularly useful to teachers who are not science specialists.

How the book is organised

The book is divided into basic units concerned with a particular scientific idea. Each contains some suggestions for pupil activities and the scientific background to those activities. They are arranged in chapters corresponding to each of the attainment targets dealing with knowledge and understanding. The scientific investigation of attainment target 1 is integrated into the activities and introductions in each chapter. Within each chapter a few specialist terms are highlighted and explained. Each chapter has sections for key stages 1 and 2, with introductions for both stages. Teachers can use the sections or chapters they need for their planning and preparation.

The chapter introductions

These introductions list the main scientific ideas and titles for the pages and the relevant items in the programmes of study. The lists are followed by some guidelines about teaching and learning within the particular attainment target. This suggests suitable strategies and draws attention to the ideas and experience which children bring to the subject. Some examples are given of how they can be investigated to extend children's learning of scientific skills. Cross curricular links are noted, with examples of topics and themes. Some illustrations are given of different ways that links may be planned to set the scientific work in the context of the wider primary curriculum. We hope these will serve to stimulate your own ideas for planning and teaching science as part of the whole curriculum. Resources are mentioned on the introductory pages in each chapter where there are particular points to make, for example about supply, safety or storage.

The activities

The programmes of study are the starting points for the practical classroom activities suggested. The activities in each spread are simply a few of the many possibilities. We hope you will want to extend them and develop your own as well. Many more activities can be found in schemes and books.

The scientific background

The science background notes are designed to give teachers the information they need to teach science with understanding and confidence. They are not intended to be taught directly to pupils. They are written in a direct style which is intended to be accessible but which children are unlikely to be able to assimilate. We hope these notes will answer many of your questions and help you answer those that children raise.

AT 2 Life Processes and Living Things

Key stage 1

Main scientific idea	Page title	Page
The variety of plants and animals	The variety of living things	7
The conditions needed for life. Caring for plants and animals	The needs of plants and animals	8
Comparing and grouping different plants and animals	Like and unlike groups	9
Plants, humans and other animals have parts which can be recognised	Naming of parts	10
Living things reproduce	Reproduction	12
We need to look after our bodies to keep healthy	Safe and healthy	13
There are patterns and stages in life	Cycles	14
There are basic life processes	Processes	16
Food supplies energy	Food	17
Human beings vary from one individual to the next	Individual people	19
You can measure the variation between people	Variation	20
Living things have distinctive characteristics	Living and non-living	22
People produce waste	Waste	23
Some waste decays but some does not	Change and decay	24

Key Stage 1

The programme of study

This states that pupils should be taught:

- the differences between things that are living and things that have never been alive;
- that animals, including humans, move, feed, grow, use their senses and reproduce;
- to name the main external parts of the human body;
- that humans need food and water to stay alive;
- that taking exercise and eating the right types and amount of food help humans to keep healthy;
- about the role of drugs as medicines;
- that humans can produce babies and these babies grow into children and then into adults;
- that humans have senses which enable them to be aware of the world around them;
- that plants need light and water to grow;
- to recognise and name the leaf, flower, stem and root of flowering plants;
- that flowering plants grow and produce seeds which, in turn, produce new plants;
- to recognise similarities and differences between themselves and other pupils;
- that living things can be grouped according to observable similarities and differences;
- that there are different kinds of plants and animals in the local environment;
- that there are differences between local environments and that these affect which animals and plants are found there.

Teaching about life and living processes

Children can begin to understand the processes of life by studying their own bodies. Their work with animals and plants gives them experience of how other sorts of living organisms carry out the processes necessary to survive, grow and reproduce. Children gain some understanding of the diversity of groups of plants and animals from first hand experience. This also provides opportunities to learn to care for them and accept responsibility. Books and television offer them insights into other species in their natural environment. Comparing different sorts of plants and animals is the basis for more systematic classification at a later stage. Sensitively handled, children's study of individual differences among themselves can be the first step toward understanding inheritance.

Cross-curricular links

Cross-curricular themes, particularly health education, link naturally with the study of living processes in animals and plants. An understanding of biology can be developed hand in hand with work on self-awareness and feelings. This can be taught as part of a health education programme or through topics such as *Ourselves, Safety, Pets, Growing, Seasons, Food*.

Resources

The children themselves are the most useful resource for many activities. Classroom pets have to be considered very carefully to make sure there are no risks to the health of animals or pupils. Invertebrates such as slugs, snails, worms or woodlice can easily be kept and observed if a suitable home is made. A plastic aquarium is valuable as a home or for observing. Hand lenses, magnispectors or other aids to viewing detail are essential. A sturdy microscope is useful, especially the binocular sort. Ensure small creatures are not damaged or dehydrated when collecting or observing them. A water spray is useful for plants too. Seeds and plants can be grown in all sorts of containers indoors and outside. Changes and contrasts are more productive for learning than perfect static displays. Get to know the parks, ponds, wasteland, woodland or whatever is locally available. Creating a small wild area will increase the variety of species and illustrate how the plants and animals are interdependent. Learning from first hand experiences and observations can be extended with good books and visual aids and software for sorting data.

Key Stage 1

THE VARIETY OF LIVING THINGS

Activities for children

Classroom displays

- Grow different sorts of plants.
- In spring vary the flowering plants and grow assorted bulbs.
- Keep cacti or other succulents, ferns and mosses alongside more familiar pot plants.
- Get children to smell and feel carefully.

The park

- On a visit to a park ask the children to find leaves from different sorts of trees.
- Look for different sorts of ducks.
- Back in the classroom help them make collages and pictures to illustrate the various living things they saw – include people.

In the playground

- In winter several species may come to a bird table, even in a city centre. To attract a wider variety of birds grow plants with seeds or berries.
- Make a small wild garden or just grow flowers that insects feed on.
- Leave a plank or a piece of carpet on the earth as a shelter for small invertebrates. Look underneath it.

Songs and games

- Sing 'The animals went in two by two' and 'Going to the zoo'. Can the children make appropriate noises for different animals?
- Use matching and sorting games to talk about different sorts of animals and plants.
- Sort pictures into two piles, animals and plants. Are there any the children are unsure about?

Secondary sources and books

- Show pictures with lots of vertebrates and invertebrates. Ask children how many different sorts of animals they can find.
- On film or TV the habits and movements of animals can be seen. Children can observe more actively if you use a video. Ask them to look out for particular creatures in a sequence. Replay it so they can check their observations.
- Display picture books about familiar environments such as a garden or pond.
- Read and show children books which illustrate the range of plants and animals in places we cannot take them – like the rain forest or oceans.
- Involve children in naming the species when you read stories like *Noah's Ark* and *Owl Couldn't Sleep*.

Science background

Nearly all living things can be grouped as plants or animals. Children may come to school with their own ideas about what is living and what is not, what a plant or flower is, what is meant by *an animal* and whether that includes people. For instance they may say that vegetables like carrots or cabbage are not plants, or they may apply the term *animal* only to examples of mammals. As you widen their experience, with careful extension of vocabulary, you can probe these ideas.

At this level you are simply helping children realise how many sorts of living things there are. They may notice different varieties of the same species (eg dogs) or different species (eg birds) or differences between broader groups (eg ferns and flowering plants). There are lots of species of insects, spiders, woodlice, centipedes and millipedes and other groups of small animals without backbones (invertebrates) which even adults may lump together. **Species** are defined by their ability to breed succesfully and/or by their structural similarity.

Humans are one species (*Homo sapiens*) belonging to a group of mammals called the order of **Primates**. The Primates include the gorilla, chimpanzee and orangutan, which are in the family of Apes, several families of monkeys, and others like bush-babies.

There is an enormous variety of plant and animal species but the number is falling rapidly as people pollute and destroy habitats. Trees and other flowering plants, birds and mammals are obvious victims. Children can be involved in campaigns to save a local woodland or field. They may care deeply about the fate of the whale, dolphin or panda highlighted by agencies like the World Wide Fund for Nature and Greenpeace. The threat to the million plus insect species is less evident and emotive.

THE NEEDS OF PLANTS AND ANIMALS

Activities for children

Out and about

- Look closely in different habitats.
- Turn over a log or stone and watch what moves.
- Put the stone back carefully and ask children what they saw.
- Talk about what it is like under stones – is it dry or damp, light or dark? What grows in cracks in a pavement or wall?

In the classroom

- Germinate various seeds, including some like sunflowers which will grow into big plants.
- Ask children what seeds need to grow. Talk about how they can test their ideas.
- Put some seeds in light and some in dark. Keep some cold and some warm. Water some and leave others. Make children responsible for watering their own plants.
- Grow tomatoes in growbags. They need lots of water and light.
- Make children's drawings and measurements into a zig zag book or strip cartoon.

Incubating eggs and raising chicks

- Arrange well ahead for an incubator and find a recommended source of fertile hen or duck eggs and a home for the birds as they grow.
- Involve the children from the start. Ask them what the incubator is for and how babies and other animals are kept warm.
- Have a rota for turning the eggs.
- Help them record the hatching on a calendar.
- Talk about how much feed to provide.
- Put children's drawings and words in a big book to record the chicks' development and changing needs.
- When the chicks leave discuss what their new home will provide.

Pets

- Do a survey of the pets children have.
- Ask how they look after them.
- Talk about what common needs they have and the special needs of each sort of pet.
- Compare this with what people need to stay alive.

Bringing things inside

- Talk with pupils about the dangers of pulling flowers, digging up plants or bringing creatures out of their habitats. Sometimes the risk is to the children, eg from poisonous berries. Usually it is the plant or animal that suffers. Often it is illegal so check on listed animals and flowers.
- If living things are brought inside children can design suitable homes.
- Make a moist moss garden in a plastic jar or aquarium. Add a cover that lets air in. Include soil and bark for woodlice.
- Look where the creatures congregate.
- Give snails and slugs cover and moisture.
- Provide fresh greens or vegetables each day.
- Children should clean the homes regularly and eventually return creatures to their habitat.

Long term projects

- Even a small area can be developed into a wildlife garden. Involve parents as well as children. Get help from local conservation associations or groups like WATCH.

Key Stage 1

Science background

Seeds need water and the right temperature to germinate; some do this quickly and are easily sprouted on blotting paper (like cress) or in a jar covered by thin cloth and regularly rinsed (like mung beans). As they grow into seedlings the effects of light or its absence begin to show in their colour, direction of growth and survival. Green plants generally need water, air, light and warmth; if your classroom corner is dusty and subject to wide temperature variations many plants will do poorly. Green plants really feed by **photosynthesis**, ie using light energy absorbed by chlorophyll to synthesise organic food from carbon dioxide and water. They also absorb minerals dissolved in water from the soil.

Animals feed directly on plants or indirectly by eating other animals. With help children can investigate the food preferences of animals like slugs and snails which eat a variety of plants; a spray is useful to increase the humidity if snails do not emerge. Animals' food sometimes supplies the water they need and some desert species, like gerbils, can survive with very little.

Fertilised hens' eggs can be bought from hatcheries. Incubate them around 40 °C and top up the water to stop the air getting too dry. Turn them frequently to keep the temperature even throughout. As they get bigger chicks become able to maintain a constant body temperature; this is what is meant by an animal being warm-blooded.

LIKE AND UNLIKE GROUPS

Activities for children

Picture matching

- Ask children to group pictures of lots of different animals and talk about how they grouped them.
- Give children pairs of pictures with slightly different animals, like a horse and a deer. Ask them to spot the differences. Then ask them to list the similarities.

What's in the soil?

- Collect some soil containing plant and animal material.
- Provide gloves and ask the children to find out what it contains. They could sort the ingredients into living, dead or never lived and suggest how they got there.
- Return any small creatures before they dry out and die.

Looking high and low

- Visit a patch where there are taller and shorter plants. A verge with a few trees or a hedge will do.
- Compare plants that climb or stand up. Find plants which stay low down.
- Encourage children to measure and count different sorts and to record their findings in drawings, charts and graphs.
- Children can make their drawings into an identification guide. Get them to describe distinctive features of each plant as concisely as they can. Introduce a simple data base.

What's that bird?

Bird watching encourages close observation.

- Ask children how they can recognise and record the different sorts of birds.
- Look for distinctive movements.
- Where do different species perch?
- Can males and females be distinguished?
- How can they tell if it is the same bird or lots of similar ones eating all the food?
- Make a data base of your birds for other children to use.

Surface features

- Compare pictures or museum specimens of vertebrates to see if they have fur, feathers, hair, smooth skin or scales.
- Provide suitable materials for children to use in collages or models of animals. Selecting and feeling them can stimulate exploration of their properties.

Key Stage 1

Insides

- Look at various skeletons.
- Use paper fasteners to make joints and investigate movements. Limbs are easiest to model and children can compare them with their own.
- Challenge the children to make simple hands with construction kits or craft materials.

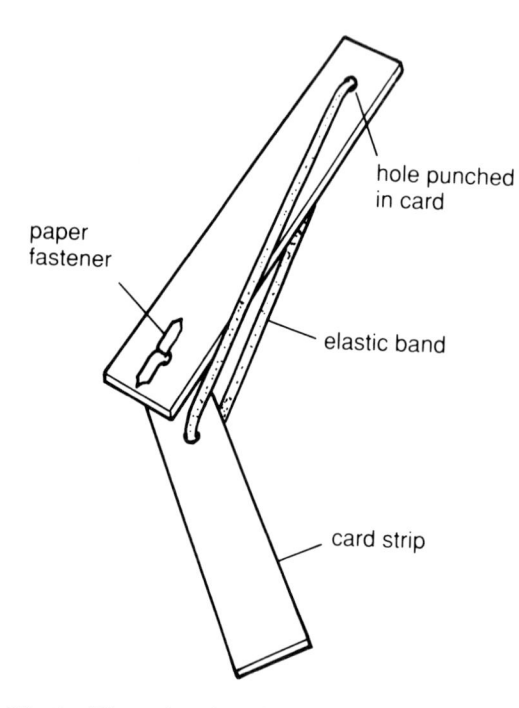

Fig. 1 *Illustration of arm joint made from card strips*

Science background

Soil contains plant material. Some may be recognisable, eg seeds and twigs. You may find evidence of small animals such as eggs or wing cases. Small creatures may emerge as it is examined. They could be species of snails and slugs, earthworms and other worms, woodlice, centipedes, millipedes, mites, spiders, or other insects. These groups of animals do not have an internal skeleton, they are **invertebrates**.

All **vertebrates** have a skeleton of bone or cartilage, including a backbone. The five groups (**classes**) of vertebrates are different on the surface. *Fish* have moist scales. *Amphibians*, eg frogs, have skin with no covering. *Reptiles* have dry scales; people are often surprised and impressed when they feel a snake or other reptile so see if you can arrange the experience for your pupils. *Birds* have feathers, but it might not be obvious to children in cases like the penguin. They may also assume all birds fly and anything which flies is a bird so discuss flightless birds like kiwis and flying mammals like bats. *Mammals* have hair but whales and dolphins may be confusing examples.

In places like hedges, verges, overgrown wasteland or unweeded gardens different plants may be found growing where it is light and shady. Many plants grow up toward the light:

- Some stand up straight and have stiffened stems. Wood strengthens the trunks of trees.
- Some plants climb or creep and may twist or have hooks to support them.
- Other plants growing lower down may spread out.

NAMING OF PARTS

Activities for children

Songs and games

- Play games and sing songs where body parts have to be named, for instance 'Simon says', 'One finger, one thumb', 'Them dry bones'.

Body pictures

- Make an outline of the body by drawing round a child laid on a large sheet of paper.
- Help children to label body parts such as arms, hands and fingers, legs and feet, head.
- Progress to less easily defined parts like the chest and to joints like shoulder, elbow, knee.

Puppets

- Make simple articulated puppets with card and paper fasteners and string. Make them move at the joints and compare this with children's movements.

Key Stage 1

- Ask children to add eyes, ears and other features. Let them use mirrors or work in pairs to observe facial features. Encourage detail and accuracy.
- Talk about the words for features such as: eyelids, eyebrows, eyelashes.

People and other animals

- Look at classroom pets or animals on a visit.
- Provide large pictures of some mammals such as cat, dog, rabbit, horse, elephant, mouse.
- Ask children to compare body parts one at a time.
  (a) What shape is the head?
  (b) Where are the eyes?
  (c) How big are the ears? What shape?
  (d) What are the teeth like?
  (e) What shape is the body?
  (f) How many legs? What sort of feet?
  (g) How is it like you? How is it different?

Plant parts

- Give children two different plants with flowers.
- Talk about what they can find on both. Draw their attention to flowers, leaves, buds, stems and stalks.
- Compare the parts, helping pupils notice similarities as well as differences
- Reinforce a simple vocabulary.

Trees are big plants

- Collect fallen leaves in autumn.
- Examine twigs to see how leaves and buds are arranged on different trees.
- Rub bark, look at cross-sections of branches.

Roots

- Look at exposed tree roots if possible.
- Grow bulbs in water so the roots are visible.
- Draw plants with intact roots.
- Pull weeds up in the garden and trace the roots.
- Use a hand lens to look at the ends of roots.

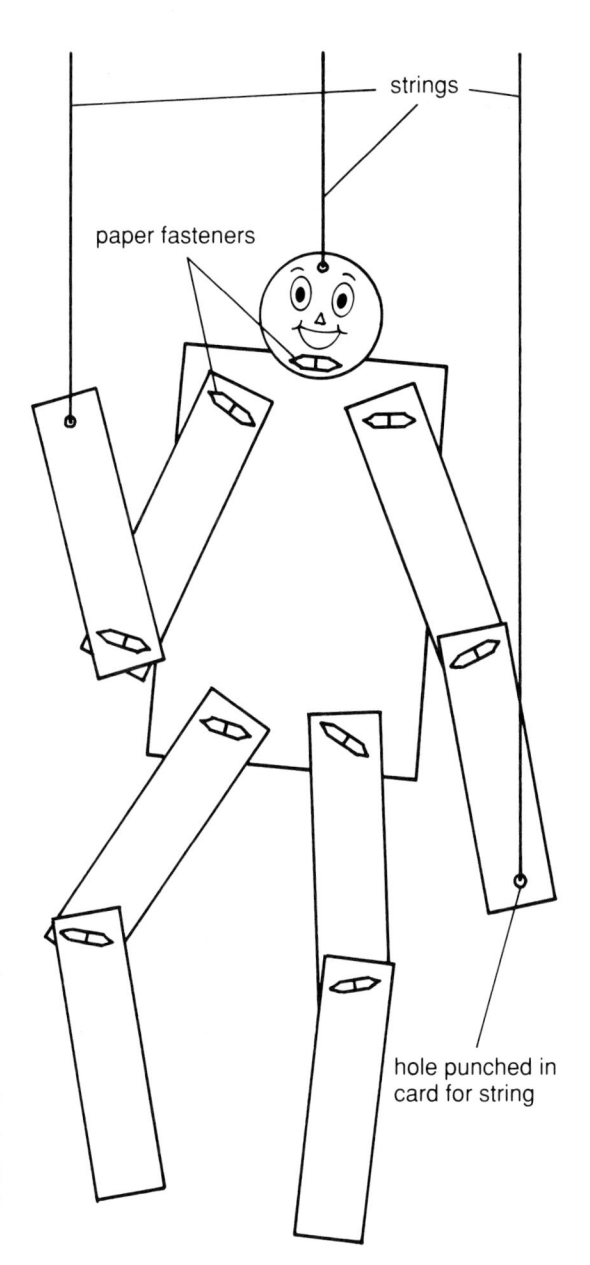

Fig. 2 *Diagram showing how to make puppets from card and paper fasteners*

- If you can borrow a skeleton, help children match the main bones to their own bodies.

Masks

- Make large masks from card or strong paper bags.

Science background

Humans and other animals have similar body parts but their appearance varies between species. Ears are visible in most mammals, and are large in some. Eyes may be on the side of the head in prey animals and prominent in hunters as well as the hunted. Teeth vary according to the diet. Limbs may be very different in size, joints, and the foot.

There are lots of words which refer to bones and other body parts but children can appreciate the arrangements without learning all the terms; they may enjoy knowing some and they should remember a few key ones like *skull*. Some terms like *chest*, *stomach* or *belly* are used very loosely by adults and children.

Despite differences in detail flowering plants from the small daisy to the huge oak have similar structures. Introduce basic terms for parts such as *leaves*, *roots*, *stem* (stalk, branch), *buds* (leaf or flower buds), *flowers*, *petals*, *fruits*.

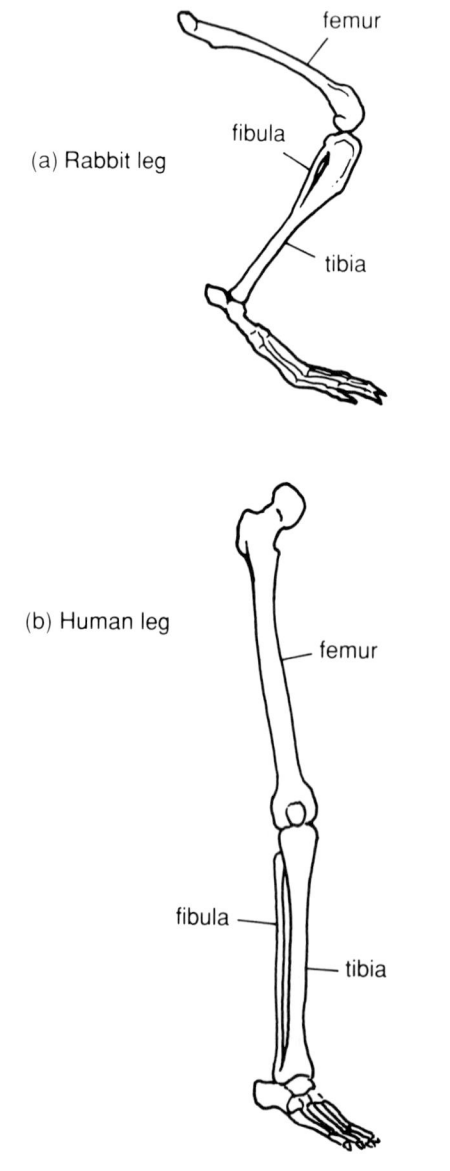

Fig. 3a & b *Bones in (a) rabbit leg and (b) human leg*

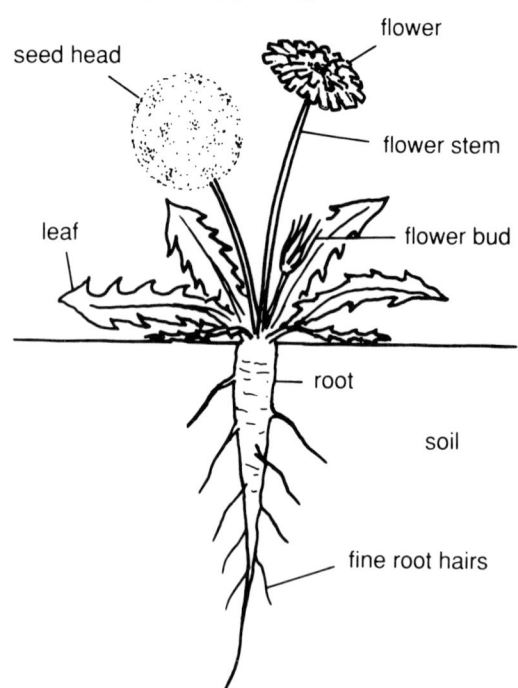

Fig. 4 *Main parts of flowering plant*

REPRODUCTION

Activities for children

Grow more plants

- Grow plants from seeds. Quick growing seeds like cress and mung beans which can be sprouted in damp conditions will show how germination occurs. Slower ones, such as hardy annuals sold for gardens, may give more idea of the way a plant can reproduce.
- Collect seeds from seedpods (avoid poisonous ones like Laburnum).

- Look for seedlings under trees like sycamore.
- Cuttings can be taken from some pot plants, eg Busy Lizzie; strawberries can be spread by runners.

Stories and rhymes

- Use stories and songs about plants or animals reproducing, from traditional ones like 'John Barleycorn', to modern classics like 'The Hungry Caterpillar'.

Little animals

- Look out for eggs laid by insects, spiders, snails and slugs. Find caterpillars and, if you can provide the right conditions, rear them.
- Warn children not to collect or disturb birds' eggs.

Science background

Flowering plants reproduce by sexual and asexual means. Sexual reproduction involves fusion of male and female cells. In sexual reproduction the seeds themselves look very different from the plant, but they contain the information to grow into another similar plant. In asexual reproduction plants spread by runners or suckers from which similar new plants grow. Gardeners take cuttings of a part of a plant and grow them into fully developed plants identical to the original.

Small animals may go through several stages in their development and look very different at each stage. Butterflies lay eggs which hatch into caterpillars (the **larvae**) that change into chrysalises (**the pupae**) before becoming adult butterflies. In some insects, for instance grasshoppers, an egg does not become a larva and then a pupa but hatches directly into a small immature adult (**the nymph**) which matures into the adult form. Frogs lay eggs and then go through a larval stage as tadpoles. Birds lay eggs which hatch into chicks that grow into adult birds without any intermediate stage. All mammals except spiny anteaters and duck-billed platypuses give birth to live young.

Many animals produce very large numbers of eggs, only a few of which survive the successive stages to mature. Animals which produce only a few eggs or young usually care for them. Most chicks and baby animals need looking after for some time while they develop.

SAFE AND HEALTHY

Activities for children

Road safety

- Teach children about how best to cope with dangers from traffic in the area.
  (a) Where is it best to cross roads?
  (b) Can you see?
  (c) Can you be seen?
- Compare different clothing to find which shows up best in the dark.

Be healthy

- Draw posters or cartoons of ways to stay healthy. Make it positive and emphasise everyday things:
  (a) cleaning teeth
  (b) exercising
  (c) sleeping
  (d) eating lunch
  (e) drinking milk or water
- Talk about why these affect health.

Stay safe and well

- Help children draw up two lists, one of things they should do to keep safe and well and another of things to avoid, such as electrical appliances or bleach.

Who helps us?

Visits to or from opticians or dentists can lead to investigations of eyes or teeth. They can also help reduce anxieties.

- Set up play areas with medical themes.
- Read stories about children in hospital.

Key Stage 1

Science background

Young animals are vulnerable and many need extended parental care until they are able to look after themselves. Humans take a long time to develop and have lots to learn as they do. Children have to learn about their physical needs and the things which can help or hinder their development. The specific opportunities and risks vary in our rapidly changing society. In general to survive and stay healthy we need to eat suitable food, have a source of water that is not infected with disease, get sufficient exercise and sleep, avoid accidents, diseases and dangerous substances.

The term *drugs* refers to chemical substances which may be useful as medicines to treat illness and improve health in particular circumstances. Children are particularly vulnerable to the effects of drugs and have to learn about the dangers of taking inappropriate medicines as well as the more notorious addictive drugs. Teaching on these topics needs to be done with sensitivity and should take account of school policies and the views of parents. There may be pupils on medication and many who take tablets such as vitamin supplements. You will need to know your children's circumstances to help them understand their health needs.

CYCLES

Activities for children

Our days

- Make large clock faces or long friezes.
- Talk about what the children do at different times. Get them to put drawings or cutout pictures at appropriate points on the clock or frieze.
- Ask which things they do every day (and night). Which things do they do only on certain days?

Special days

- Use a festival, holiday, birthday or story (Christmas ones abound, for example). Talk about what happens on that special day.
  (a) What time do they wake up?
  (b) What happens first?
  (c) Do they take time dressing up specially?
  (d) Are there special meals that take a long time?
  (e) Do they stay up late?

Stages in life

- Display pictures of children and their families (and teachers) at different ages.
  (a) Can the pupils recognise their friends as babies?
  (b) Can they recognise their teachers as children?
- Make big folded books or strip cartoons with children's drawings or cutout pictures to show stages from birth to adulthood.
- Invite grandparents in and prepare pupils to interview them about their childhood.

Life cycle

- Draw a life cycle for an animal species. (This is best if the animal is being reared, for instance chicks incubated, caterpillar bred).
- Help children draw life cycles for other animals.
- Use cutout pictures to make a human one. Make sure they do not depict it as if one individual cycled round for ever! (See opposite.)

How have I changed?

- List the things the children can do now which they could not do as a baby. What could they do
  (a) When they were born?
  (b) When they were two years old?
  (c) When they began school?
- Invite a parent in with a baby. Ask the parent to bathe or feed the baby.
- Invite a parent and a toddler in and ask pupils to entertain the toddler.
- Talk about what pupils do with their younger or older siblings.

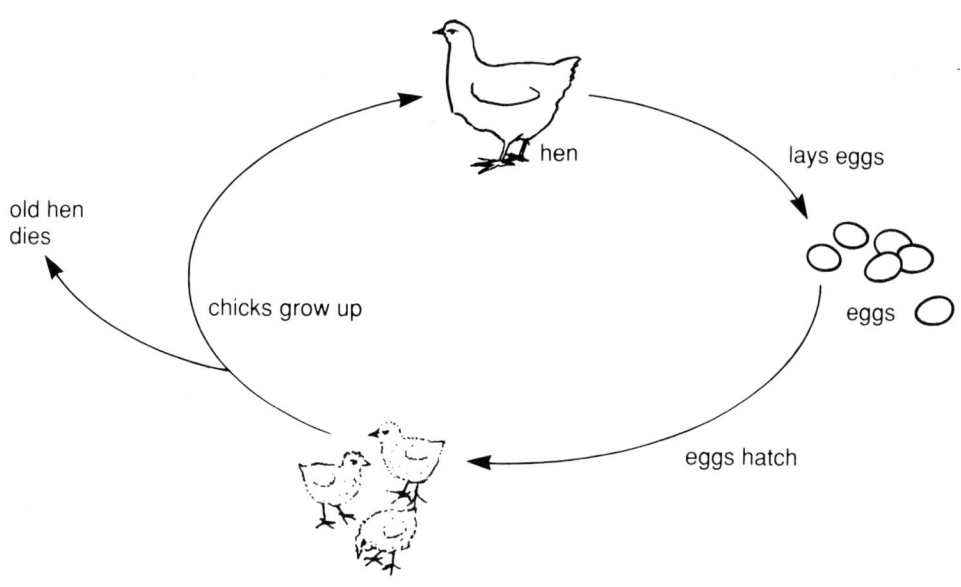

Fig. 5 *Life cycle of a hen*

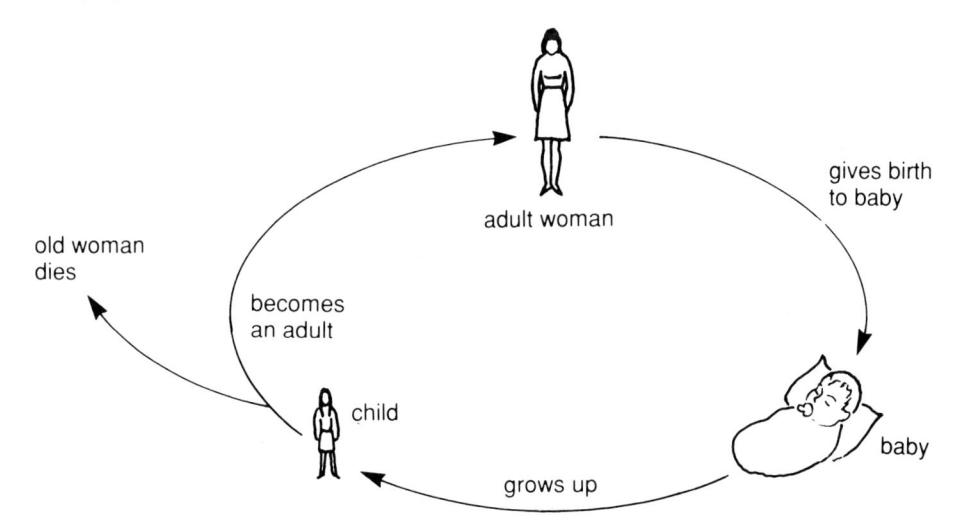

Fig. 6 *Life cycle of a human*

Science background

Animals and plants have daily and annual patterns of behaviour or growth which are partly a response to changes in light or temperature. People also respond to these and exhibit other rhythms, for instance monthly cycles. We have some basic internal rhythms and their disruption can impair our health. Disturbed sleep patterns for instance can make people inefficient or unwell.

The study of human development will be done in the context of the school's policy on sex and health education. Changes from birth to their own age will be most obvious to children – eg increase in height and weight, changed proportions, greater strength and new skills. Older pupils may be concerned about the onset of puberty and need more detailed explanation of the changes that will happen to them. Their growth in size and strength is accompanied by changing body proportions, secondary sexual characteristics such as deepening voice, body hair or developing breasts, and primary sexual characteristics as the sexual organs develop.

Individuals go through similar changes in life but at different rates and this may seem critical to young people when their friends change sooner or later. The changes are directed by the level of *hormones* in the body and influenced by external factors such as the the amount and sort of food eaten. Malnutrition, for example will reduce growth rate and delay onset of sexual maturity.

Childhood and other stages in the human life cycle are socially defined rather than discrete steps marked by sudden physical changes such as those that occur when some animals metamorphose (eg when tadpoles turn into frogs).

Life cycle diagrams show the stages through which a species regularly passes in each generation.

PROCESSES

Activities for children

Alive

- Find out what pupils mean by 'alive'.
    (a) Sort pictures or items into 'alive' and 'not alive'.
    (b) Do they need a third category for 'no longer alive'?
    (c) Ask what living things can do that dead or non-living things cannot.

Moving

- Explore all the ways that children can move.
    (a) Which parts move?
    (b) Which directions can they move at elbows, knees, wrists, shoulders, necks?

Bones and muscles

Look at a skeleton and see where the joints are.

- Move parts of the skeleton and get pupils to move the same parts of their bodies. What makes their bodies move?
- Feel the muscles as they contract.
- Model limbs with card tubes or wood or construction kits for bones and simulate muscles with elastic bands.

Breathing

- Breathing is only really obvious after exercise.
- Get children to feel their chests after running.
- Explore which parts move, which way, how often?
  NB In any investigations of exercise check no pupil is at risk because of asthma, heart condition, etc.

Eating

- Talk about what food children eat.
    (a) Which food has to be chewed a lot?
    (b) Which teeth do we use to bite, to chew?
    (c) What happens when we swallow?
- Use models, OHP overlays or simple diagrams to explain how food and air go down separate tubes.

Sight

Sight can be investigated easily by young pupils as long as eye safety is stressed.

- How far away can they read letters?

Touch

- Can the children identify things in a feely bag?
- Can they make up a test to compare how well they can feel with fingers and toes?

Hearing

- Ask pupils to develop tests to find out:
    (a) What is the quietest noise they can hear.
    (b) How well they can tell where a sound comes from.

Science background

Living things (organisms) feed to get their nutrients, respire to release energy, excrete waste, grow and repair themselves, can sense changes in their environment, move parts or the whole of their body, and reproduce. These are basic processes which maintain life in plants and animals. In humans and other mammals feeding, breathing, growth and reproduction, sensing and moving are carried out in very similar ways.

We breathe by moving the ribs and the diaphragm to change the volume of the chest cavity so air enters and leaves. After exercise more air is exchanged at a greater rate to increase the supply of oxygen. This is done by breathing faster and deeper and happens involuntarily, although we can breathe deeper on purpose. Most movements pupils investigate will be voluntary, caused as they deliberately contract and relax muscles which move bones relative to one another at joints. We move our lower jaw to chew food. After we have swallowed it, involuntary waves of muscle movement carry it down the oesophagus to the stomach. The oesophagus lies behind the windpipe (the trachea), which is the tube through which air passes. As the food is swallowed the windpipe is closed off.

Many of our muscular movements are made in response to information carried from our sense organs. Our sense of touch can tell us about changes in position, pressure, and temperature which we may respond to voluntarily or as an involuntary reflex. Eyesight and hearing are the most obvious examples of senses for which there are specialised sense organs.

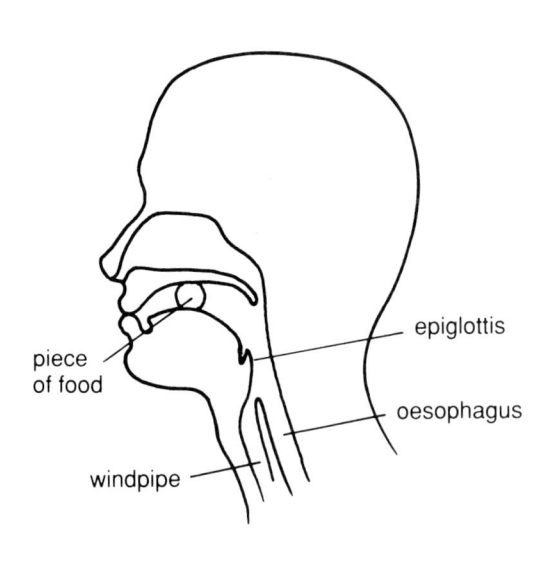

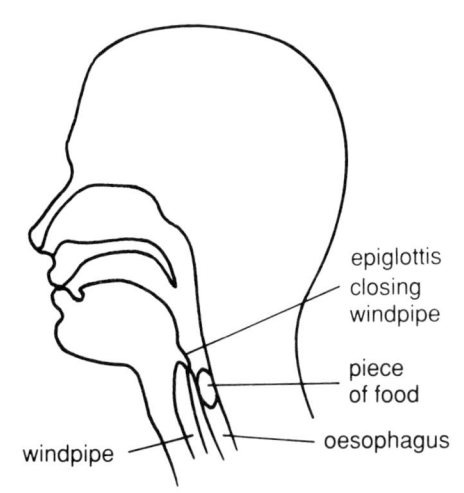

Fig. 7 *Cross-sections of a human skull and neck showing the passage of food*

FOOD

Activities for children

Feeling hungry

- Sing songs like 'Hungry, hungry', 'Food, glorious food'.
- Talk about how we feel when hungry and discuss what sort of things make us feel hungry.
- Set up a kitchen or café play area.
- Use contemporary examples of food shortages to explore how people are affected by insufficient energy.

What's in food?

- Display foods that supply lots of energy:
  (a) The carbohydrates in your pupils' diets such as breads, potatoes, pasta or rice.
  (b) Snacks and sugary foods.
  (c) Fatty foods and oils.
- Let children cut out pictures from magazines to make a collage of different sorts of food.
- Older children can examine food packets that list the energy values and other ingredients.

Key Stage 1

Energetic

- Draw pictures of energetic activities.
- Use drama to link exercise with the need to eat.
- Emphasise how active adults and children need lots of energy.

Science background

We get the energy for our bodily processes from food. Food is really just a special form of chemical energy and we can refer to it as our fuel.

Green plants trap energy from the sun when they **photosynthesise**. This stored energy in a plant may become food for an animal. Some animals get their food directly from plants, others eat animals which have in turn eaten plants. The flow of energy from sun to plant to animals can be represented in food chains.

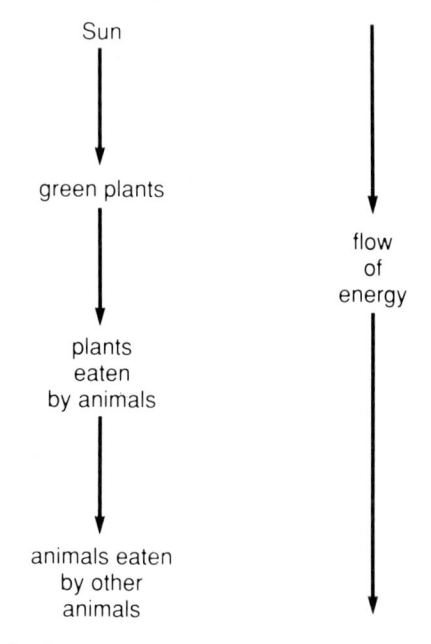

```
Sun
 │
 ▼
green plants              │
 │                        │
 ▼                      flow
plants                    of
eaten                   energy
by animals                │
 │                        │
 ▼                        ▼
animals eaten
by other
animals
```

Fig. 8 *Food chain*

The energy from food is stored in chemical bonds which can be broken down in the body to release energy. In respiration this occurs slowly. It can be released rapidly by burning. We can burn foodstuffs, just as we burn other fuels. The energy available in foods can be calculated by burning them. The amount of energy available in foods is labelled in *kilojoules*; 1 *kilojoule* (kJ) = 1,000 *joules*. Joules are the standard units used to measure energy but some people may refer to the older units – *calories*.

Table 1 *Energy value of food*

Energy value of food

	Energy value (kJ)
One smartie	24
One peanut	25
One slice of bread and butter	500
100g chips	1000
100g crisps	2250

However, a diet high in fatty foods such as chips and crisps can lead to obesity and ultimately other problems such as heart disease. Food also supplies other things that our body needs to work and stay healthy such as **protein**. Here we are referring only to the energy needs and not to the need for a balanced diet.

Some foodstuffs in our diet are rich in **carbohydrates**, such as starch and sugar, which supply most of our energy. Sugar can be used very rapidly as a source of energy. The level of sugar in our blood is normally kept steady but a drop in level will be associated with a feeling of hunger.

Fat is a source of energy. It is not digested as rapidly as carbohydrate. If we have more energy supplied in our food than we need it is stored as fat. If we need more energy than our food can supply fat stores are used. If our food or stores of fat cannot supply sufficient energy then our body protein may be broken down to release energy. Lack of food may produce an overall shortage of energy.

Children may be able to see the link between energy and being able to move and keep warm from their own experiences, advertisements and everyday usage of the phrase 'short of energy'.

Many of the investigations, such as burning foodstuffs, that develop a deeper understanding of this topic may be tackled in key stage 2 but the foundations can be laid from the start of key stage 1 as children survey foods, consider their diets, explore the needs of themselves and other animals for energy, and develop their vocabulary.

INDIVIDUAL PEOPLE

Activities for children

Blind catcher

- Play blind child's buff. Clear a safe area. Blindfold one child who has to catch someone. The blind catcher has to guess the person by either:
  (a) feeling their face, or
  (b) listening to them squeak.

Guess who?

- In spare moments tell the children 'I'm thinking of a person in our class. Can you guess who?' Give the children **one** guess for each clue.

Going out in groups

- Ask the children to leave the classroom according to characteristics. For instance:
  (a) children with brown eyes can go out to play;
  (b) children with curly hair can get their milk.

What has a human got?

- How would aliens from another planet describe people to other aliens?

Which hand?

- Ask the children which hand they use. Many of them won't know their right from their left. You might want to label one hand in some way.
- Record the results in a simple chart like the one below.
- Do the same for feet.

Science background

People can vary in two respects:

(a) **Inherited characteristics** are those characteristics we get from our parents. These include the shape of our face, the colour of our eyes and the shape of our ears. These are the characteristics which are passed from generation to generation.

(b) **Acquired characteristics** include things like scars and abilities. No one is born able to rollerskate and some people will never have this as a characteristic. You pick up or acquire these characteristics as you go through life. You cannot pass them on to the next generation.

Table 2a *People like to use different hands: left hand, right hand*

People like to use different hands	
Left	Right
Joanne, Mark	Ahmed, Tim, Ben, Sushma, Cheryl

Key Stage 1

Key Stage 1

VARIATION

Activities for children

Hair colour

- Give each child a small square of paper on which they draw a face with their colour hair.
- Stick these onto a very simple chart.

Who is tallest?

- Ask the children to line up in order of height. They can measure each other's height using hand spans for instance.
- Measure people sitting down. How can we make this fair for everyone?

Big foot

- Ask the children to draw round their shoes and then write their name on the outline. Stick these onto a chart in size order.
- Visit a shoe shop and ask the assistant to show the children how feet are measured.

Table 2b *Hair colour*

Table 2c *Size of feet*

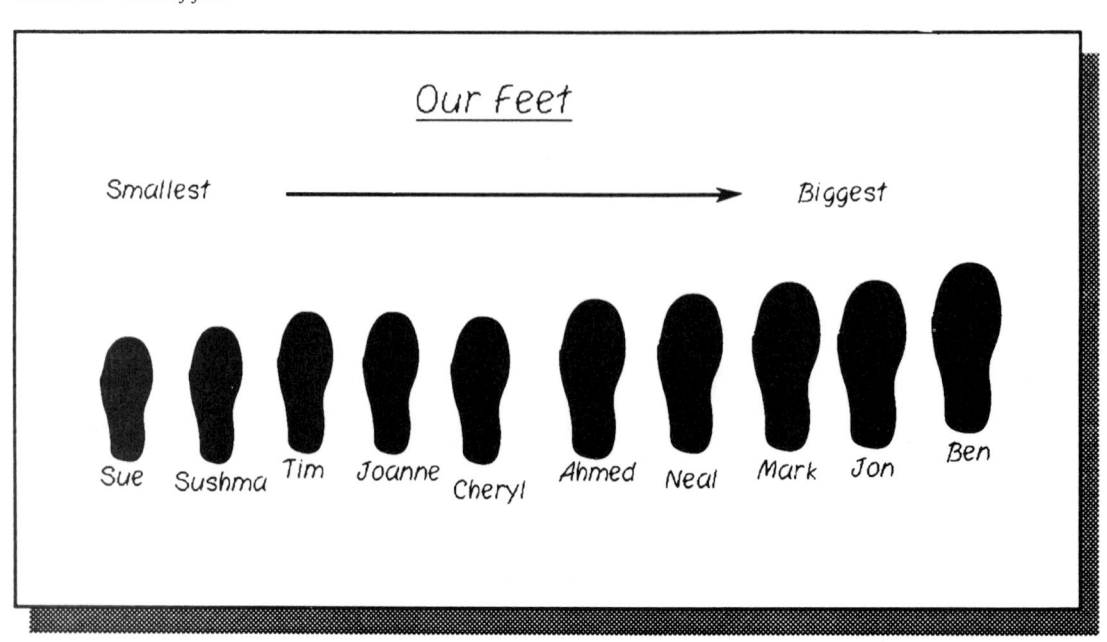

Table 2d *Size of head*

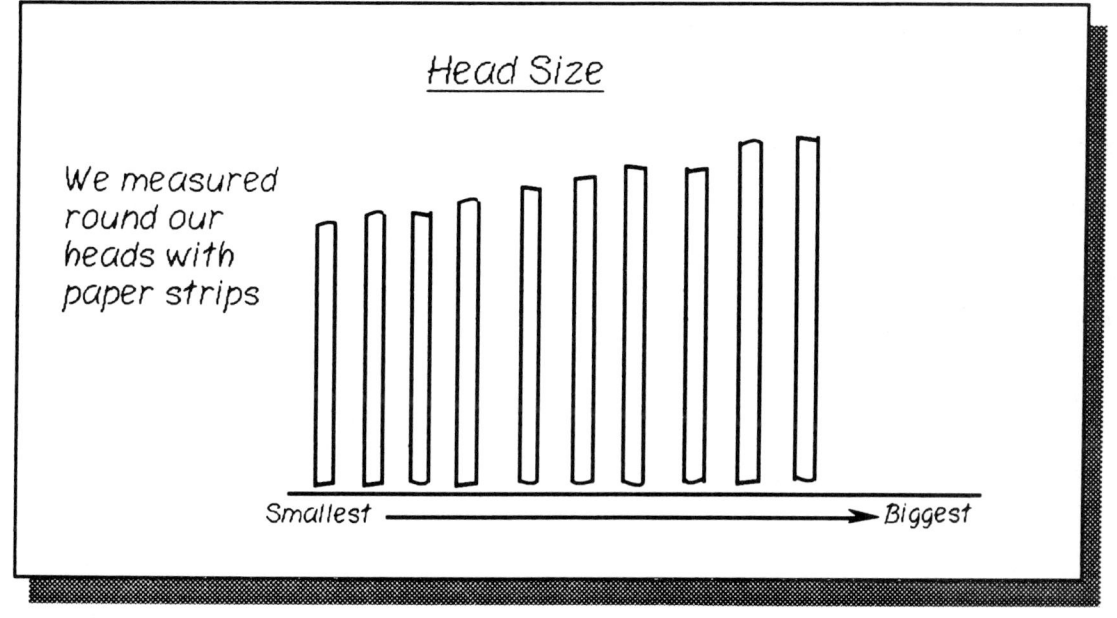

Head Size

We measured round our heads with paper strips

Smallest ⟶ Biggest

Hat size

- Put out a collection of hats.
- Who does each hat fit best?
- Measure round the children's heads using tape, a strip of paper or string.
- Cut to size and stick on a chart.

Teeth

- How many teeth have the children got? Record the answers in paintings, drawings and writing.

Science background

Measuring simple differences might reinforce the notions of biggest, tallest or strongest being best. You might want to select attributes which do not reinforce this idea.

All the characteristics investigated above have a normal distribution in the population at one age. The graph of the characteristic would be shaped like the one below which shows weight variations.

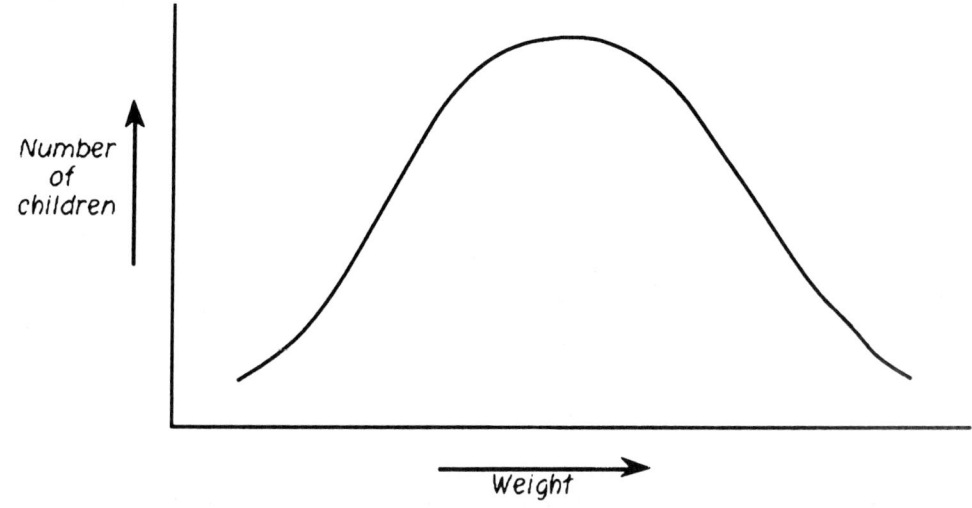

Number of children ↑

Weight ⟶

Fig. 9 *Normal distribution of children's weight*

Key Stage 1

LIVING AND NON-LIVING

Activities for children

Odd one out

- Draw three objects one of which is living and the others non-living. Get the children to say which is the odd one out in each set.

How do you know?

- Show the children pictures of living things or actual animals or plants and ask them how they know each is alive.
- Draw pictures of living things and write a short caption saying why they think they are alive.

Twenty questions

- Start off sessions with the phrase 'I am thinking of a living thing/non-living thing that has never lived'. Ask them to guess what it is.

Circle and map

- Give the children a page with a number of living and non-living things drawn on it. Down the side of the same sheet write phrases which describe the characteristics of living things. Get the children to draw a line from a living thing to an appropriate phrase.

Table

- Ask the children to suggest some non-living and living things. List them on a big sheet of paper. Ask the children to write the name of objects in the correct column of the table below.

Once alive	Never alive	Living

Fig. 10 *Table*

Seeds and bulbs

- Ask the children whether they think seeds and plant bulbs are dead or alive. Germinate seeds and talk about the changes which occur to the apparently lifeless objects.

What is it made from?

- Collect objects that are made from things which were once living. Talk about what each one is made of and where it came from.

Table ⟶ trees
Belt ⟶ cows
Mat ⟶ rushes

Museum

- Make a small museum of the remains of living things. These could include shells, bones, seeds, bark, fossils, snake skin and dead insects. Display them in clear plastic boxes such as cotton wool bud boxes and chocolate boxes (a famous Italian make is best).

Science background

The distinction between living, non-living and never alive can form the basis of productive classroom discussion. Children will frequently be confused about things such as flames, for instance, which exhibit some of the characteristics of living things. Living things exhibit seven characteristics which distinguish them from dead or non-living things.

Grow: Living things are capable of getting larger as they get older. Some living things, seeds for instance, spend a long time without altering their size.

Reproduce: Living things can make copies of themselves. These copies can be identical clones, such as plant cuttings, or they can be similar to the parent as in the case of human children or plants grown from seed.

Sense: Living things react to changes in the environment. Plants grow away from gravity and towards light. Animals use senses which may include touch, smell, taste, hearing and sight.

Move: Living things can move. Plants' leaves move to maximise their exposure to light. Apparently immobile animals like clams can move certain parts of their body.

Feed: All living things take in food to give them energy and provide them with the raw materials from which to make their body parts. Plants make food from water, carbon dioxide and sunlight.

Respire: Living things, including plants, take in oxygen from the air and give out carbon dioxide. Plants take in carbon dioxide during the day as they photosynthesise.

Excrete: Animals and plants excrete a range of solid and liquid waste.

WASTE

Activities for children

NB Always wear protective gloves when handling rubbish. Beware of sharp objects.

Which is waste?

- Give the children a selection of objects including some waste items (eg a bottle top, scrap paper, an empty crisp packet) and some items of value (eg a coin, a small toy, a metal spoon).
    (a) Which would they put in a bin?
    (b) Which might be put in a skip for recycling?
    (c) Which might be dangerous if left lying around?
- Give the children pictures of different objects. Talk about which they would put in the waste bin.

Classroom litter

- Look at the types of rubbish thrown away in the classroom bin.
- Tip the rubbish out onto a large sheet. Sort and talk about it.

Containers and wrappers

- Bring in a collection of wrappers and containers for the children to talk about and sort into groups.
    (a) Which containers held liquids?
    (b) Which held powders?
    (c) What other ways can the children sort the containers?
- Using large PE hoops, sort the containers, and wrappers into groups.

What do you throw away?

- Devise a way of keeping a list of the wrappers, tops, bottles and boxes that the children use then throw away. (The list might be a tally chart of previously agreed items.)

This week we threw away:			
Wrappers	Boxes	Drink cans	Bottles
✓✓✓	✓✓	✓✓✓	✓✓✓
✓✓✓		✓✓✓	✓✓
		✓✓✓	✓
		✓✓✓	
		✓	

Fig. 11 *Graph showing the amount of litter that the children threw away in a week*

A litter survey

- Walk around the local streets and look where litter collects. Talk about who drops litter and what the children can do to help.
- Prepare a map which the children can use to mark the position of litter bins and concentrations of litter.
- Children can make a tally chart showing the most frequent items of litter.
  Cans   / / / /
  Bottles   / / /
  Crisp bags / / / / / / / / /
- This can be turned into a simple graph.

Talk to the disposal workers

- Many local councils will be pleased to send

officers to talk to the children or to suggest ways to involve the children in keeping their town or city clean. They may be able to suggest safe visits to landfill sites, road sweeping depots and bin lorry depots.

Design ways of keeping the place tidy

- The children could design ways to encourage people to drop less litter. These might include simple ideas such as a poster or a more ambitious set of ideas for bin design and maps showing the best place to site them.

Science background

People use a wide range of materials much of which we dispose of as rubbish. A small proportion of this rubbish is not disposed of properly and becomes litter.

CHANGE AND DECAY

Activities for children

Food decays

- Seal some pieces of food in jam jars. (Use a paper or cloth cover rather than a metal lid to avoid misting up.)
- Watch the way that mould grows on the food.
- Keep accounts of the changes in the form of a class diary.
  (Carrot, bread, apple, cake, cheese and tomato all produce satisfactory changes.)
  NB Some rotting foods can be toxic. Do not open the jars. Dispose of the containers safely.

Leaf decay

- Look for leaves under holly bushes or other evergreens. At any time of year you should be able to find leaves in different states of decay. (In the autumn you should be able to find a sequence of decay under almost any tree.)
- Get the children to arrange these in order from most decayed to least decayed.

Burying waste

- Ask the children to design a test to see what happens to waste products which have been buried in the soil. They will have to take into account how to find the buried objects and how to compare them with the original. Items like apple peel, orange peel, paper, and metal objects will be worth including.

Metal change

- Collect scrap metal items such as bottle tops, scraps of foil, nails of different types, drawing pins, screws, copper pipe, electric cable, wire wool, paperclips.
- Ask the children to design investigations to see what would happen to these pieces of metal in different conditions. For instance:
  (a) What would happen if they were kept wet?
  (b) What would happen if we covered them with soil in a box?
- Ask the children to predict what they think will happen.
- Keep a diary of the changes noticed.

Plastic bag decays

- Some stores say that their bags will break down when buried in the soil. Challenge the children to test this claim. (These tests will probably take about six months to complete.) Smaller pieces of bags could be dug up at intervals to look at the progress of the different plastics.
- Write reports of the experiments to the bag providers and manufacturers.

Science background

People use a wide range of materials, much of which we dispose of as rubbish. A small proportion of this rubbish is not disposed of properly and becomes litter. All food items will decay over a relatively short period of time. Paper, wood and other plant based items decay readily.

Some plastics are so stable that they will not show appreciable change over centuries.

Children may think that all metal rusts. In fact only iron and steel rust. When rusting takes place there is a **chemical reaction** between the metal and the oxygen in the air. The iron **oxidizes** and forms a new compound called ferric oxide. Iron and steel are sometimes coated with other less reactive metals such as chromium to prevent air reaching the iron. Painting or coating with plastic has a similar effect. Other metals such as aluminium will oxidize but this oxide forms a protective coat around the metal so preventing any further rapid oxidization.

Key stage 2

Main scientific idea	Page title	Page
Seasonal and daily changes	Changes	29
Comparing and identifying plants and animals by close observation	Groups of plants and animals	31
Factors in decay	Decay and preservation	32
Classifying with biological keys	Keys and classification	34
Plant and animal communities found in different habitats	Habitats	35
Predators and prey; food chains	Feeding	36
Plants and animals have organs which carry out specific functions	Insides	37
Health is affected by diet, drugs and lifestyle	Health and illness	39
Sexual reproduction and growth in flowering plants and mammals	Reproducing and growing	41
Living organisms are made up of cells; microbes are microscopic living organisms	Cells and micro-organisms	43
Living things in one group vary from one individual to the next	Measuring variation	45
Inheritance is controlled by genes	Genetics	46
Waste products can be recycled	Recycling	47
Water is used to dispose of waste materials	Water pollution	48
Air pollution has many causes and effects	Air pollution	49

The programme of study

This states that pupils should be taught:

- that there are life processes, including nutrition, movement, growth and reproduction, common to animals, including humans;
- that there are life processes, including growth, nutrition and reproduction, common to plants;
- the functions of teeth and the importance of dental care;
- that food is needed for activity and for growth, and that an adequate and varied diet is needed to keep healthy;
- how blood circulates in the body through arteries and veins;
- the effect of exercise and rest on pulse rate;
- that humans have skeletons and muscles to support their bodies and to help them to move;
- the main stages of the human life cycle;
- that tobacco, alcohol and other drugs can have harmful effects;
- that plant growth is affected by the availability of light and water, and by temperature;
- that plants need light to produce food for growth, and the importance of the leaf in this process;
- that the root anchors the plant, and that water and nutrients are taken in through the root and transported through the stem to other parts of the plant;
- about the life cycle of flowering plants, including pollination, seed production, seed dispersal and germination;
- how locally occurring animals and plants can be identified and assigned to groups, using keys;
- that different plants and animals are found in different habitats;
- how animals and plants in two different habitats are suited to their environment;
- that food chains show feeding relationships in an ecosystem;
- that nearly all food chains start with a green plant;
- that micro-organisms exist, and that many may be beneficial, eg in the breakdown of waste, while others may be harmful, eg in causing disease.

Teaching about life and living processes

Children need to become aware of the wide variety of living things with which they share the world. Their awareness of similarities and differences needs to be accompanied by an understanding of how different species, including the human species to which they belong, are interdependent. It is important to help children at this age build a sound basic understanding of their own anatomy and physiology as a foundation for healthy living. Of course this should be a part of a programme of health education and personal and social education.

Pupils will already have some understanding of how their bodies work and of how similar processes occur in other animals. They will also have learnt something about plant growth and reproduction. If they have kept animals or grown plants then they may be quite knowledgeable about those. Television may have given them vivid detail of particular species, environments or processes such as feeding. However their knowledge is likely to be uneven and may mask some basic misunderstandings – for instance about the location of organs in the body, or the characteristic properties of living organisms, or the distinctions between plants and animals. As teachers we can build on their existing range of knowledge by a combination of first hand investigation and use of good secondary sources. There are many opportunities for children to plan and conduct investigations at the appropriate level, progressing for instance from simple observations of the conditions needed for the growth of seedlings, to advanced investigations of the range of variables they think may explain differences between the plant communities found in two locations.

Genetics is the study of the way in which information in the form of **genes** is passed on from one generation to the next. Each individual organism, whether it is a human or a dandelion plant, inherits characteristics from its parents. The ability of the organism to respond to changes in the environment is, to a large extent, determined by this inheritance. A group of organisms as a whole will share many characteristics but there will be considerable variation within the group. This was as true of an extinct group like the dinosaurs as it is true for existing animals and plants. Extinctions must be linked in some way to the inability of a group of organisms to respond to changes in their environment.

Environmental awareness and concern about environmental issues is likely to be high in this age group. Scientific understanding is needed to underpin this and to inform the decisions they will make as adults. Children can be actively involved in local and global debates about loss of habitats, recycling, or water pollution for example. They can express their commitment in actions, such as helping to make conservation areas, as well as finding out more. There is no shortage of information about pollution and conservation but the underlying scientific ideas are not always well understood. Some, such as the processes of decay, lend themselves to investigations by pupils.

Cross-curricular links

The study of life and living processes has traditionally formed an important part of the primary curriculum. In many schools it has been linked to local studies, seasonal work, observing and caring for plants and animals, and in some to community involvement and improvement of the environment. Sponsorship from industry and association with environmental organisations has been increasing. Health education programmes and publications have recognised that the biological studies are but one element of the child's education as a healthy and responsible citizen. Studies of 'Ourselves' or 'My Body' can be extended to incorporate effective learning and awareness of family, social and cultural issues. The scientific study of life can be planned in association with cross-curricular themes of environmental education, health education, education for citizenship, or education for economic and industrial understanding. It links easily with the foundation subjects of geography and technology.

Topics in which life and living processes can be studied include: *Ourselves, Gardens, Pollution, Senses, Water, Change, Movement, Growth, Homes.*

Opposite is a topic web with which a teacher began to plan work on the familiar primary topic of homes.

Resources

Animals and plants can be encouraged by creating a small wild area. If animals are to be kept in classrooms check regulations and guidance from the local authority or consult publications such as *Be Safe* from the Association for Science Education to ensure there are no risks to the health of pupils or the animals. Do not bring wild birds or mammals into the classroom, alive or dead.

Prepare containers and media to grow plants. To assist observations of small animals you will need containers, nets, droppers, suitable magnifiers and a sturdy, low power microscope. A good range of reference books for identifying and grouping plants and animals will be needed. Sensors and software for compiling databases or tabulating and graphing results will be valuable if available.

Local museums as well as the Geological and Natural History Museums in London sell some beautiful reproduction fossils. Educational suppliers like Geosupplies (16 Station Rd, Chapeltown, Sheffield S30 4XH. Tel 0114 2455746) supply sets of attractive fossils. Usborne offer a good range of popular books about prehistoric animals with dinosaurs being the clear favourite.

Information about genetics and selection can be obtained from anyone who breeds animals or plants. If you live in a rural area the local farmer might talk to the children about how plant or animal varieties are bred. In the city a pet shop owner, pigeon fancier, budgie breeder or goldfish specialist will have a fund of useful information. You might be able to visit a rare breeds centre.

This aspect of science above all the others relies on teachers knowing the local environ-

Key Stage 2

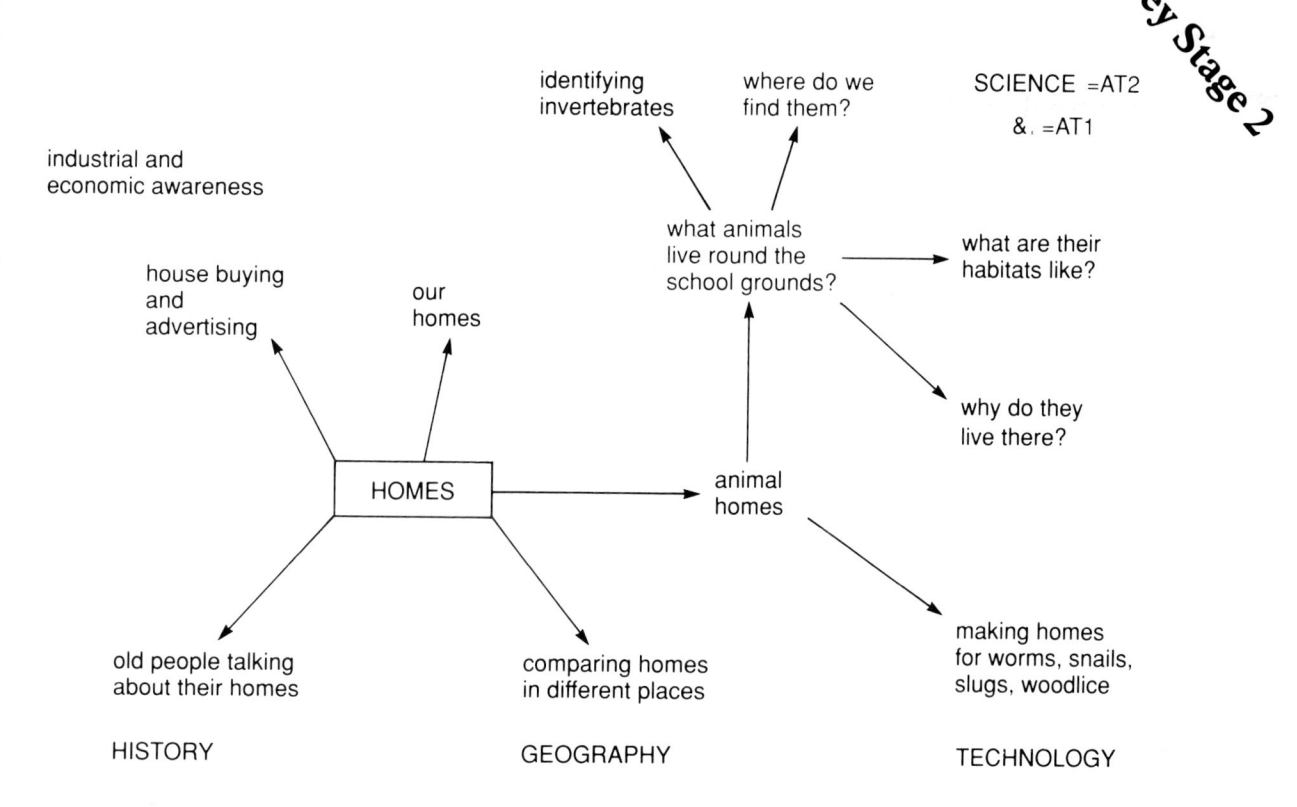

Topic web showing HOMES at center with branches:
- industrial and economic awareness
- house buying and advertising
- our homes
- identifying invertebrates
- where do we find them?
- SCIENCE =AT2 &. =AT1
- what animals live round the school grounds?
- what are their habitats like?
- why do they live there?
- animal homes
- making homes for worms, snails, slugs, woodlice — TECHNOLOGY
- comparing homes in different places — GEOGRAPHY
- old people talking about their homes — HISTORY

Fig. 12 *Topic web*

ment. The problem of litter and dog fouling will be all too apparent in a town whilst the impact of large scale agriculture will press in on some rural areas. If there are extractive industries near you their management may be keen to forge local community links. Most council planning offices are keen to respond to enquiries from teachers and children. Contact Tidy Britain (Wigan Pier, Wigan) for curriculum packs and other resources.

CHANGES

Activities for children

Animal rhythms

- Get children to survey when their pets eat and sleep. When are they active?
- Discuss how to record the results.

Signs of spring

- What signs of spring can children notice on a walk in a park?
- Ask such questions as:
  (a) When do dandelions flower?

(b) Can they find sprouting sycamore seedlings?

(c) What are birds doing?

Buds in spring

- Ask children which local trees come into leaf first. Encourage them to watch and to chart the order.
- Draw leaf buds and flower buds on trees or other flowering plants. Display a sequence of drawings at different stages.

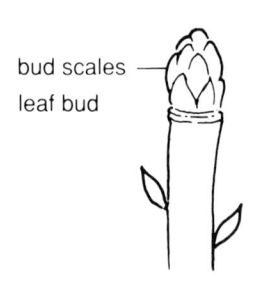

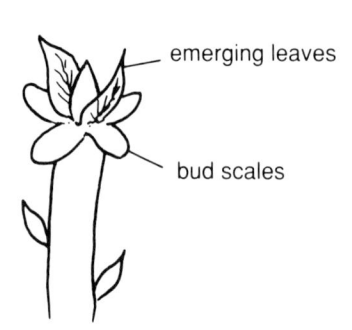

Fig. 13 *Leaf buds opening*

Plant growth

- Investigate the growth of seedlings.
- Count weeds as they emerge on soil or the flowers children sowed in a seed bed.
- Encourage the children to keep regular records of the numbers and size of seedlings. The results can be made into bar charts.

- Discuss what factors they think might affect their growth.
- Help them test their suggestions and relate their observations to the changing conditions outdoors.

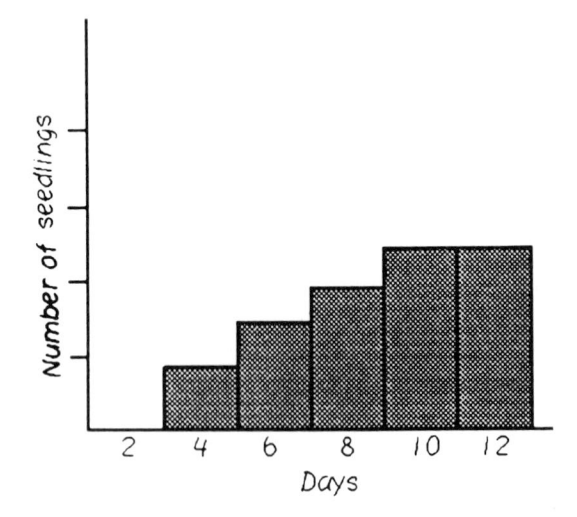

Fig. 14 *Bar chart of seedling growth*

Coping with winter

- Ask children which animals they see less of during winter. Where do they think they go?
- Look under leaf litter and sheltered spots for insects and other small animals. How do hedgehogs cope?
- Which animals really do hibernate and which are just slower? Use books to find out.
- Which birds come and go? Keep a diary.
- Find out about migration from books, films and by writing to schools abroad.

Science background

People vary in their response to the length of day and light levels. Plants and animals, including humans, have diurnal (daily) and seasonal (annual) rhythms. Annual and daily patterns vary round the world and children can begin to appreciate this when they have become familiar with their own.

Several factors may combine to influence plant growth, including temperature, daylight and moisture. Plants also have characteristic times and rates of growth.

A combination of innate behaviour and environmental stimuli may control seasonal and daily patterns of animal behaviour such as migration, singing and flocking by birds. Birds which stay over winter when days are short may have difficulty getting enough food and keeping up their body temperature in cold weather.

Some animals, for example the dormouse, build up fat over the summer; their bodies then cool and slow down so much that they can survive winter without feeding – this is hibernation. They may sleep when it is cold but come out if there are warm spells, as do hedgehogs. Amphibians, like toads, also hibernate and will not emerge until it is warm enough. Some insects, for instance ladybirds and some butterflies, survive by sheltering and others may enclose themselves over winter as a chrysalis.

Since squirrels eat lots of nuts or berries, their food is actually in shortest supply during spring rather than autumn and early winter. They survive by burying food when it is abundant, but have also become very adept at taking food put out for birds in winter.

GROUPS OF PLANTS AND ANIMALS

Activities for children

Comparing and sorting plants

- In spring and summer look at flowers. Ask children how they could group them:
  (a) by colour
  (b) by the number of petals
  (c) by the way the flowers are arranged on the stem
- Drawings can be made into a class book for reference.
- In summer and autumn collect leaves from trees or weeds. Sort them into groups by size, by outline shape, and by features such as:
  (a) smooth/toothed edge
  (b) simple/compound

  Use hand lenses to look for small differences like hairs.
- Identify the plants by matching their leaves against pictures in a reference book.
- Rub or press them and make a book to use for identification.
- In winter and spring look at twigs.
  (a) How are the buds arranged?
  (b) What colour and shape are they?
  (c) How do they feel?
  (d) What marks are there on each twig?

    Look at the tree to see how they branch.

A patch of grass

- Give pairs of children small patches of grass. They can be outlined by a PE hoop or rope.
  (a) Challenge them to see how many sorts of plants they can find.
  (b) Can they find different grasses?
  (c) How are they different from the other plants?

  Provide a hand lens. Gardening books or lawn food publicity may be useful for reference.

Life in the garden

- On a warm day weed and tidy a patch.
  (a) What sorts of plants are being grown?
  (b) What are weeds anyway?

  Look out for small animals. A magnispector will encourage closer observation and careful comparison.

Bigger things

- Use pictures to sort big animals (old wildlife magazines are useful).
- Design a zoo where similar groups are located near to each other.
- Visit a garden centre and let children plan their own with plants grouped. (They might use symbols or cut out pictures from plant catalogues.)

Science background

Trees are woody perennial plants (shrubs are small woody plants – conventionally below 6m) which can belong to various groups of plants. Flowers are found on most trees as well as those plants we often refer to simply as 'flowers'. In some plants (like dandelions) what we term the *flower* is really lots of small flowers. Leaves may occur singly or be grouped. If a leaf is divided into smaller leaflets it is termed **compound**. If not it is termed **simple**.

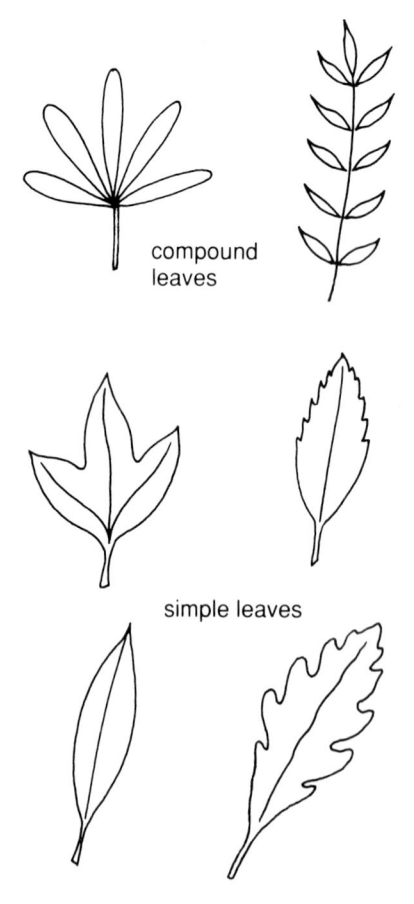

Fig. 15 *Compound and simple leaves*

Rough grassland can contain a surprising variety of broadleaved plants as well as grasses. The flowers of grasses are only obvious in June. Children with hayfever should not be asked to work with them.

Children may not realise there are different sorts of grasses, mosses or ferns. Non-flowering plants may have different parts which are equivalent to flowers such as cones in conifers, spore cases in mosses and ferns. These may not be obvious.

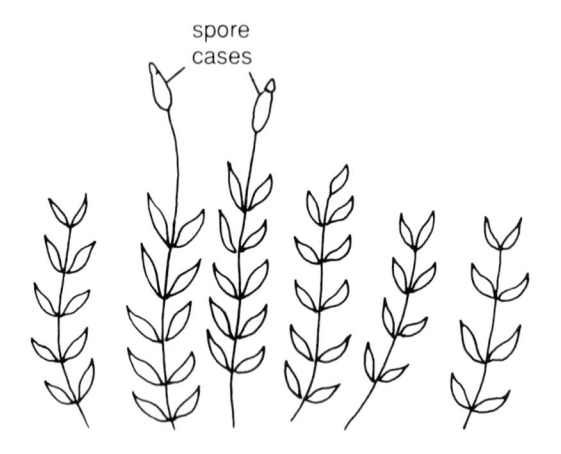

Fig. 16 *Spore cases in moss*

Weeding, turning over stones and looking in long grass can yield different groups of invertebrates such as woodlice and centipedes. There may be more than one species belonging to the same large group – different sorts of spiders for instance. Magnification and drawing will encourage children to look more closely and systematically at the sections of their bodies, the mouthparts, hard and soft parts, the number and arrangement of any legs or wings.

DECAY AND PRESERVATION

Activities for children

Autumn in the woods

- Collect leaves to press and preserve.
- Look for fallen leaves at different stages of decay.
- Examine old leaf litter which is decomposing. Get children to feel it.
- Dig a small hole to see how far down decayed material is found.

Key Stage 2

A rotten log

- Find fallen branches or logs to feel and see how they change.
- Lay a log on newspaper or a sheet and take off some bark.
- Ask children to look for plant life. They may find moss, ferns or fungi. Watch out for small animals.
- A group could make a display or collage featuring their labelled pencil drawings and concise descriptions.

Rotten fruit

- Show some fruit which is starting to rot.
- Ask children how they can keep fruit fresh.
- Help them plan fair and hygienic tests. These can be done in a jar if a small hole is punched in the lid and cotton wool taped over it.

Find out about fossils

- Borrow a set of fossils from the museum. Draw them and use reference books to find what they are and how they were formed.
- *Make a fossil*
  1. Warm a slab of Plasticine.
  2. Make a 'wall' round the edge of the slab using more Plasticine.
  3. Press a shell, small bone or leaf into the slab to make a shape.
  4. Remove the shell, bone or leaf.
  5. Mix plaster of paris into some water in a cup or bowl.
  6. Pour the creamy plaster into the shape.
  7. Leave it to set.

Science background

Fungi are sometimes classed as plants and sometimes placed in a kingdom of their own. They require close observation and careful handling. Check a field guide to learn which are poisonous and teach children safe habits. Mushrooms and toadstools belong to the group of fungi which have gills. They reproduce by **spores** released from those gills. Fine root-like **hyphae** may be found running from the base of a toadstool and for much of the time these are the only sign that there is a fungus there.

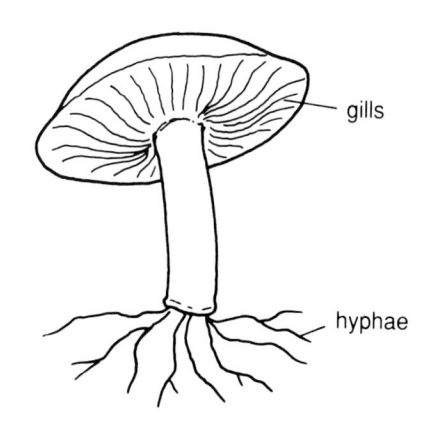

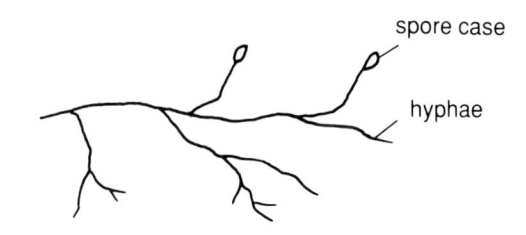

Fig. 17 *Fungus with gills and pin mould under lens*

Moulds are simpler sorts of fungi composed solely of hyphae. **Yeasts** are fungi composed simply of cells which divide when the yeast multiplies. **Bacteria** are very small, simple living things (micro-organisms). Some bacteria and fungi can be harmful to people and other living organisms. On the other hand, some have useful effects. Children should not cultivate moulds on food in case they grow harmful ones.

Decay

When things die they begin to break down. This is accelerated by the action of weather and animals. Certain fungi, moulds and bacteria decompose them, but warmth, moisture and air are also needed for this process of decay. Decayed leaves and twigs make humus which enriches the soil. Removing the conditions for decay by freezing, drying, excluding air or by adding chemicals helps to preserve food.

Fossils

Living things which die are sometimes preserved naturally for short or long periods. A few plants and animals which died millions of years ago did not decay but were fossilised. This happened in several ways.

- Some were frozen – eg woolly mammoths in Siberia.
- Some were trapped in bogs which were too acid for bacteria and fungi – eg the bog people in Denmark.
- Some were squashed under layers and slowly changed into fossils in rocks – eg ammonites.

Fossils can be parts of a plant or animal or even a mark left by one: for example dinosaur footprints.

Fossil remains are clues to the sort of environment and the life existing at different periods in the past. They also provide evidence of how the variety of living things have evolved. However some living things were more likely to be fossilised than others and the fossil record is therefore uneven.

KEYS AND CLASSIFICATION

Activities for children

Making and using keys

- Give children a few objects to sort. Divide them into two piles by a question to which the answer is yes for some and no for the rest. Divide one of the piles again by asking another question. Do the same with all the piles until each contains only one item.
- Let children try this with collections of other objects, eg assorted pens and pencils. Help them choose questions which distinguish the objects. Get them to record what they do on large sheets of paper.
- Show children how to use software like Branch and Sort (from NCET), to sort a few leaves or twigs.

Using keys

- When the children have made these simple keys they can swop them and use one another's to separate and name objects. Encourage them to suggest improvements and try different ideas.
- Give them simple published keys to identify familiar birds or flowers.
(ref *Clue* books, SNSS publications)
- Provide pictures of animals from each of the main groups of vertebrates – ie mammals, birds, amphibians, reptiles, fish – and from some groups of invertebrates – eg worms, molluscs, and insects. Challenge the children to put them in the correct group by using a simple branching key.
- Do the same with plants, including algae, mosses, ferns, conifers and flowering plants. Use real specimens rather than pictures if possible.

Science background

Biological keys are a systematic way of identifying things. The simplest are branching trees which sort things out on the basis of yes/no questions about observable features. Making their own may help children understand how to use published keys later. It also disciplines observations and questions. Databases reinforce and apply this. They can be very useful when children need to record and identify what lives in a rich environment. Most keys need to be more complicated than simple branching trees. They may combine yes/no and either/or choices with questions where there are several answers – eg 'How many petals has the flower?' They often use numbers – eg 'If the answer is three go to clue no 4'.

Living things are classified into groups. The basic unit is the **species**. Closely related species are placed in the same **genus**. Related genera are placed in the same **family** and so on in bigger and bigger groups up to the animal and plant kingdoms. Fungi, bacteria and viruses do not fit easily into either kingdom.

Table 3 *Main groups in the animal kingdom*

protozoa		single celled animals like amoeba
flatworms		e.g. tapeworm
annelid worms		e.g. earthworms
anthropods		animals with jointed limbs, including insects, spiders, woodlice, millipedes, centipedes and crabs
molluscs		e.g. snails, slugs, squids, cockles
vertebrates		animals with backbones; fish, amphibia, reptiles, birds and mammals

Table 4 *Main groups in the plant kingdom*

algae		Simple plants such as seaweeds and thread-like pondweeds; some are very small
mosses and liverworts		small plants without true roots which reproduce by spores
ferns		plants with true roots and stems which reproduce by spores
seed-bearing plants which include		conifers which have cones not flowers, flowering plants which all have reproductive organs called flowers

HABITATS

Activities for children

Different environments

- Find two contrasting environments, such as:
  (a) shady and sunny parts of a garden
  (b) mowed and uncut patches of grass
  (c) wet and dry meadow
  (d) a piece of ground which has been partly covered by a stone or old carpet

  Ask children what differences they can spot. Encourage any observations and questions.

- To focus their investigations give groups of children contrasting patches by laying down hoops or marking out squares. Ask them to find out how many different plants and animals live in their patch.

- Ask them to decide how to record how many of each sort there are.

- Ask the groups to compare what their patches were like and what they found in each. What differences and similarities do they notice? They may include:
  (a) temperature, light, moisture, compaction of soil
  (b) the presence of other plants and animals

Life on a tree

- Take children to a nearby tree. Find out what lives under it, on the bark, in the foliage and flowers.

- Give children books and keys and hand lenses to help with identification.
- They can record their findings by drawing the plants and animals they find to display on a large tree picture.
- Go back at different seasons to compare what can be found.

Science background

The place where a plant or animal lives is called its **habitat**. A group of different sorts of animals and/or plants sharing a habitat is called a **community**.

A particular habitat provides an environment which suits some sorts of plants and animals better than others. The factors in an environment which influence what lives there include:

- *Physical factors* such as amount and type of soil, how wet or warm it is, how much light there is.
- *Biological factors* such as plants competing for light or food, plants providing shelter or food for animals, people working the land.

The communities found in habitats can reflect a combination of factors. Children will find it easier to begin by studying two habitats with marked differences in one factor – eg wetness or light level. Extend their understanding by studying the community at regular intervals along a line **transect** from wet to dry or dark to light.

As things grow they cause changes in the environment so the community changes in turn; this is known as **succession**. The community is also influenced by changing conditions over a year: eg climate, day length, growth of food or shelter.

A large tree provides several small habitats:

- The branches may be visited by birds and squirrels.
- Insects may live on or in the leaves. Others may visit the flowers.
- The bark can be home for various invertebrates.
- The community living on the ground under the tree's **canopy** will differ from that further away. A transect can be made from the trunk out to trace the changing frequency of plants.

Some trees like oaks support more varied communities than others like sycamore. If there are several trees near your school give each group one to adopt.

Interactions among the communities and seasonal changes are especially obvious in spring and summer. The growth of plants and of the tree's own leaves may be followed by signs of insects eating them and then by creatures feeding on those insects.

FEEDING

Children's activities

Gardening

- Grow grass or wheat in trays. Put some
  (a) in soil
  (b) in a multipurpose compost
  (c) in soil plus a general purpose fertiliser

  Keep the soils moist. Ask children to predict what will happen.
- They can measure the growth of plants in each tray and look out for any other differences.
- Discuss what they find and whether they think the tests were fair.
- Encourage them to devise other tests. Grow tomatoes in growbags.
- Ask children to plan fair tests of the effects of different liquid fertilisers.

What eats what?

- Make or buy cards with pictures of plants and animals that live in a habitat like a jungle or a wood.
- Ask children to find a big, fierce animal and say what it eats. What does that get its food from?
- Continue to make a sequence of cards back to a plant or plants.
- Challenge pupils to make up a card game or a

strip cartoon or a folding picture for young children.

- Show them how to draw a food chain with arrows that show how food energy is transferred as something is eaten.

Pond life

- Visit a pond in spring or summer. Supervise children closely.
- Get them to look at what grows on the bank and in the pond. What animals can they spot?
- Show them how to dip with a net and put any animals gently into flat white containers. (If you don't have nets and droppers use sieves and plastic spoons.)
- Help them to pursue their own questions, for instance 'How do they move?' Can they identify them with a simple key? Can they find out what they eat?

Science background

To grow and be healthy plants need nitrogen, phosphorus and potassium which they absorb from the soil. Soil kits can be bought to test the concentration of these substances in the soil. If it is poor or heavily cultivated it may be low on some elements. This can be corrected by adding a fertiliser containing the elements needed.

A high nitrogen content encourages growth and green foliage which is useful for lawns, green vegetables or new plants. Potassium is needed for succesful fruiting. The balance of elements may be important. Their concentrations in proprietary fertilisers are listed on the labels. Check beforehand that these are harmless. Fertilisers themselves will not harm children but there may be other risks from additives such as weedkillers or from infection via organic material like bonemeal.

Organic fertilisers such as compost, manure or seaweed provide the elements slowly over a long period and may also improve the soil structure. Inorganic, chemically manufactured fertilisers supply elements quickly over a short period. Different sorts of fertilisers contain different amounts of each element.

Although liquid fertiliser is often referred to as plant food it does not supply food energy to plants. Plants trap energy from the sun. Some are eaten by various animals which may in turn be eaten by other animals. This transfer of food energy can be shown in a **food chain**:

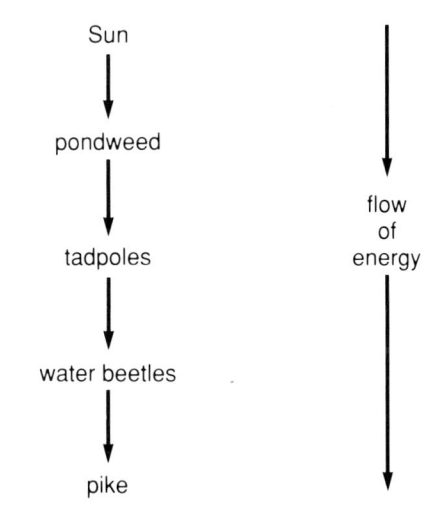

Sun → pondweed → tadpoles → water beetles → pike

flow of energy

Fig. 18 *Food chain, Sun → pike*

In any community there are likely to be a few larger fierce animals (**predators**) eating several sorts of smaller ones (their **prey**). However prey animals may be eaten by different predators. Some may be **carnivorous** themselves and compete for yet smaller animals. Many will be plant eaters (**herbivores**) who could be competing for similar plants or have very specific foodstuff. To properly represent these feeding relationships we may therefore need a more complex diagram known as a food web. A pond illustrates these relationships and how the conditions in a particular habitat are reflected in the species found there. Ponds need to be checked to ensure children can dip safely and without causing damage.

INSIDES

Activities for children

Heartbeat and pulse

- Help the children locate their heart and feel it beating.

Key Stage 2

- Show children how to feel their pulse at the wrist. Ask them to beat it out with the other hand so you can check they are feeling it.
- Chart and graph the pulse rate of all the pupils before and after exercise.
  NB If any pupils have asthma or heart conditions beware of overexerting them.

What's inside you?

- Ask pupils to list what they think is inside them.
- Get them to point to where they think their stomach, lungs and kidneys are.
- Use models, cutouts or overlay pictures to help them see how the internal organs fit into their chest and abdomen. Life-size pictures, 3D models, pop-up books and video make it more realistic.

What happens to your food?

- On a large silhouette locate and connect cut-out pictures of the main parts of the digestive system: mouth, oesophagus, stomach, small and large intestine. Get children to trace the route of food and label what happens at each.

Nerves and messages

- Sit the class in a circle holding hands. Pass a squeeze from one child to another until it goes round the circle. Practise to see how fast the message can be sent.
- Talk about how the message is sensed, passed through nerves to and from the brain to the muscles in your other hand.

Inside plants

- Cut a variety of stems across and lengthways. Let pupils draw what they see with a magnifying glass. Trace stems as they branch and join leaves.
- Stand celery or cut flower stalks in ink.

Leaves, buds and flowers

- In spring carefully take buds apart and draw the parts.
- In summer and autumn rub and draw large leaves to show the veins and compare the top and underside.

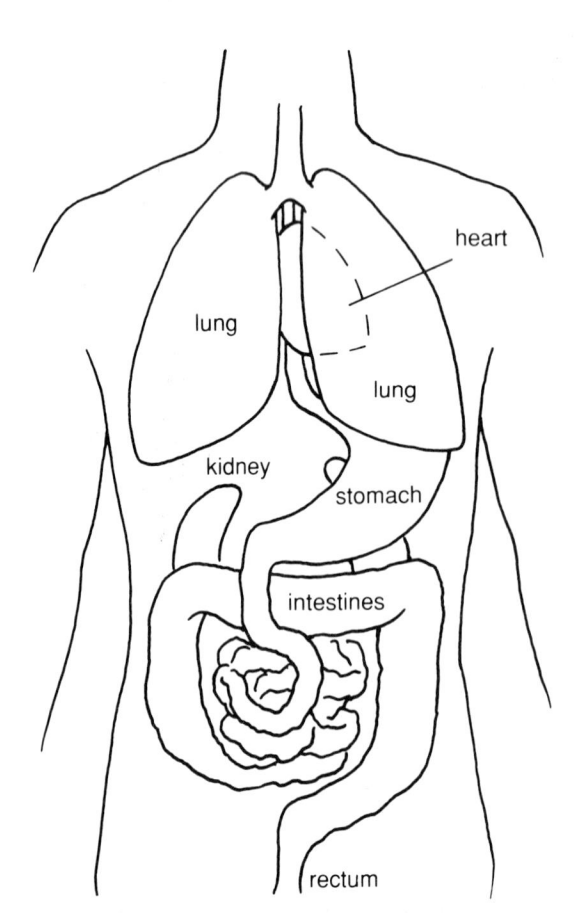

Fig. 19 *Cross-section of body*

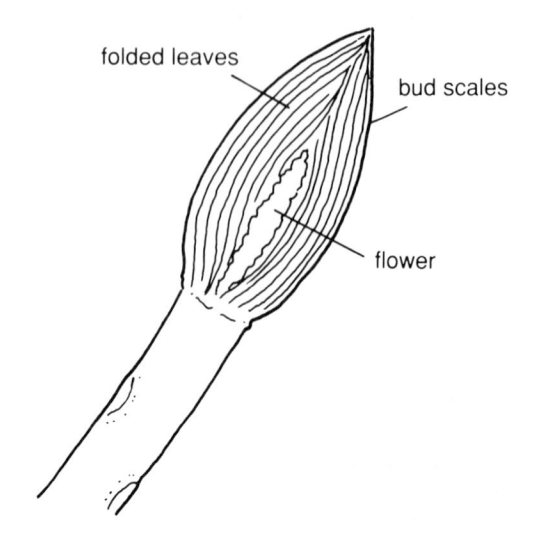

Fig. 20 *Cross-section of horse chestnut bud*

- Dissect and draw large flowers like tulips.
- Make large model plants with materials like wire, paper or cloth for leaves; join straws or card tubes joined for stems.

Science background

Mammals have internal organs which carry out special functions, for instance the kidney removes substances from the blood and regulates the fluid in the body, passing urine to the bladder. The heart pumps blood through arteries. We can feel it passing through the arteries at pulse points such as the wrist. Arteries branch until the blood eventually passes through fine capillaries which rejoin into veins whence the blood returns via the lungs to the heart. Air in the lungs is in contact with a huge number of capillaries so the blood leaving the lungs has more oxygen and less carbon dioxide dissolved in it. The lungs fill up the chest cavity and as it expands, they do, so more air enters. If we breathe deeper and faster more air passes in and out of the lungs so more oxygen and carbon dioxide can be exchanged. The heart also beats deeper and faster, pumping more blood round. This happens when we exercise.

Food has to be broken up physically and by **enzymes**. This begins in the mouth where it is chewed, the saliva makes it soluble and starch is broken down. The process continues in the stomach where the acid helps digestion. In the passage through the intestine digestion is completed, soluble substances are absorbed into the blood and the food becomes drier waste which we excrete.

Our senses detect changes in the environment and send messages along nerves. Different sense organs detect light, sound, temperature and pressure. In the circle activity above, a message from pressure detectors in one hand is interpreted in the brain whence another message goes along different nerves and causes muscles to contract in the other hand. If messages from our sense organs automatically lead to a muscular reaction we call it a reflex action.

When muscles contract they pull on bones to which they are connected by tendons. The combination of muscles contracting and relaxing causes movements of bones which are joined together in the skeleton. Some bones are long cylinders and their action is like a lever. Some joints allow movement like a hinge, others may allow rotation or side to side movement. Some joints between bones become fused before or after birth – eg in the skull.

Flowering plants have specialised structures for support and for transport of water and dissolved minerals (essentially roots and stems with tubes which carry water and which are strengthened if the plant is upright and heavy), for trapping and converting light energy from the sun by **photosynthesis** (green leaves) and for reproduction (flowers). As water evaporates from the leaves more will rise up the tubes in the stems. Ink may be carried to the leaves and flowers in this way, revealing the pattern of the transport system in the plant.

HEALTH AND ILLNESS

Activities for children

Good health

Any work in this area should be part of a school policy on health education which will take account of home circumstances.

- Identify things which make for healthy growth and emphasise positive action by pupils:
  (a) eat and drink enough but not too much
  (b) take regular exercise
  (c) sleep well and long enough
  (d) clean teeth thoroughly
- Pupils could make posters, slogans and pictures of role models.

Balanced diet

- Survey the foods pupils eat in a day, a week. Sort them in various ways suggested by pupils.
- Use charts and packets to find out what is in the foods they eat.

Key Stage 2

- Plan menus and survey school meals to emphasise the need for a balanced diet.

Fig. 21 *Healthy eating*

Good teeth

- Use dental health material and a visiting dentist to explain the structure of teeth and how they develop.
- Use disclosing tablets to show how to brush properly.
- If you can get a real tooth put it in cola for a week.

Drugs

- Ask pupils what they associate with the word *drug*.
- List uses of drugs as medicines to treat illness. Compare with abuses of drugs that harm us, such as nicotine and alcohol.
- Point out that some drugs in small doses may be medicinal if correctly used but deadly if used wrongly or excessively.
- Discuss the effects of alcohol and nicotine.

Body defences

- Discuss examples where the body resists disease or damage and mends itself:
  (a) how children's cuts have healed
  (b) how they recovered from illness
  (d) how they may now be immune if they had a disease
- List diseases they know and how they may be caused.
- Find out what they understand by the term *germ*.

Science background

The body is sensitive to damage, disease and harmful substances which affect the processes of life. Children need to understand how important their habits now may be for their health later. For instance regular exercise of the right sort helps maintain a healthy heart and lungs. The effects of some of their actions, like cleaning teeth regularly, are easier to see than others, like eating a balanced diet.

A balanced diet is one which provides the right amounts of the different sorts of foodstuffs. We need carbohydrate and some fat for energy, proteins for building and repairing the body, and small amounts of vitamins and essential mineral salts such as calcium and iron. Poverty often leads to a shortage of all sorts of foodstuffs in the diet and particularly protein. Children in affluent societies may have an imbalanced diet which is high in fats and sugars. Too much of those may lead to obesity and to heart disease later. Excess of certain fats from animal products (**saturated fatty acids**) is thought to be particularly unhealthy. Children may get lots of fat, sugar and salt in snacks and drinks. These may also contain added colourings, flavourings and preservatives which are unhealthy or which cause side effects in some children.

Drugs are substances which exert chemical effects in the body. These may be quite specific and can be used to treat illness or symptoms. For instance drugs like aspirin can bring down the temperature when there is a fever. However many have undesirable side effects – aspirin can sometimes damage the stomach lining. The dosage of a drug is usually critical and overdoses of some useful drugs can be damaging or lethal. Many drugs which dull pain and tranquillise can eventually depress breathing. Alcohol seems to stimulate but actually works by inhibiting nervous action so a high dose may depress breathing until the person dies. The other side effects may happen first and cause the drinker to be sick and feel bad as the breakdown products of alcohol accumulate in the blood. There are longer term effects of heavy drinking of alcohol, including liver damage and for some people addiction. Some drugs may be addictive because the body gets used to them and unpleasant symptoms occur if the drug is withdrawn. Nicotine has physical effects on nerve endings and blood vessels and smokers may find it hard to do without these but they are not all physically addicted. Tobacco contains other ingredients which are harmful. Any information about drugs, including those children may be at risk from on the streets, should be accurate and should ideally be given as part of a systematic drugs education programme. This can be positive if children are learning to take care of their health and seeing how the body does maintain itself and resist attacks on the delicate balance of its processes.

The body has feedback mechanisms which help it maintain the balance, this is termed **homeostasis**. For example the level of blood sugar is normally kept within a narrow range and our body temperature remains constant. Illness may affect these mechanisms.

Our bodies also have defence mechanisms such as the ability to heal, to increase the number of white blood cells which capture bacteria, and to develop immunity to disease. Malnutrition, some illnesses and drugs may impair these defences. AIDS is a condition which arises if a particular virus (HIV) impairs the immune system.

REPRODUCING AND GROWING

Activities for children

Germination

- Ask pupils to investigate conditions which they think affect germination of plant seeds (for instance temperature, moisture, light).
- Use rapidly germinating seeds such as cress and then other less rapid ones like hardy annuals or vegetables (try radish, lettuce) which can be grown on subsequently.

Grow seedlings

- Investigate whether the growth of seedlings depends on the same factors as the germination of seeds. Grow them in small pots.
- Help children to control and measure variables as appropriate:
  (a) standardising the amount of water added
  (b) measuring the height and noting other changes

- Compare growth in sand, gravel, poor soil, soil with added liquid fertiliser.

Plants make seeds

- Grow plants to fruition and collect seeds. Use bought plants or some already grown in school. Hardy annuals such as candytuft or marigold can be grown in pots or in borders or chequerboard gardens. Beans raised outdoors or in big pots or growbags need more attention but give striking results.

Flowers

- Dissect flowers, comparing several sorts. Draw them and label the parts to emphasise that they are reproductive organs with male and female parts as well as petals which attract insects to aid pollination. Study flowers which are pollinated by insects and by other means such as wind.
- Look at flower heads with ripening seeds.
- Collect seeds and start the cycle again!

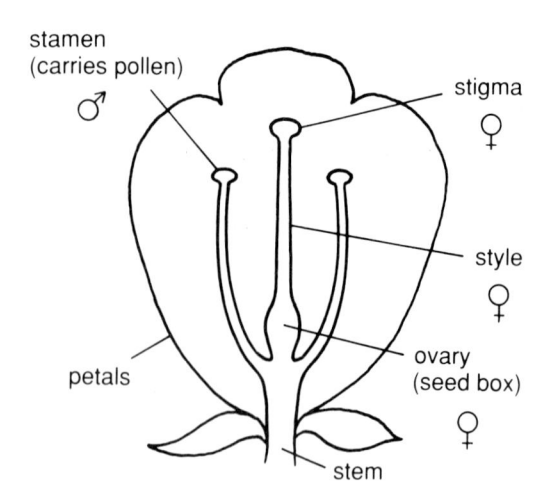

Fig. 22 *Cross-section of a flower*

Science background

Sexual reproduction in plants and animals involves the combination of male and female sex cells. Animals and flowering plants have special organs for this process.

In flowering plants these are in the flowers. The male cells are in the **pollen** on the tips of the **stamens**. The female organ is termed the **carpel**; it is made up of an **ovary** joined to a sticky **stigma**. During pollination pollen grains are transferred, in some species by insects attracted by coloured petals or scent. Pollen grains which land on the stigma of a plant of the same species may send pollen tubes down to ovules and fertilise a seed. (See figure at top of page.)

Fertilised ovules develop into seeds. These ripen and are spread, some by wind or water, some by animals eating the fruit they are in or brushing against sticky seeds, or by exploding fruits such as broom or balsam. If seeds have suitable conditions they will **germinate**. Some seeds need particular conditions, such as preliminary freezing. In general they need sufficient warmth and moisture. The seed contains some food which is used initially as the first parts develop. (See figure above.)

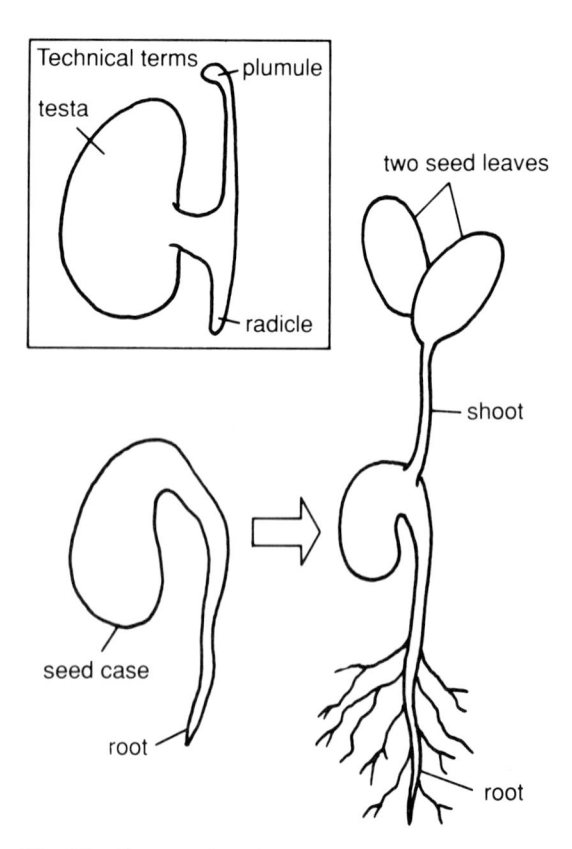

Fig. 23 *Cross-section of a bean*

As the seedling grows it develops different parts and requires slightly different conditions – light for instance. Its growth will be affected by the amount and direction of light, the temperature and by watering; if the soil is lacking in essential minerals its development will be impaired unless these are added in fertilisers.

Mammals have organs (**testes**) that contain the male cells (**sperms**) and transfer them to the female where an **egg** (the **ovum**) may be fertilised and develop inside the female into an embryo which is eventually born into the outside environment.

Children will need to learn about the particulars of the human menstrual cycle and the internal and external organs of reproduction in the context of a sex education programme which includes the social aspects of maturity and parenthood.

CELLS AND MICRO-ORGANISMS

Activities for children

How small?

Help pupils get an idea of how small cells and microbes are.

- Begin by asking them what is the smallest thing they can think of. Make a chart or scale and arrange things in order of size.

Under the microscope

Use whatever microscope is available.

- How much does it magnify? (Multiply the magnifying power shown on the eyepiece by that on the objective; look at a transparent ruler under the microscope.)
- How small an object can be made visible?
- What sort of detail can children see in:
  (a) thin pieces of plant tissue, such as onion skin
  (b) a hair from your head
  (c) tiny plants or animals in a drop of pond water (do not let this touch the microscope lens, and do not let the animal dry out or overheat)
  (d) a thin film of 'live' baker's yeast

Make a cell

- Make large collages or 3D models of cells, referring to pictures in books for details. Work out how many times bigger than the real thing they are.

Microbes

- Make some bread or yoghurt.
- Use reference materials or visits to find out how bread, yoghurt or some other foodstuff are produced using microbes such as yeast or bacteria.
- Explain that microbes are minute living things, such as fungi and bacteria, some of which cause disease but others are useful.

Safety and health in the classroom

- Consult LEA recommendations or the ASE booklet *Be Safe* for guidance.
- Do not grow moulds in open containers.
- Do not scrape cheek cells or take blood samples.
- Cutting thin plant sections as suggested in many books can be difficult and might be risky as sharp scalpels are needed.

Science background

Plants and animals are made up of microscopic units called cells. Different sorts of cells carry out different functions. Very large numbers of similar cells group together to make tissues. Different sorts of tissues are grouped together in organs.

In plants there are cells carrying out different functions such as supporting, transporting, **photosynthesising**.

Plant and animal cells are a little different as only plant cells have proper cell walls and contain vacuoles filled with sap. If they are photosynthesising cells they contain **chloroplasts**.

However, both animal and plant cells have a nucleus which contains the genes.

Microscopic plants or animals (microbes) may be made of very few cells. Some are made of just a single cell – for instance bacteria, amoeba. There are millions of bacteria and other microbes of which some sorts are helpful, for instance because they aid digestion in our gut, play an important part in decay, or are used in food production. There are others which are harmful because they cause illnesses, for example typhoid. Some other diseases are caused by viruses. They are too small to see with light microscopes. Viruses are not proper cells and do not have a nucleus. They can only develop and multiply if they enter other cells. The minute size of micro-organisms and of cells may be difficult for children to appreciate so introduce them to the relative scale of things by working down from the world seen through the hand lens to that revealed by the classroom microscope and to ever smaller worlds.

Sizes range from a typical animal cell at around 1,000 μm to yeast at about 20 μm, to a bacterium at around 1 μm (1,000 μm = 1mm).

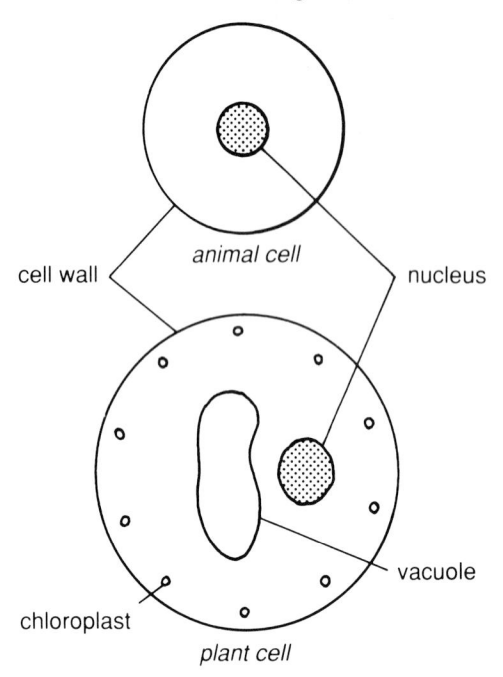

Fig. 24 *Animal cell and plant cell*

Here are some of the sorts of cells in the human body.

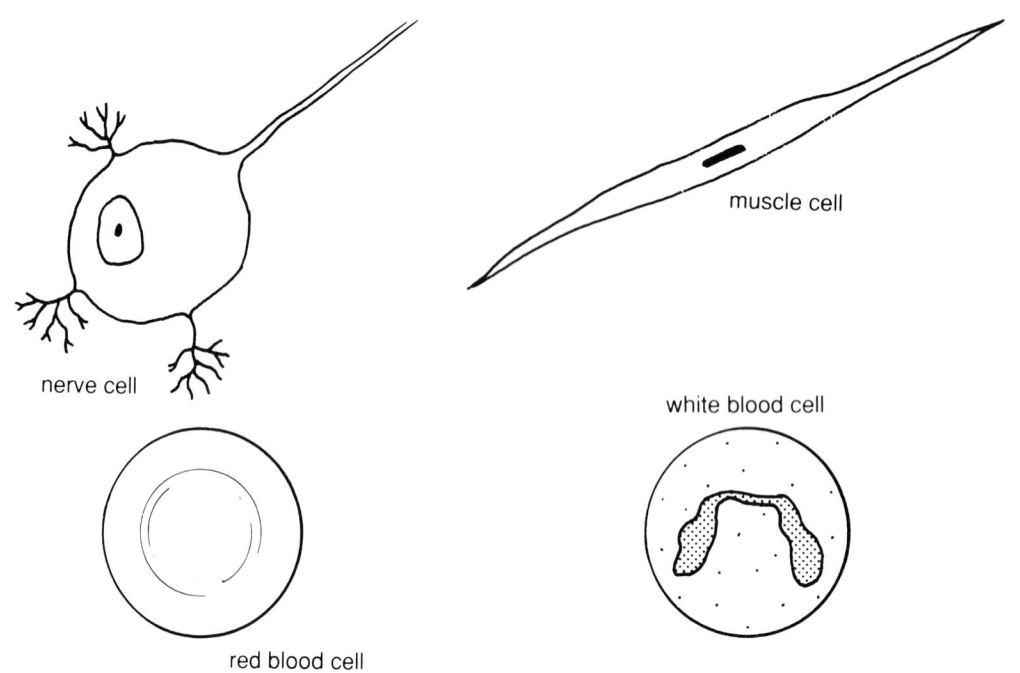

Fig. 25 *Human nerve, muscle and red and white blood cells*

MEASURING VARIATION

Activities for children

Tree leaf size

- Visit the local park. Which is the biggest leaf of a particular variety of tree that anyone can find?
- Collect 10 leaves of one kind at random. Back in the classroom the children can measure their width and length and record them in a table like this:

Leaf type	Width (cm)	Length (cm)
Sycamore	11	6
Sycamore	9	4

- Discuss the results. What reasons for the variation in size can the children suggest?
- What other things could they measure?

Seedling growth

- In a seed tray sow about 50 seeds of a rapid growing plant like cress. Keep it light and well watered. Ask the children to suggest ways in which we can be sure that each seed gets equal water and sunshine.
- After a week carefully remove each seedling. Accurately measure the length of each seedling.
- Use the information to fill in a table and complete a graph showing the variation in seedling length.

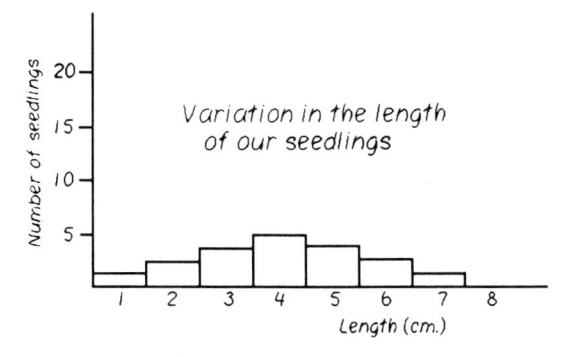

Fig. 26 *Graph showing variation in the length of seedlings*

- Talk about the pattern of results. Do you get similar results with other seed types? What could account for the variation?

Worm length

- Collect worms by digging a patch of well cultivated ground. Keep the worms moist and dark during their captivity.
- Measure the length of the worms. This may take some ingenuity since worms can be very active. Ask the children to design a fair way and kind way of measuring the worms.

Snail or slug size

- Collect some slugs or snails from the locality. Look after them carefully. Potato and apple are good foods.
- Ask the children what differences they notice. What measurements could they make? For instance they might count and tabulate the number of turns on the snail shell. You might count the number of snails with their opening on the right and those which open on the left and see which is the most common.
- Measure the length of slugs.

Science background

Individual living things of one type will vary in many ways. This is because of their **inheritance** and their environment.

The clearest example of an experiment which examines largely inherited characteristics is that of the seedling growth. Here, as long as the other variables like moisture and light are controlled, the main variable is in the seed itself. Similarly, the way in which a snail's shell turns is controlled by **inheritance**. Most snails open on the right hand side.

All the other features observed in the experiments are likely to be caused by environmental factors. Age is the main factor influencing size, with food supply and space also of importance.

Reproduction occurs in all living things. It can be **asexual** or **sexual**. In asexual reproduction the new individual is genetically identical to its parent because only one parent is needed. Asexual reproduction is common in very simple plants and animals. When we take cuttings of plants, we assist in asexual reproduction.

In sexual reproduction there is a guarantee of variation because two parents are needed and the genes of one individual are combined with another in an unpredictable way. Sexual reproduction takes place in more complex animals and plants. When gardeners sow seeds they are using the products of sexual reproduction.

Simple animals like snails, worms and slugs are **hermaphrodites** and contain both male and female elements in one body. They can, however, mate sexually with other individuals.

In **sexual reproduction** every new individual inherits characteristics from both its parents. This information is contained in the chemical composition of the **genes** which are carried on the **chromosomes**.

Normal body cells contain pairs of chromosomes. In humans there are 46 chromosomes arranged in 23 pairs. In male **sperm** cells and female **ovum** cells there are only 23 single chromosomes. In sexual reproduction the ovum and the sperm come together. When the sperm and the egg are fused the two half sets of chromosomes join forming an individual with the normal number of chromosomes.

GENETICS

Activities for children

Pedigree animals

- Ask a breeder of any type of pedigree animal to talk to the children. Breeders will often have fascinating information about how they select for certain characteristics in their animals. Ask them for instance how they try to enhance such features as speed in racing dogs and pigeons, and colour in budgies.

The farmer

- When visiting a farm ask the farmer how breeding animals are selected. For instance, why are undersize animals or cows with a poor yield not used? What differences are there in the crops which are grown today compared with those grown twenty years ago.

- Visit a rare breeds centre and research cattle, pigs or sheep to find out who their wild ancestors were. How has their appearance changed by use of selective breeding?

Science background

In **asexual reproduction** each new individual is identical to its one parent because there is no new combination of genetic information.

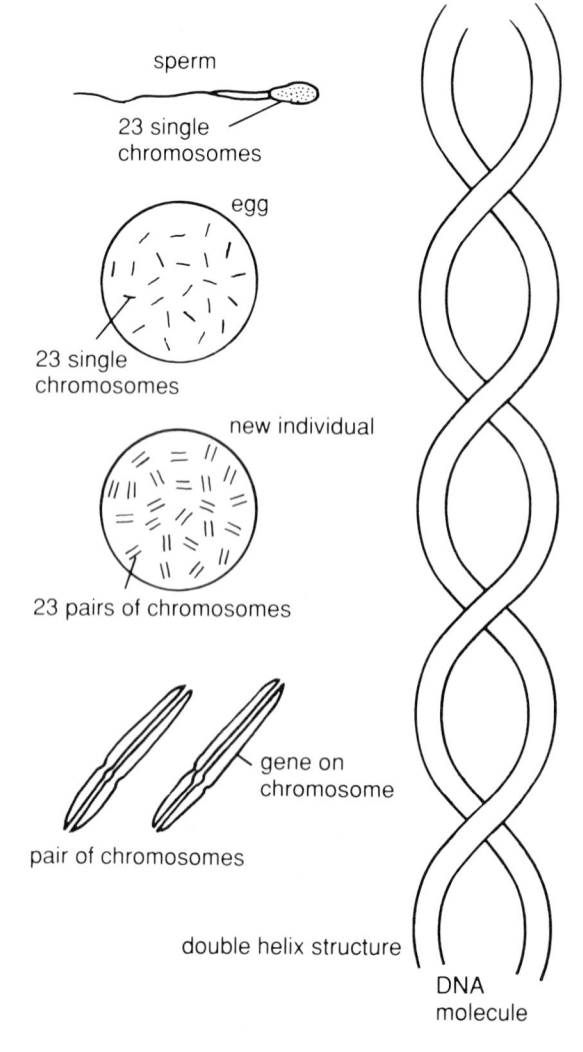

Fig. 27 *Cells for sexual reproduction*

Where the parental genes carry the same message the baby will have the same characteristic, e.g. where both parents have blue eyes. However, where the genes carry different messages the dominant gene will mask the recessive gene. This happens where the gene for brown eyes will mask the gene for blue eyes.

Each gene carries information coded in a chemical called **DNA**. This occurs in the form of a very long double helix molecule.

Ethical problems

Dealing with inherited characteristics of children is a minefield; this is why we have recommended looking in the main at animal breeding. With a very high divorce and illegitimacy rate it is no longer easy to discuss any human inherited characteristics without causing embarrassment. This is especially true of simple characteristics such as tongue rolling. If neither parent can roll their tongue and the child can, or vice versa, some difficult questions might result because this characteristic is always dominant. So if the gene is present it will always reveal itself. Eye or hair colour may be less problematical since it is a much more complex characteristic and an amount of unexpected variation can be expected.

RECYCLING

Activities for children

Recycling paper

- (1) Start by ripping up the paper you want to recycle into small pieces. Tissue paper is the best. Avoid newspaper as the ink is very messy indeed.
- (2) Soak it in warm water and mash it into a pulp. Sieve the pulp.
- (3) When most of the water has been removed roll out the pulp onto a wad of newspaper. Place a piece of clean paper between the newspaper wad and the pulp to stop it picking up unwanted ink. Dry the new paper.
- (4) Investigate:
    - (a) Which paper gives the best results.
    - (b) Which recycled paper is best to write on.
    - (c) Which is the most absorbent recycled paper.

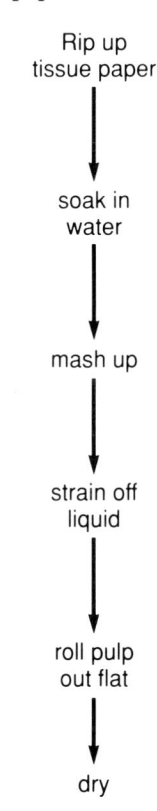

```
Rip up
tissue paper
    ↓
  soak in
   water
    ↓
  mash up
    ↓
 strain off
   liquid
    ↓
 roll pulp
  out flat
    ↓
    dry
```

Fig. 28 *Recycling paper*

Recycling water

- Make some water dirty by adding soil and then challenge the children to clear the water.
    - (1) Use plastic pop bottles cut in two to act as collecting jars and funnels. (Use a small hacksaw and scissors to cut the bottles safely.)
    - (2) Give the children a selection of cotton wool, broken pieces of plant pot, gravel, coarse sand, fine sand, limestone chippings, filter paper and any other materials which you have to hand which might prove useful. These can go into the funnel.
- Devise a system where the children have to buy materials for making filters with tokens.

Key Stage 2

1 scoop of fine sand might cost 4 tokens, 1 scoop of coarse sand might cost 3 tokens. The children should spend time evaluating the effectiveness of the different materials in helping to recycle water.

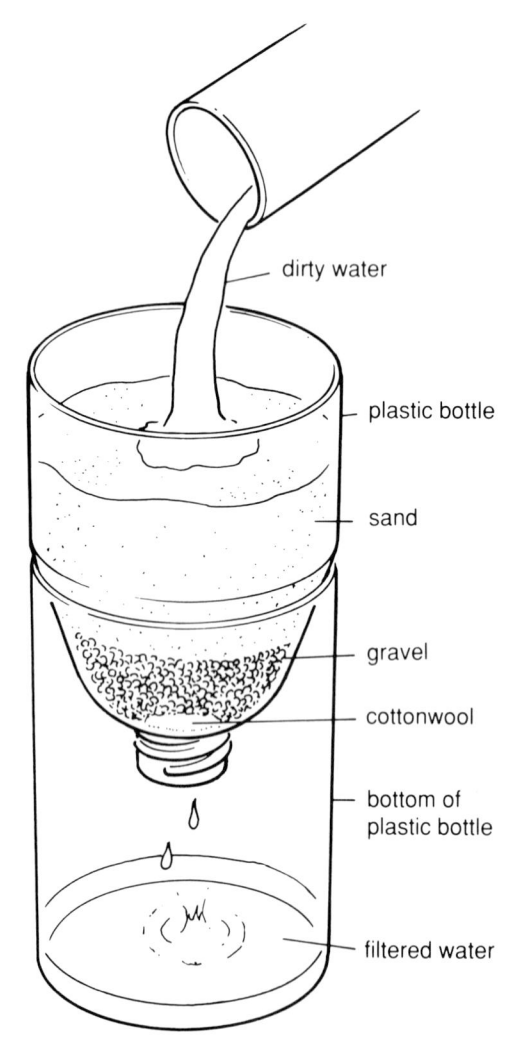

Fig. 29 *Recycling water*

Science background

Much paper is now recycled to avoid both cutting down trees and using the extra energy needed to make new pulp. Water recycling has been going on for years in treatment plants. The River Thames is said to be drunk about thirty times between its source and the sea.

WATER POLLUTION

Activities for children

Water plants

- Collect some water plants such as duckweed. Ask the children to plan tests to see what happens to the plants when the water in which they are growing is polluted. Keep a clean control jar. Label the jars.
  Safe pollutants might include: salt, washing up liquid, washing powder.
  NB Do not use bleach.

Fertilizer pollution

- Collect samples of water from ponds and rivers. Ask the children to plan tests to investigate the effect of adding some liquid plant fertilizer to one sample and not to an identical sample. Keep both jars in bright sunlight.

Oil pollution

- In the context of the environmental impact of oil spillages, observe what happens:
  (a) when oil is poured onto water
  (b) when oil and water are mixed up
  (c) when you add detergents and then shake the mixture
- Coat some feathers with car oil. Investigate the most effective ways to clean them.
  NB Supply plastic gloves and put plastic sheets on tables.

Science background

Biodegradeable materials can be broken up by bacterial action into simple chemicals. Oil is biodegradeable but some of the substances made from it, eg plastics, are not. Oils will not dissolve in water but when mixed with detergents they form tiny particles **suspended** in the water.

Soap powders and soaps are made by reacting fats or vegetable oils with sodium hydroxide. They are biodegradable. Soapless detergents such as most automatic washing powders are made from refining crude oil. Soapless detergent washing powders often contain **enzymes** which break down the proteins which form stains on clothes; they also contain brightening agents to make white clothes appear whiter. Some soapless detergents are not biodegradeable.

Adding fertilizer to water containing algae or larger plants causes them to grow rapidly. This depletes the oxygen in the water. The smelly mud at the bottom of ponds is the result of the breakdown of plant and animal remains by bacteria which work without oxygen. Rivers may become seriously deficient in oxygen because fertilizers washed out of farmland contain **nitrates** and promote excess aquatic plant growth. These nitrates can also find their way into ground water and so into drinking water supplies.

AIR POLLUTION

Activities for children

Acid rain

- Use universal indicator papers to find out the acidity of rain. The paper will change colour in an acid solution.
- What happens to seedlings watered with weak acids? The children can plan tests using different dilutions of vinegar.

The ozone layer and the greenhouse effect

- Teach the children about the greenhouse effect and its possible impact on climate.
- Ask the children to suggest how they could use less energy and so reduce the amount of carbon dioxide in the atmosphere.
- Ask the children to design posters which tell people about the problems which could arise from the possible changes in climate.
- Help children to untangle the issues about the ozone layer from the greenhouse effect.

Atmospheric pollution

- Set up, at points around the school, pieces of card on which you have glued sticky-back plastic with the sticky side out. Take the cards in after several days and see which site has the greatest amount of dirt in the air.
- What other ways of measuring the air pollution can the children suggest? Where do they expect to find the worst air pollution? Do their observations support their hypotheses?

Science background

Rain is normally **acid** because it dissolves carbon dioxide from the air. Its pH is about 5 or 6. When there is a lot of sulphur dioxide from burning fuels this is dissolved by the rain and its pH can get as low as 3 or 4. This results in damage to plants, especially evergreen trees.

The **greenhouse effect** is caused by the way in which several gases, including carbon dioxide and methane, trap heat near the surface of the Earth. Without any greenhouse effect the Earth would be far too cold to sustain life. However the extra amounts of carbon dioxide produced by burning, and methane produced by agriculture, are resulting in an enhanced greenhouse effect which will lead to a warmer planet. Carbon dioxide makes up a tiny proportion of the air at 0.035%, having risen from 0.028% a hundred years ago.

The ozone layer is a layer of the upper atmosphere rich in **ozone** which is a form of oxygen with three atoms (O_3). It absorbs many of the harmful ultraviolet rays from the Sun. CFCs are a group of gases which when released into the atmosphere combine with ozone in the upper atmosphere robbing the earth of its protective layer. One of the main sources of CFCs is the refrigerant found in domestic refrigerators.

Car exhausts produce large quantities of unseen carbon dioxide and carbon monoxide. They also produce soot (carbon) as a result of the inefficient burning of fuel. When car engines are cold they are less efficient and produce more soot than when they are warm. In some places smog is common. Smog is an acidic mixture of fog and smoke. It is common in very congested cities with high levels of car use.

AT 3 Materials and their properties

Key stage 1

Main scientific idea	Page title	Page
Simple properties of objects	Exploring objects	51
Simple properties of materials	Exploring materials	53
Characteristics of materials and grouping based on simple properties	Groups of materials	54
Collections of natural materials can be sorted by appearance	Sorting natural collections	56
Effects of heating and cooling	Heating and cooling	57
Natural and manufactured materials	Raw materials	58
Soils are formed through natural processes and vary from place to place.	Soil	60

Key Stage 1

The programme of study

This states that pupils should be taught:

- to use their senses to explore and recognise the similarities and differences between materials;
- to sort materials into groups on the basis of simple properties, including texture, appearance, transparency and whether they are magnetic or non-magnetic;
- to recognise and name common types of material and to know that some of these materials are found naturally;
- that many materials have a variety of uses;
- that materials are chosen for specific uses on the basis of their properties;
- that objects made from some materials can be changed in shape by processes including squashing, bending, twisting and stretching;
- to describe the way some everyday materials change when they are heated or cooled.

Teaching about materials

Young children find it difficult to distinguish between an object and the material from which it is made. Children should be encouraged to use all their senses when exploring objects and materials. For instance, smell is important when investigating some foodstuffs and the sound of an object when tapped can give a clue to whether it is made from wood, plastic or metal.

Play with materials like sand and water provides opportunities for exploring their behaviour. Comparisons between the feel of materials like flour and salt lays the foundation for more systematic grouping of materials based on their properties.

Cookery provides unrivalled opportunities for children to change materials. Children may take these changes for granted if they are not pointed out to them by a skilled teacher. With guidance and supervision they can investigate the changes which occur, for example when eggs are beaten, or the way that cakes will only rise if self-raising flour or baking powder is used. Melting and solidifying introduce the effects of heat, which may be reversed in some cases. The fact that virtually all the changes in cooking are not reversible may be something that pupils have not considered before.

Cross-curricular links

Much of the children's scientific learning about materials can be developed from the first hand experience and topics familiar in infant classrooms. Topics where materials could be studied include: *Changes, Hot and cold, The park, Clothes, Houses, The home corner, Opposites, Shops, Water, Helping at home, Cooking,* and *Shoes.*

Resources

Make collections of different types of materials readily available centrally within the school to facilitate this sort of work. For instance central stocks of different types of building materials would be helpful. A wide selection of natural objects and materials should be available. Collect shells, feathers, interesting pieces of wood, seed heads, dried flowers and grasses, rocks and crystals, for instance. There should also be a good range of materials and objects which have been manufactured, for example from different plastics and metals.

Aids to close observation, such as a range of lenses and a low power microscope, are essential. The best microscopes for key stage 1 will magnify up to ten times. Children will find it difficult to use any which are stronger than that.

EXPLORING OBJECTS

Activities for children

Making collections and displays

The regular classroom events and displays should involve children in matching and identifying objects by various attributes:

- Use colour themes when the class has, for example, a red week and they bring items in.
- Make displays of objects which have similar shapes, such as round things.
- Provide collections to feel and sort, for instance into rough and smooth sets.
- When you take children out ask them to look for particular things to collect – for instance one time it could be different sorts of rocks, another it might be just shiny objects.

Extend the range of displays and play materials so children can discuss their experience of various physical features:

- Provide flexible and elastic things which children can try to squeeze, bend or stretch; later change these for more rigid objects.
- Vary the consistency of clay or Playdough which they use.
- During cooking draw their attention to how ingredients look and feel as they are opened, poured and stirred.
- Supply different sorts of paper for them to paint on and to examine when wet and dry.
- In craft activities ask them to compare different glues or paint mixes.

Games to play

At odd moments games can be played with individuals or a large group. Examples are given below.

- Which of the three objects you show them is the odd one out?
- Can they find out what you have in your hand by asking questions about it?
- Can they describe something so other children can guess what it is?
- Introduce a simple version of Kim's game where they have to remember a small collection of objects you show; choose objects with different properties.

Shop play

- Set up a shop with items the children can sort onto shelves, sell and package. Encourage the 'shopkeepers' and 'customers' to refer to the wares by properties such as size, shape, colour, how they feel and their strength.

Washing up

A simple activity like washing up the dishes after cooking can be used to develop ideas about materials.

- Use utensils made of various materials – metal and wooden spoons, plastic and pottery plates, for example.
- Ask them which things might break, which are strongest, what should we wash first.
- Get children to talk about how the dishes look and feel before they are cleaned – sticky, crumby, greasy, slippy.
- Provide different sorts of washing-up liquids or soaps, cloths and scourers.
  (a) What do the soaps look and smell like?
  (b) What happens if we add different liquids to bowls of warm water?
  (c) Do the children think the plates will come clean with soaking or do we need to rub them?
  (d) Which scourer is roughest?
  (e) Which cloth is best for drying?

Smelly stuff

Pupils' awareness of different smells during cooking could be developed into a more directed investigation.

- Put samples with distinctive smells into small pots with pieces of cloth like muslin held on the top with elastic bands. (Try small pieces of apple and banana, herbs and spices.)
- Have each child smell one at a time and say what they think it is. Encourage them to describe the smells and to discuss their ideas.

An adult will need to direct the activity. With help the children may be able to test each other and organise the taking of turns. Afterwards open the pots and let them check their ideas.

NB Warn them not to smell or taste unknown substances.

Key Stage 1

Science subject knowledge

Teachers will not need any special scientific ideas to use these familiar activities. They will need to think about the scientific potential of experiences which may previously have been used to promote language or maths. Children should be helped to observe familiar and unfamiliar objects, to notice a variety of physical properties, and to describe and communicate their observations. The talk involved in all these activities is important for the children's scientific learning. The children's descriptions and the new vocabulary can be added to displays.

EXPLORING MATERIALS

Activities for children

Sand and water play

The water trough and the sand tray provide essential play media at this stage.

- Colour the water in the trough for added interest.
- Add bubbles to water.
- Different equipment can be provided to stimulate exploration including filling and emptying beakers of different size and shape, pouring through funnels and lengths of pipe, making water wheels turn and soaking up water in sponges.
- Encourage the children to see that some materials sink and others float by making boats from polystyrene and different types of wood.

Equipment can be varied in the sand tray to help children explore how it pours and fills and may be piled up or shaped.

- Does wet sand or dry sand make the best pies?
- Does all the sand in the pit go through a sieve or are there pieces in the sand?
- Put small beads or similar objects in the sand and challenge the children to find them all.
- Other everyday materials can be compared to see what else behaves like sand, for example salt or semolina.

Collections

- Display collections of different materials. For instance: rocks, feathers, leaves, metal things, plastic things, wooden things, natural materials collected on a walk in the park.
- Add words and phrases which the children use to describe the objects.
- Encourage the children to explore and observe carefully, using their senses and talking to one another. Help them to distinguish between an object and the material it is made from.

Using our senses

Touch

- Encourage the children to touch a variety of materials including wood, metal, plastic, stone and rubber things.
- You can emphasise the sense of touch by placing objects in a box or bag inside which the children can put their hands to feel the objects. Encourage them to describe the feel of the material as well as the objects. Change the objects regularly and leave the box or bag to be used throughout the day. Introduce something made of more than one material, for instance a plastic pen with a metal clip.

Sound

How do materials sound when they are tapped?

- Put out a set of objects to be tapped. These might include wooden objects and blocks of different sorts of wood, and various types of plastic and metallic items from the classroom or home. Ask the children if they can recognise the object from the sound it makes when tapped. Do this with small groups or the class as a whole. They could close their eyes whilst you tap various objects.
- Show the children how to test each other. This can be done by one child standing behind another and tapping objects and seeing if their friend can guess what it is.
- Encourage the children to talk about which

Key Stage 1

objects were easy and which were hard to guess.

Science background

Infant teachers will be familiar with most of these activities. They lay the foundations for understanding the physical properties of material. At this stage we are concerned to encourage children to notice a wide variety of features. Subsequently they can begin to recognise the important properties by which materials may be distinguished and grouped. Their play can be structured so they explore the appearance and behaviour of discrete materials like sand, where small particles are visible, and continuous materials like water.

Children may find difficulty distinguishing between an object and the material of which it is made. Their exploration of collections will help with this as well as extend their awareness of the properties of objects. Different materials (substances) can be distinguished by properties such as their hardness. Objects may have features which are independent of the substance they are made from – eg their shape. Many objects are made of more than one substance.

GROUPS OF MATERIALS

Activities for children

Sheets

These investigations refer to fabrics but paper could be used just as easily.

- Set out a collection of about five or six contrasting fabrics and ask a small group of children to examine and compare them. Encourage them to talk about the fabrics and sort them in any way they suggest. Ask them how they could group the fabrics. You can extend and focus their observations and investigations by posing questions such as:
  (a) Which fabrics can you see through?
  (b) Which fabrics are rough?
  (c) Which feel thick?
  (d) Which are stretchy?

- To make a permanent record the children could be encouraged to cut small squares of fabric which can be stuck onto a sheet of paper. (See Table below.)

- Ask the children to plan tests on the fabrics. For instance what effect does water have on the fabrics?

See through fabrics	Not see through

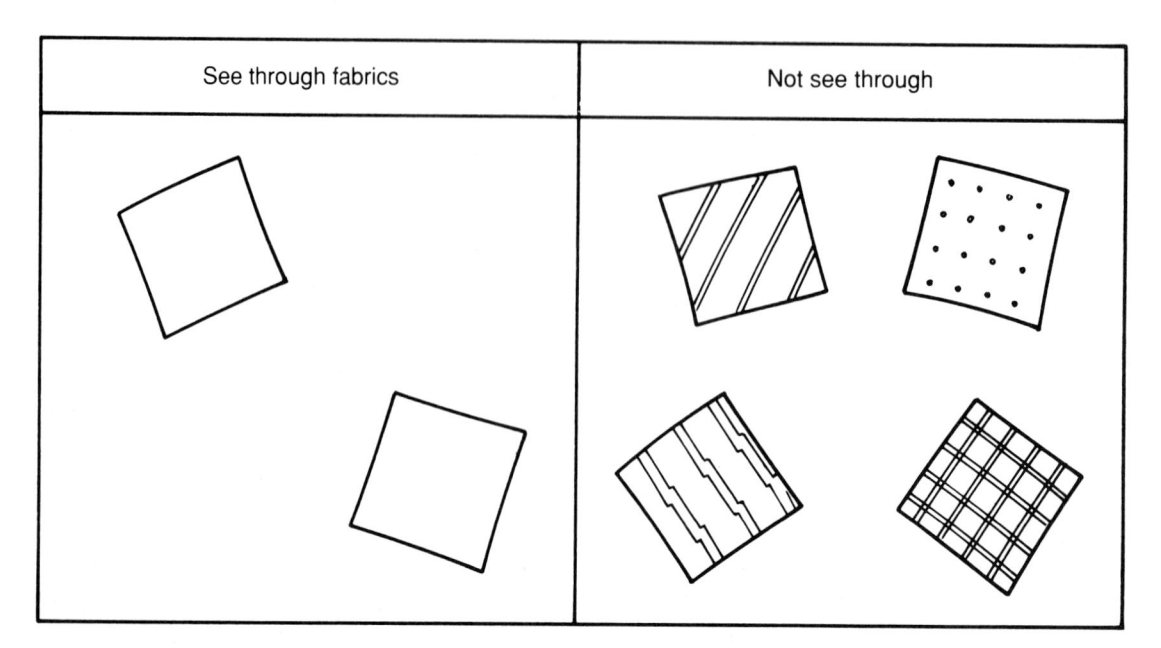

Table 5a *Table showing see-through/non-see-through fabric*

Table 5b *Table showing water-proof fabric*

Water soaked into these fabrics	Water stayed on the surface of these fabrics then soaked in	Water stayed on the surface of these fabrics

(a) Put out squares of fabric, beakers of water and droppers.
(b) Record the results in a simple form by sticking them in groups onto a piece of paper. (See above.)

Making a hat

- Children could apply their findings by choosing a fabric and making a rainhat for a toy such as Paddington Bear or Postman Pat.

Metal, wood and plastic

- Make three separate displays or collections for children to examine: one of wooden things, one of metal things and one of plastic things. Talk about what the objects in each group feel like; focus children's attention with questions like:
  (a) Does the material feel cold or warm to the touch;
  (b) What sound does it make when you tap it;
  (c) Is it easy to bend?
- Pupils could add their own objects to the appropriate display.
- You could provide a mixture of wooden, metallic and plastic objects for them to sort out. This could be an undirected individual activity or you could use it as a simple quiz at odd moments with the class.

Science background

Fabrics are made from a wide range of synthetic and natural fibres. The cloth may have been made by weaving or knitting or pressing the fibres together. Individual fibres can be teased out of many fabrics to examine under a hand lens or microscope. Knitted materials tend to be more flexible than the equivalent woven fabric. The ease with which water soaks into fabrics can depend on the closeness of the fibres as well as the nature of the fibres themselves; it may be affected by the presence of natural oils or the addition of waterproofing agents. Some fabrics will repel water until they are thoroughly wetted and then the water will soak through. New fabrics have been developed which are highly waterproof.

Wood is light for its size. It splinters and pieces can be broken off. Pieces of wood from different trees have differing grains and properties. Some woods like balsa are very soft and are easily marked by fingernails. Wood feels warm to the touch and makes a hollow sound when tapped.

Metal is generally heavy for its size. Some metals like aluminium are lighter than others like iron. Although metals can be bent and stretched most are too hard for young children to shape or cut. Metal is cold to touch. It makes a characteristic bright, clanging metallic sound when tapped.

Key Stage 1

There are lots of different types of plastic – for example polythene, PVC, polystyrene. Some are rigid and others bend easily. In general plastic is light, often soft and warm to the touch. It is relatively easy to cut and it can be made into a vast range of shapes and colours.

SORTING NATURAL COLLECTIONS

Activities for children

Collecting natural objects

- Collect safe natural and manufactured objects such as: pine cones, acorns, rocks, pebbles, nails, snail shells, pieces of paper, pieces of brick, feathers, twigs.
  (a) Ask the children to sort the objects in any way they like.
  (b) Next, ask them to sort the objects in two sets: natural and manufactured.

20 Questions

- Play 20 questions. The children try to guess the object you are thinking of by asking questions. You can only answer 'yes' or 'no'. Encourage them to question whether the object is natural or manufactured.

Sorting tree

- Handle the objects you have collected and played 20 questions with.
  (1) Start by sorting the set of objects into two sets.
  (2) Take one of the sets and sort that into two sets.
  (3) Take one of those sets and sort that into two and so on.
  (4) The children can draw the resulting tree.

Compare similar natural materials

- Give the children two natural objects or materials. Ask them to compare them noting:
  (a) all the ways they differ
  (b) all their similarities.

  You could do this with: feathers, snail shells, twigs, leaves, nuts or fruits, samples of soil, pebbles or rock samples.

Birds' nests

What materials are birds' nests made from?

- Obtain a nest after the birds have flown and allow the children to take it apart. Note the material used in its construction.
- Challenge them to remake the nest afterwards!

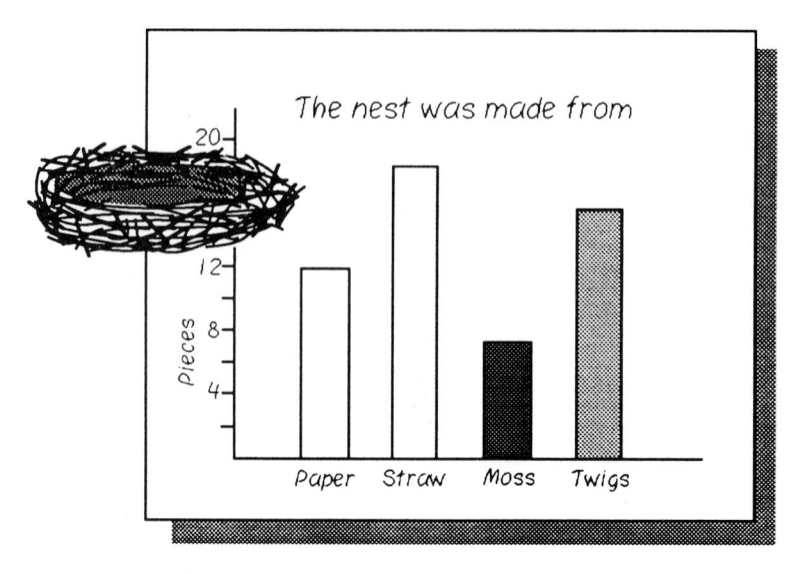

Fig. 30 *Graph showing composition of nest*

Feathers

- See how many different kinds of feathers the children can collect. Describe the differences and make careful observational drawings.
- Gently tease apart a feather. Zip it back up. What happens?
- Look at what happens when you put a drop of water on the feather.
- Look at feathers under a strong lens or microscope if the children can use one.
- Try to make a quill pen using a strong flight feather.

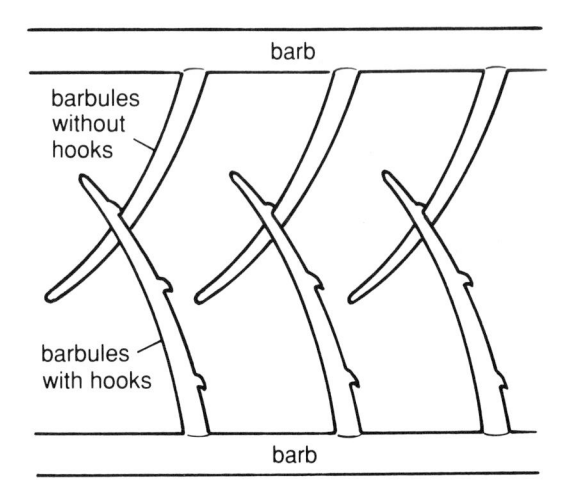

Fig. 31 *Flight feather*

Science background

The use of branching keys is an important first step in the more formal classification used by biologists. It is also a useful way to sharpen children's observation and their ability to ask questions.

Bird feathers are made of a substance called **keratin**. There are three types of feathers:

- The large flight feathers have a large rigid quill with feathery barbs which hook together to form a continuous surface.
- Contour feathers cover the main part of the body.
- Down feathers are feathery and have no barbs to hook together.

HEATING AND COOLING

Activities for children

Heating and cooling materials

- Ask the children how they think heat affects things like modelling clay and how it can be tested. They might suggest things like: placing some in a fridge, some in the room, some on the radiator or in the sun.
- Extend their observations with questions:
  (a) What differences do you notice?
  (b) Which is the easiest to shape and mark?
  (c) What happens when you try to roll it out?
- Ask the children to reflect on their experience of handling and eating chocolate from the fridge and comparing it with chocolate left in a hot room or even a pocket!
- The effect of heating foods can be investigated if it is contained in small, clear plastic food bags which could be stood in warm and cold places.
- Foods can also be floated in foil containers in bowls of hot water.
  NB Teacher demonstration only.
- Other foodstuffs such as margarine or jelly can be melted and solidified in a similar way. This work could be part of a topic on food or change.

A snowy day

- Melting and solidifying can be explored most easily when icicles and snow are around so the experience and the language arise naturally. Problems like 'How can we keep our icicle?' can be posed.

Key Stage 1

- Snow can be collected and a simple pictorial record made as it changes in the warmth of the classroom.

From the freezer

- Children can compare the behaviour of solid and liquid water whatever the weather if you can make ice. Different sizes and shapes of ice can be made in the fridge – if necessary a cold-bag can be used to bring them to the class. Large blocks of ice can be made by freezing water in a balloon or plastic sandwich box.
  (a) Get the children to look at this before it goes in the freezer.
  (b) They can look at it and feel it at intervals until it is solid.
  (c) They can handle and talk about the block as it melts.
- In the summer ice lollies are the ideal stimulus. Look closely at how they change as they warm up. Make lollies using different juices and mixtures.

Toasting

- Children can make simple observations as bread is toasted.
  (a) They can feel the fresh bread.
  (b) They can compare it with the toast at different stages until it burns.
  (c) They can predict what will happen when margarine and other spreads are put on the toast.
  The children can record the sequence in words or drawings.
- Let the children compare the effects of burning toast to the effect of burning wood.
- List materials that children don't think will be affected by heat.

Baking

- Scones are simple to make.
  (a) Get the children to stir and look at the ingredients.
  (b) Ask the children if they could get the flour and fat back from the scone.
  (c) Talk about what the dough is like before it is cooked.
  (d) Test what some scones are like when they have been cooked for only five minutes.
  (e) What happens to overcooked scones?
- Ask the children to draw the scones at different stages.
- Fold a piece of paper into four and get the children to show in pictures how the scones were made.

Science background

Heating materials changes some of their properties. Substances which are solid at room temperature may be made easier to work by heating. Cooling reverses this change.

A substance can change from a **solid** to a **liquid** if enough heat is supplied. It has to be raised to the temperature at which it melts. Each substance has a characteristic temperature at which this change will occur. When the reverse happens and the liquid is cooled it will solidify (freeze).

Water **freezes** and ice melts at 0 °C so children witness it changing state in the British climate. They need to see other substances melt and solidify and begin to recognise this as a general phenomenon. Cooking provides temperatures at which this can be shown. It also introduces other sorts of changes which cannot be reversed. Toasting initially dries the bread. When bread is burnt it is reduced to carbon. Carbon is also formed by burning wood to get charcoal.

RAW MATERIALS

Activities for children

Distinguishing natural and manufactured materials

- Make collections which include both manufactured and natural objects.
- Encourage children to classify the materials

Table 6 *Materials classified into groups*

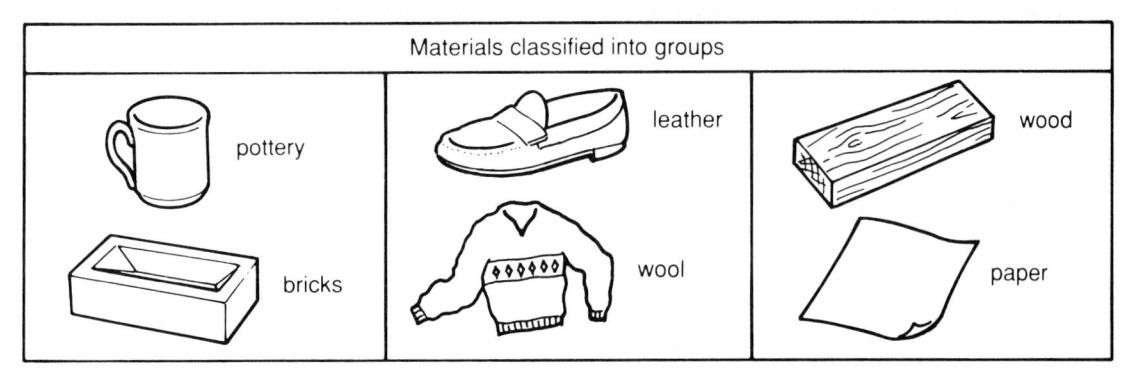

Materials classified into groups		
pottery / bricks	leather / wool	wood / paper

into several groups. They can record their ideas in tables like the one above.

Examples of raw materials

Examine a range of raw materials. These could include some of the following:

Clay is easily processed by the children.

- They can change it into bricks by shaping and drying. Ask the children to say what changes they would expect to see in the process. If you do not have a kiln ask to use that of the local secondary school to fire your bricks.
- Ask children to devise tests for hardness, water absorbency and strength.

Raw wool is obtainable in some areas where it has caught on fences.

- Wash the fleece. What changes are there after you have washed it?
- Can the children form strands from the wool?
- You could introduce simple spinning and knitting. If you know anyone who spins or weaves ask them to demonstrate and to show children different sorts of wool.
- The class could make a display of garments made from various natural and synthetic fibres.

Cement is turned into concrete by mixing it with sand and water.

- Ask the children to design tests to see the effect of mixing sand and cement in different ratios. Cast the different mixes into small containers.
- Ask the children to devise a simple test for the strength of the blocks.
- Get them to plan investigations into the strength of concrete coloured with powder paint.

Science background

Most of the materials children meet will have been physically changed by some treatment or made by some chemical combination of substances (synthesised).

Some of the most important natural materials are extracted from the ground. These include all metals which occur in rocks in the form of ore. Most metals have to be processed to free them from the surrounding rock. A few, gold included, are sometimes found **native**. This means that they are pure in the natural state. Children encounter different metals in everyday objects, eg steel or aluminium in cans.

Cement is made from limestone which is heated and then mixed with clay. When it is mixed with water it forms long strong **crystals** which bind with the sand or pebbles in the **concrete**. If too much sand is mixed with the cement the resulting concrete is weak. Adding coloured powder paint will probably result in a very weak block.

Raw woollen fleece is coated in lanolin which helps it to resist water. So called 'Natural' woollen garments retain some of this oil. The spinning process relies on twisting together short strands of wool which are then held together by the force of friction. The way in which garments are made can be seen under a microscope. Weaving produces strong but relatively inflexible cloth. Wool is most often knitted. The resulting pattern of strands produces fabric with a great deal of flexibility.

Clay is the basis of pottery and bricks. It is heated in large ovens called kilns to above 600 °C where the clay partially melts. Domestic ovens are incapable of reaching such high temperatures.

Wood is the basis of most papers although rags and other vegetable matter can be used. The wood is pulped and then mixed with large quantities of water. Chemicals are added to break down the cellulose in the wood fibres.

Oil is the raw material used to produce the majority of plastics.

SOIL

Activities for children

Look at soil

NB Take care that the children wear gloves or wash their hands after handling the soil.

- Use a small trowel to collect a small plastic bag of soil. Spread it out on a plastic sheet.
  (a) What can the children find in the soil?
  (b) What animals and plant materials can they see?

  Draw small pictures of any individual items of interest.

- Allow small samples to dry out and then spread them very thinly on white paper. Rub it with your fingers and look at them using a strong magnifying glass or microscope.
  (a) What shape are the larger pieces of stone?
  (b) Can you see any strands of plant remains?

Compare different soils

- Collect small samples of soil from different places, eg from a flower bed, from under a hedge, from waste ground or from a marshy place. Ask the children to suggest ways to compare them.
  (a) Are the samples all the same colour?
  (b) Do they all feel the same when you rub them?
  (c) Do they all have the same amount of water in them? How could you find out?

Grain size

- Investigate whether all the soil samples have the same amount of gritty and fine pieces using either
  (a) a graded set of sieves, or
  (b) a jam jar half filled with water. Add two spoons of soil. Shake. Allow to settle. Draw the resulting layers.

Topsoil and subsoil

- Take a sample from the top layer of soil. Carefully remove and set aside any large plants. Dig a neat hole down as far as you are able and look at the layers of soil. Take a sample from the bottom of the hole. Make comparisons between the two samples of soil.

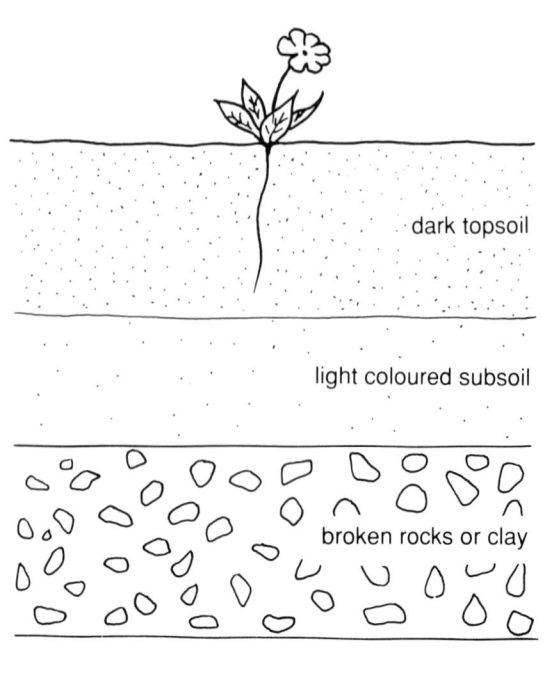

Fig. 32 *Cross-section through soil*

Soil development

- Look at walls where lichens or green algae grow. Are they growing in soil?
- Look at the mosses on the walls. They need a tiny amount of soil in which to grow.
- Look at places where dust collects near the base of walls in particular. Do any plants grow there?

Making soil

- Challenge the children to make a variety of soils and to test them. Give them pieces of soft rock such as soft sandstone if you can find it (gritty sand if you cannot) and peat or garden compost.

Science background

Soil supports growing plants. It holds the water they need and supplies the minerals that are essential for growth. It is *not* the source of plant food. The only source of food is sunlight.

Soil is made from ground up pieces of rock mixed with plant remains. The type of soil in your locality will depend principally on the underlying rock type, the amount of rainfall and the vegetation. Soils from different locations will show considerable variation in the proportion of large gritty pieces and fine clay particles. These variations are shown up in the test where the soil is mixed with water and allowed to settle. The largest particles fall through the water most rapidly and form the bottom layer. The very fine clay particles sink very slowly and form the top layer. The stuff floating on the surface of the water is plant remains which form the **humus** in the soil.

Worms play a large part in creating the characteristic **soil profile** as they ingest small grains of soil and bring them to the surface in worm casts.

In a town you are unlikely to find lichen growing on the walls. Instead look for the green algae which is a microscopic plant and looks like a green stain on the walls. Algae and lichens can grow directly on rocks without any soil. Moss can grow in the soil created by the decayed lichen and algae mixed with the brick or stone particles worn from the wall. Lichens were probably the first land plants on Earth and began the process of soil creation. They get their minerals from the air and the rock on which they are growing.

Key stage 2

Main scientific idea	Page title	Page
Comparing the properties of materials	Solubility	65
Weight, mass and density	Weight and volume	65
Comparing properties of materials	Strength of materials	66
The properties and uses of materials	Using materials	67
Changes of state	Solid/liquid/gas	70
Ice, water and steam	Water, ice and steam	70
The properties of gases	Gases	71
Oxygen combines with materials when they burn. Iron combines with oxygen in rusting	Breathing and burning	73
Acid, alkaline or neutral	Acids and alkalis	74
Separating and purifying mixtures	Mixtures	75
Many raw materials are dug out of the ground	Using the land	75
Rocks can be sorted and grouped	Rocks	76
Air is all around us. Wind and rain can be measured	Air, wind and rain	77
Sensing devices detect changes in the environment	Sensing the environment	78
When water evaporates it forms water vapour. Water condenses to form droplets of liquid water. It forms clouds which fall as rain	The water cycle	79
Landscapes are the result of complex processes over a long period of time	Landforms	81
Earthquakes and volcanoes result in characteristic landforms	Volcanoes and earthquakes	82

Key Stage 2

The programme of study

This states that pupils should be taught:

- to compare everyday materials including hardness, strength, flexibility and magnetic behaviour, and to relate these properties to everyday uses of the materials;
- that some materials are better thermal insulators than others;
- that some materials are better electrical conductors than others;
- to describe and group rocks and soils on the basis of characteristics, including appearance, texture and permeability;
- to recognise differences between solids, liquids and gases, in terms of ease of flow and maintenance of shape and volume;
- that mixing materials can cause them to change;
- that heating or cooling materials can cause them to change, and that temperature is a measure of how hot or cold they are;
- that some changes can be reversed and some cannot;
- that dissolving, melting, boiling, condensing, freezing and evaporating are changes that can be reversed;
- about the water cycle and the part played by evaporation and condensation;
- that the changes which occur when most materials are burned are not reversible;
- that solid particles of different sizes, eg those in soils, can be separated by sieving;
- that some solids dissolve in water to give solutions but some do not;
- that insoluble solids can be separated from liquids by filtering;
- that solids which have dissolved can be recovered by evaporating the liquid from the solution;
- that there is a limit to the mass of solid that can dissolve in a given amount of water, and that this limit is different for different solids.

Teaching and learning about materials

This area of work affords many possibilites for open-ended investigations at the appropriate levels. For example:

- Children can be involved in planning fair tests, such as deciding which wood makes the best chopping board, or which is the best soap powder.
- They can plan investigations where the relevant variable is identified, such as the width of paper samples in strength tests.
- They can plan investigations which involve a range of variables, such as: those which influence the rate of carbon dioxide formation by yeast, or the factors which influence the strength of paper (thickness, type, width, wetness, for instance).
- The idea that all matter is made from particles is a powerful tool to help explain the behaviour and properties of materials. However, at this stage most children are likely to think of these particles as pieces of the substance which are too small to see. More sophisticated ideas about molecules and atoms are unlikely to be useful at this stage.

Weather and atmosphere

Although not specifically included in the science programmes (1995) investigations of the weather can develop pupils' skills of observation and measurement as they make increasingly accurate, quantitative observations of wind, rain and temperature. They can begin to see patterns in their results and interpret other data. There are opportunities for them to use records from secondary sources, the media and weather stations. Information technology can be used to capture and handle data.

Our daily weather changes can to some extent mask the underlying climate. Children's studies of the local weather conditions should introduce them to the link between the climate and the Earth's atmosphere. They can begin to see how important the climate is for human activities and how it may change as a result of human activity across the globe.

Rocks and soil

The processes which result in the formation of rocks and soil operate on such a long time scale that many adults, let alone children, have difficulty in comprehending them. The enormous forces involved in earthquakes and volcanoes are staggering and dwarf even the destructive power of nuclear weapons.

This area of work can present challenges to teachers concerned to develop an active scientific approach. However, few children are not fascinated by crystals, fossils, minerals and unusual rocks. A jar of soil contains a microcosm of animals, plant remains and pieces of rock which reveal the way it was made. The differences in soils from place to place are considerable and have a major impact on the plants and animals which can live there. Observation of rocks and soils can be a starting point for questions and investigations by pupils. They can progress from simple comparison of hardness of rock sample to more advanced controlled investigation of properties of different soils involving a range of variables.

Cross-curricular links

The properties and behaviour of materials can be investigated in the course of many cross-curricular topics such as: *Changes, Hot and cold, Forces, Detectives, Water, Paper, Food,* and *Kitchens*.

Topics in which the Earth and environment can be studied include: *Rocks, Water, Underground, Air, Mining, Farming, Time*. The most obvious links are with physical geography and geographical skills. Scientific and geographical work on the physical environment will be part of the wider environmental education of pupils. Activities may be part of a long-term monitoring of weather, or arise from local studies, fieldwork during visits, comparison with other places, issues and events of topical concern.

Resources

Collections of rocks may be borrowed from local museum services or bought from suppliers such as NES Arnold. Trowels and containers will be needed if soil samples are to be collected. Sieves and a selection of gravels, sands and composts will be useful. Many of the resources for studying soils can be acquired with little cost.

Simple measuring equipment can be made for recording the weather. Scientific skills and technological capability can be extended as anemometers or rain gauges are developed by pupils. Equipment can be bought to make more accurate measurements and full weather stations are offered in catalogues. Many schools create their own and make use of visits to introduce children to more sophisticated ones. Sensors with accompanying software are becoming available from suppliers such as Philip Harris. These will allow pupils to log environmental features such as temperature.

At key stage 2 children will need strong ($\times 8$) hand lenses and microscopes which magnify up to $\times 20$. They will need access to a range of measuring devices such as spring balances, simple top pan balances, scales, calibrated beakers and a range of standard masses. Weight carriers are useful but a simple homemade version is shown in this chapter. Indicator papers for testing acidity and alkalinity should be available. Homemade indicator paper can be made by dipping blotting paper in red cabbage water and leaving to dry. The most important resource is a good variety of materials for investigations. These need to be stored so they are easily available and there should be a system to ensure they are returned or replenished. A range of simple kitchen chemicals is useful. A freezer is needed to produce ice but this can be brought in a non-glass thermos flask. (Chunks of ice may shatter glass ones.)

SOLUBILITY

Activities for children

Which things dissolve?

- Set out a range of substances such as flour, sugar, salt, sand, coffee, baking powder, tea and sodium bicarbonate. (A spoon or lolly stick in each container will prevent contamination.) Then ask the children which substances they think will dissolve in water. Test each substance in turn and record on a simple chart.

How much will dissolve?

- Challenge the children to find out how much salt can be dissolved in a measured amount of cold water. You might use level measures of a 5 ml medicine spoon to measure out the salt. Ask to see the plans for their investigation before they begin.
- Try to find out if 400 ml of water dissolves twice as much salt as 200 ml of water?
- Allow some salt solution to evaporate slowly and examine the resulting crystals using lenses and microscopes. Do the same using alum.

Dissolving in cold and warm water

- Ask the children to plan investigations as to whether warm water from the tap will dissolve more or less salt than cold water.

Science background

In a **solution** the solute (usually a solid) is broken down into tiny particles (**molecules** or **atoms**). These particles are spread evenly throughout the solution. The atoms and molecules are so small that they will go through the finest filters.

Common salt is made up from atoms of sodium and chlorine. These atoms are broken apart when the salt is dissolved. The atoms are spread evenly throughout the liquid. A dissolved solid will not sink to the bottom.

Children often confuse **suspensions** with solutions. In a suspension the solid is broken up into pieces which are still visible to the naked eye. They cloud the liquid and will eventually settle at the bottom. Suspended solids can be filtered out. Flour is an example of a solid which goes into suspension.

When a solution is allowed to evaporate, the dissolved solid will come out of solution. In the case of the salt or alum the atoms form regular shapes called crystals. When evaporation is slow and steady the crystals have time to form and so grow large. If evaporation is rapid the atoms cannot arrange themselves and so only small crystals are formed.

WEIGHT AND VOLUME

Activities for children

Solids

- Weigh a variety of objects using different weighing devices such as scales, spring balances and beam balances.
- Weigh the same object with all the weighing devices you have. Record the different readings on a table. Are all the readings identical? Which device seems to give the most accurate reading?

Volume of irregular shapes

- The volume of irregular shapes can be worked out. Half fill a see-through litre measuring jug with water. Place the object into the water. The amount by which the water in a measuring beaker rises is the volume of the object.

Weight of liquids

- Do all liquids weigh the same? Ask the children to predict if they think they will.
- Make strong solutions of salt water. (Use food colours to help you tell them apart.) Measure equal volumes of brine and fresh water. Weigh them.

Science background

There is a difference between **mass** and **weight**. Mass is the amount of matter in an object and it does not change wherever you take it. Mass is measured in kilograms (kg).

Weight is the effect of the pull of the Earth on a mass. Weight should be measured in **newtons** (N). A newton is a measure of force. Force is best measured using a spring balance which is effectively a forcemeter.

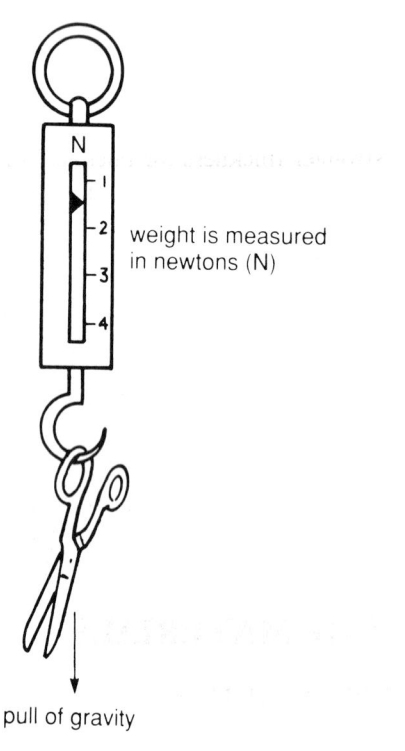

Fig. 33 *Spring balance*

Objects of the same size weigh different amounts if they are made from materials with different densities. **Density** is the mass of one cubic centimetre of a material.

One cubic centimetre of pure water weighs one gram. The density of water is 1 g/cm^3 (grams per cubic centimetre). So 100 cm^3 of pure water weighs 100 g.

When salt or any other solid is dissolved in water it increases the density of the water. The more salt which is dissolved the greater the density becomes.

STRENGTH OF MATERIALS

Activities for children

Strength of hair

- (a) Take strands of hair from willing volunteers. A smart tug should remove one strand at a time quite painlessly. To avoid possible problems with hair pulling, you could carefully collect strands before the work begins. Keep these secure with a bulldog clip. Label the clip with the name of the donor.
- (b) Make a loop of hair on the edge of a table. Secure this with sticky tape.
- (c) Make a weight carrier from a margarine container or yogurt pot. Hang it from the hair using a bent paper clip. Add weights carefully until the hair breaks.

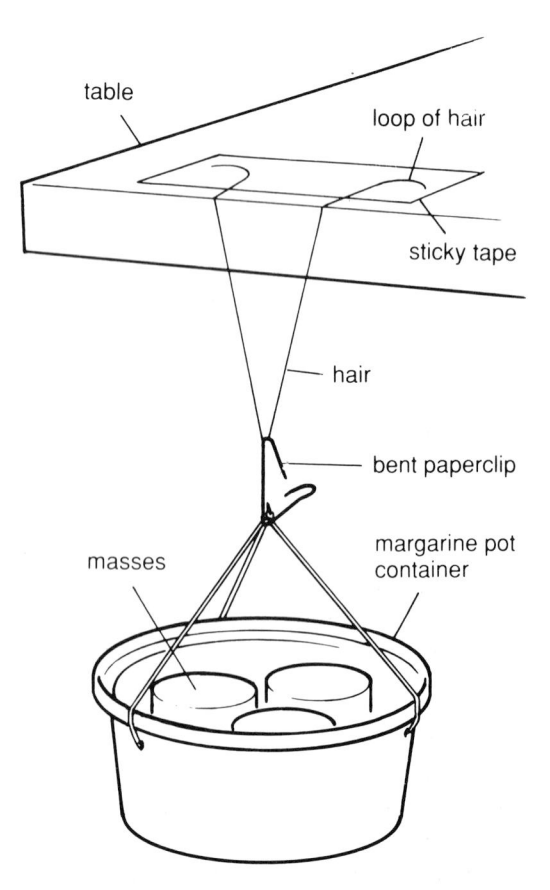

Fig. 34 *Testing the strength of hair*

(d) Encourage the children to do at least three tests on each hair type. They can record the results in a table similar to the one shown below or they can devise their own.

	Hair from (name)	Hair colour	Description of hair	Weight carried
1	Ronald	black	crinkly	40g
2	,,	,,	,,	50g
3	,,	,,	,,	45g

- A similar technique can be used to test the strength of strands of steel wool (obtain this from hardware or decorators' shops) or threads.

Strength of threads

- Considerable weight is needed to snap strands of cotton. Less weight will be needed to snap individual strands of wool when untwisted. Take care to protect floors, desks and toes when testing strong threads.

Strength of newspaper

- Cut strips of newspaper about 3 cm wide. Wrap both ends around pencils and secure them with bulldog clips. Hang a strip from a convenient stand. Hang a margarine pot weight hanger from the lower bulldog clip. Then investigate these variables:
  (a) Does the weight carried depend on the width?
  (b) Do different newspapers use paper of different strength?
  (c) Does the weight carried depend in any way on the direction of the strip torn from the sheet? ie Is newspaper torn from top to bottom as strong as the same paper torn sideways?

Strength of different papers

- Does the weight carried vary with the type of paper? Collect a range of papers such as newspaper, tissue paper, kitchen paper, wrapping paper and writing paper. Ask the children to make their tests fair.

Science background

It is important to do at least three tests where possible to get an average reading. In the case of hair for instance, the strength of the hairs on an individual's head will vary. If your children cannot calculate easily, take the median (middle reading) of the results. For instance if the results for the hair from one person are 50 g, 80 g and 70 g, then 70 g is the median.

Strands of hair are elastic. Watch the way that strands spring back after they are stretched. Hair is made of keratin which is the same fibrous protein from which fingernails and horn is made. Many natural substances are immensely strong. Spiders' webs for instance are a good deal stronger thickness for thickness than steel. You will probably find that on average hair is about as strong as the strands of steel wool you test in the classroom.

The strength of a strip of paper depends on its width. Twice the width gives twice the strength. The strength of a piece of paper is proportional to its width.

The strength of a strip of paper also depends on the orientation of the fibres in the paper. In tissue paper this is seen most clearly. It is very easy to tear in one direction but much more difficult to tear in the direction at right angles.

USING MATERIALS

Activities for children

Plastic for carrier bags

One everyday material which needs to be strong is the plastic of plastic bags.
NB Warn children of the dangers of suffocation if they put plastic bags over their heads.
Obtain plastic carrier bags from a variety of stores.

- Test the strength of a plastic bag by suspending it from a stout piece of wood supported on the backs of chairs. (See overleaf.) The bag should be tested to destruction.
NB A substantial weight is needed so beware toes and polished floors.

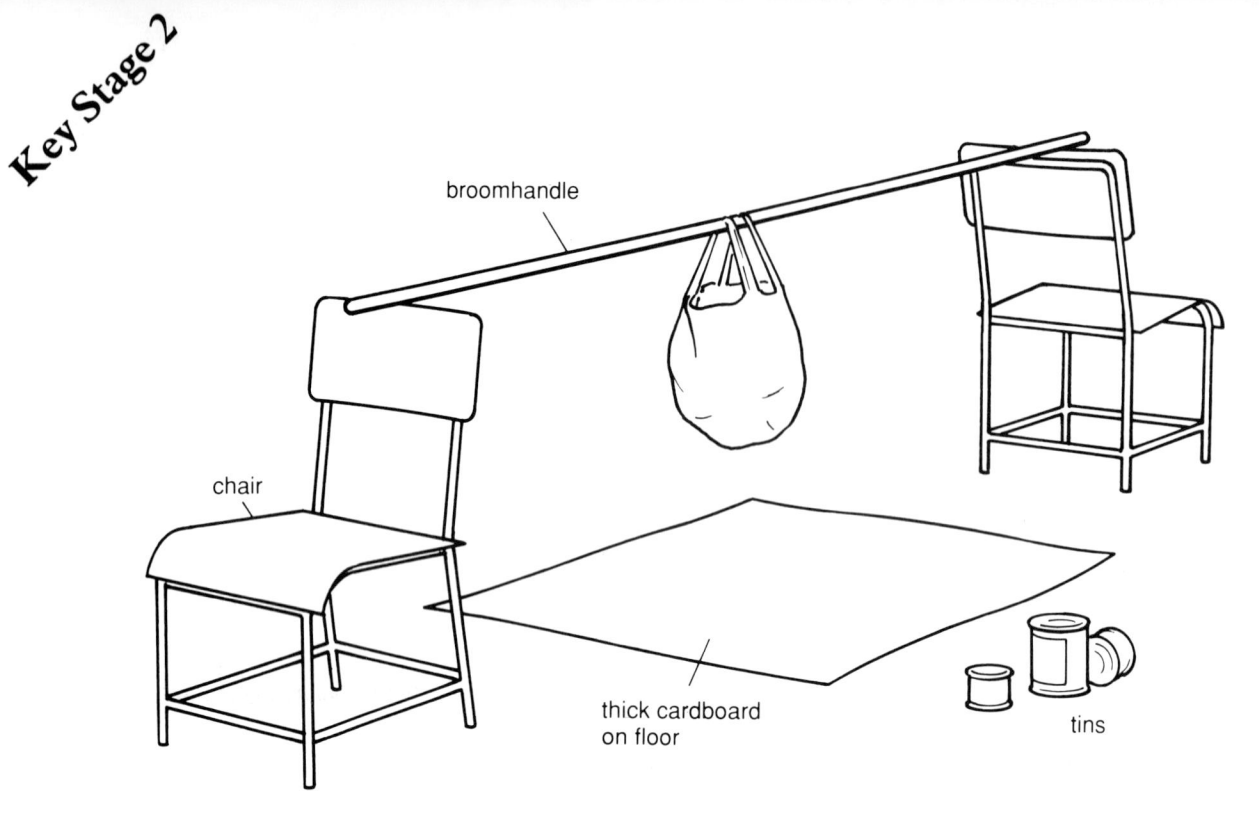

Fig. 35 *Testing the strength of a plastic carrier bag*

A good alternative to testing whole bags is to cut strips from the bag and use the technique for testing paper.

Wood for kitchen chopping boards

- Collect different wood samples eg plywood, pine, chipboard, hardboard, formica covered board.
- Compare the suitability of different materials as kitchen chopping boards.
- Encourage the children to design their own tests.
- Tests for absorbency are helped if food colour is added to the water.

NB One safe way of testing hardness is to drop a dart onto the sample and see how far the point sticks in. Use a cardboard tube to guide the dart. Another way is to scratch each sample 10 times with a sharp point but do not use a sharp knife.

Wallpapers for kitchens

- Collect a wide range of wallpaper samples.
- Ask children to suggest the qualities they would expect from a kitchen wallpaper.
- Encourage them to design their own tests on the papers. They may need substances like jam, oil, and cleaning materials for their tests.
- Record the results using the actual paper samples stuck onto a table.

The best tissue

- Ask children what qualities do they need in tissues? They could investigate:
  (a) Which make of soft tissue is the most absorbent?
  (b) Which is the strongest when wet?

The best soap powder

Which soap powder is most effective for cleaning dirty washing?

- Ask the children to dirty several fabric samples (they will enjoy this). Can they make them all equally dirty?

Table 7 *Results of testing washing powders*

Original sample	Persil	Radion	Daz	Plain water
▨	○	○	○	▨

- Encourage them to devise a fair way of testing the cleaning power of different powders.

Science background

Many of these experiments are based on the idea of consumer tests such as those reported in the magazine *Which?* You might get children to read up some of the more suitable articles and then write their reports in that style.

Carrier bags will generally, but not invariably, break at the handles where there is less plastic. You can feel that the plastic is much more stretched at the handles. There is more stress here because the downwards pull of the shopping is concentrated by the narrow width of the material.

If the bag has been cut this marks the place where the plastic is likely to fail. The deeper and narrower the cut the more it is likely to break at that point. This is the result of the concentration of force at that point.

Modern kitchen worktops are made from a layer of patterned paper sandwiched between a thick wooden base and a clear, tough plastic coating. The most suitable woods for chopping boards are hardwoods with a close grain like beech. Softwoods like pine are generally unsuitable because they absorb water more rapidly than the closer grained woods.

Many wallpapers are misnamed. They are really plastics. A vinyl paper is really a thin layer of plastic glued onto a paper layer. Being plastic it is waterproof so highly suitable in kitchens and bathrooms. Tissues are highly absorbent because of the loose way in which the fibres have been put together. **Capillary action** causes water to be attracted into the tissue. One effect of a soap powder is to break down the surface tension of water. This allows more thorough wetting of the fabric.

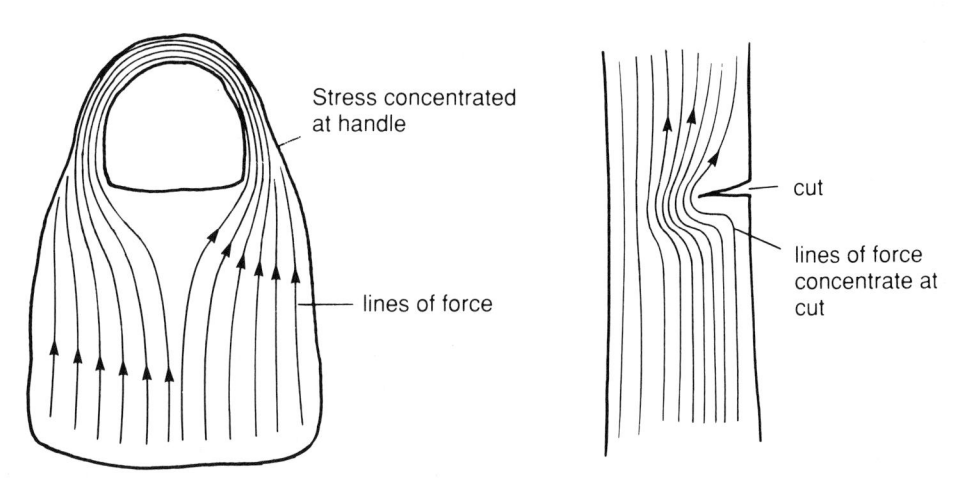

Fig. 36 *Stress within a plastic bag*

Key Stage 2

SOLID/LIQUID/GAS

Activities for children

Observing wax changing

NB Ensure that all spare paper is off the table and tie back all loose clothing and hair.

- Watch a candle burn. Make sure it is in a firm holder – a large piece of modelling clay works well. Place the candle and holder on a sheet of wood or a metal tray.
- Ask the children to draw the candle flame. One effective method is to use pastel crayons on black paper.
- Draw attention to the small pool of liquid wax below the wick. If this liquid wax falls onto a cool surface it freezes to become solid wax again.
- Squeeze and shape cold and warm wax and talk about the differences in pliability.
- Blow out the candle. The wax vapour appears in the form of white 'smoke'. Ask the children what they think the stream of white 'smoke' is.
- Relight the candle. After a few moments blow out the candle again, but this time relight the 'smoke'. The candle will instantly relight.

Solids, liquids and gases

- Ask the children to classify a variety of substances. They might make a table like this. Interesting discussion can arise from considering substances like thick custard or warm chocolate.

Solid	Liquid	Gas
Wax	Melted wax	Wax vapour
Margarine	Melted margarine	
Ice	Water	Water vapour

Science background

Wax is a **hydrocarbon** which burns when it is in **gas** form. Hydrocarbons are chemicals made largely from carbon and hydrogen. Many children will think that it is the wick which burns and that the wax is there to support the wick. The wick provides a large surface area for the heated wax to evaporate from.

Changes of state involve energy. Heat energy is needed for a substance to be changed from solid to liquid and from liquid to gas.

This heat energy is needed to break the bonds between the molecules. Once the bonds have been broken the **molecules** can move more freely.

WATER, ICE AND STEAM

Activities for children

Different states of water

As part of a demonstration, talk with the children about the simple properties of water.

- What is it like as a liquid?
- Contrast it with ice.
- Look at steam from a kettle. (This is a teacher demonstration.)
  (a) What happens to the water?
  (b) Can they always see the steam or does it seem to disappear?
  (c) What do they think happens to the steam eventually?

Evaporation

- Ask the children to find out which puddle in the playground dries up first? What do they think happens to the water?
- Set out saucers of water. Ask the children to place them in different positions in the classroom. Which dries up first?
- Ask the children to devise fair tests for drying pieces of cloth. How can they speed up and slow down evaporation?

Science background

Molecules are tiny particles of matter. Each molecule of water is made up of one atom of oxygen and two of hydrogen.

The molecules in ice are bound very tightly together and stay in the same position relative to each other. In its liquid state the molecules which make up water are bound loosely. Individual molecules can move freely around within the container. This gives water its ability to cover surfaces. The molecules of water in vapour form are not bound to each other. They are free to move and will take up any available space. Water vapour is invisible. It is present in air most of the time. The steam we see is condensed water vapour.

- **Condensation** is the change from a gas to a liquid (at 100 °C in water).
- **Freezing** is the change of state from a liquid to a solid (at 0 °C).
- **Evaporation** is the change from a liquid to a gas at boiling point (100 °C).

Evaporation of liquid water is affected by three factors: temperature, air movement and the amount of water vapour in the air. Evaporation takes place most readily in dry moving air at high temperatures. If the air is humid (wet), cold and still, evaporation will take place very slowly.

Warm air can hold more water vapour than cold air. The air next to the cold surface such as a window becomes cool. It is less able to hold water vapour than the warm air away from the surface. The excess water is deposited on the window as condensation. The 'ghosts' we make with our breath in winter are the result of the warm wet air from our lungs becoming cooled rapidly when it comes into contact with the cold air.

GASES

Activities for children

Investigations and discussions on gases could arise in various ways:

- They could be planned as part of a topic on air or a health project on breathing and lungs.
- Children might have observed phenomena out of school that they want explaining. For instance they may have seen hot air balloons.

What are pupils' ideas about gases?

- Ask your children to make word lists or flowcharts to indicate what they associate with 'gas' or 'air'.
- Ask them to draw pictures and posters where gases are involved, eg breathing in space or under water, bubbles in drinks, poison gases and pollution, evaporation and condensation.

Carbon dioxide

- Investigate the action of yeast. Add some warm water and sugar to fresh yeast. (NB Some dried yeasts do not work in these conditions – check packet.) Watch the bubbles produced and collect them in a balloon over the neck of the container.
- Investigate the effect of adding vinegar to sodium bicarbonate or baking powder.
- See what happens to the flame of a short candle in the jar with the sodium bicarbonate and vinegar.
- Arrange a visit to a fire station and a demonstration of fire extinguishers.

What's burning?

Set up a candle so two pupils can watch it safely.

- Cover the candle with a jar and watch it extinguish.
- Try putting the same jar over another candle immediately. What happens?
- Now refill the jar with fresh air. What happens when you place this over a burning candle?

Balloons

Provide some identical balloons for pupils to blow up.

- Ask them what is inside an empty and an inflated balloon. Let them find ways of showing their answers – for instance by releasing air into water.

- Ask them which they think is heavier – an empty or a full balloon.
- Challenge them to devise ways of testing their answers. They could use a balance or sensitive scales or simply hang two inflated balloons on either end of a cane and then pop one of them.
- Make a similar balance with two empty balloons. Blow one up and return it to the balance.

Science background

The ideas previously introduced in Solid/liquid/gas are important precursors to these activities. Gas molecules are free to move around and take up as much space as is available. These molecules are widely spaced in comparison with those of liquids or solids but nonetheless they do have mass.

Very light gases

Some gases are heavier than others. Hydrogen is the lightest gas but it is also very flammable. It was the gas used to fill airships. After disasters such as the R101 and the *Hindenberg* in the 1930s hydrogen was thought to be far too hazardous. Helium is the next lightest gas and is now used to fill airships. Helium is inert and will not burn.

Hot air balloons

Hot air balloons float because hot air is less dense than cold air. It is less dense because hot air expands and the same number of molecules take up more space. This means that there are fewer molecules inside the hot balloon. Fewer molecules means less weight.

Hot air balloons and helium balloons both float in air because they displace air. The displaced air is heavier than the combined weight of the balloon and the hot air or helium. Airships float in air for just the same reasons that ships float on water.

Natural gas

This is the gas we burn at home. It is mainly methane. Air is a mixture of gases. The main ones are:

- *Nitrogen* (78%) – which is part of all living things.
- *Oxygen* (21%) – essential for all respiration in both plants and animals. Plants produce this gas in large quantities during photosynthesis.
- *Carbon dioxide* (less than 1%) is the product of respiration, it is an essential component for plants to produce sugars in their leaves during photosynthesis. It is used to make drinks fizzy. It is produced when anything is burnt and is thought to contribute to **global warming** as it helps to hold the Sun's heat near the Earth.

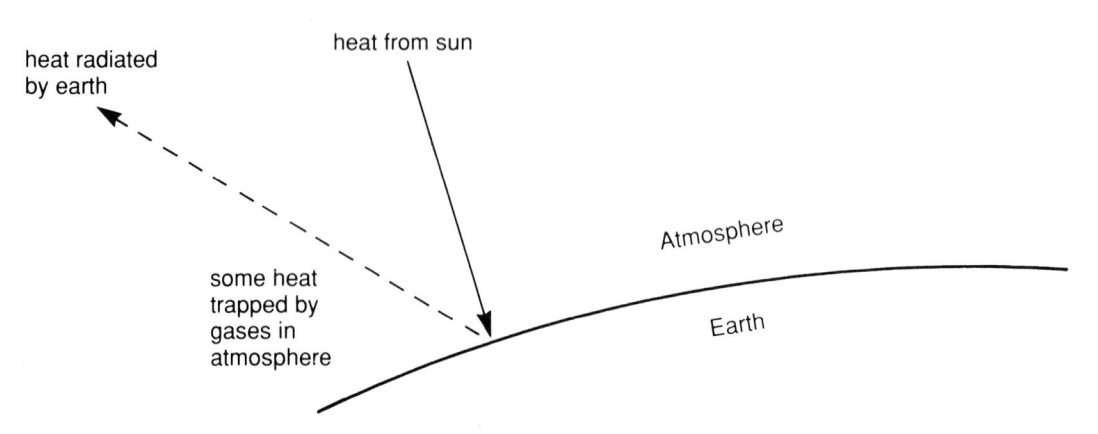

Fig. 37 *Earth showing radiation of heat*

BREATHING AND BURNING

Activities for children

NB Extra care is needed where investigations involve flames.

Candle in a jar

- (a) Ask the children to predict which candle will burn longest.
  (b) What reasons do they give?
  (c) Ask how the test can be made fair.
  (d) Use a table to record the results.

Jar	Length of burning time
a	
b	
c	

- Do the experiment again to check your results.
  (a) What happens if you do not allow fresh air into the jar?
  (b) What reasons do the children give?
- Investigate the effect of using a candle with a bigger flame.
- Ask the children to devise an investigation which tests if a candle burns for as long in air which they breathe out.

We use air

- Count the number of breaths taken in one minute when
  (a) sitting
  (b) running
  (c) jumping on the spot.
- Work out the average for a group of children.

Plants use air

- Sprout some bean seeds (such as mung beans) in a sealed jar. When the seeds have sprouted remove the lid and quickly put a lighted splint into the jar. What happens to the flame?
- Does the same thing happen when you put it into a similar jar without sprouting beans?

Rusting

- Ask the children to devise tests to find out what causes iron to rust.
  (a) Ask them to show you their plans.
  (b) Compile a list of ideas.
  (c) Set up the experiments and record the progress of the iron. (Nails are easiest to obtain.)
- Wet some steel wool and push it into a tall jar. Put the jar in a dish of water. What do the children predict will happen? What does the steel use when it turns into rust?
- Record using word equations such as:

  Iron + water + air = rust

Burning

- Place a candle in a holder on a piece of wood. Make small spoons from pieces of aluminium foil. Hold the foil in spring pegs. Place a very small piece of food on the foil spoon. Then record the changes in the appearance of the food
  (a) before heating
  (b) as it begins to change
  (b) once all changes have finished.

Science background

Combustion takes place when a substance combines with **oxygen**. This can take place rapidly as in **burning** or slowly as in **respiration**. Combustion releases energy stored in fuels. It produces waste products such as gases which go into the atmosphere.

Large candle flames combine wax with oxygen more rapidly than do small ones. Large flames use oxygen more rapidly and are hotter. When people exercise we combine products from food with oxygen more rapidly than when we are sitting. This leads to a higher breathing rate and warmth generated by exercise.

Rusting occurs where iron combines with oxygen. Rusting can be prevented by preventing air from coming into contact with the iron. This can be done by painting or coating with a metal which will not react with oxygen so easily.

- The chemical symbol for iron is Fe.
- The chemical symbol for water is H_2O.
- The chemical symbol for rust (hydrated iron oxide) is $Fe_2O_3H_2O$.

ACIDS AND ALKALIS

Activities for children

SAFETY FIRST – Pupils need to realise that strong acids or alkalis are dangerous and to be aware of their corrosive effects. Teachers need to distinguish weak from strong acids/alkalis and ensure their pupils work safely. Children should not work with any suspect cleaning fluids such as bleach.

Cabbage colour

NB Teachers only.

- Cut some red cabbage finely and boil it in water for 5 to 10 minutes. Stir and squash it and drain the liquid when cool. Dilute it with more water. Put a little of the red cabbage water in clear glass or plastic containers. Add a few drops of kitchen substances such as lemon juice, white vinegar, fruit juice, washing powders, tea, cola, sodium bicarbonate, baking powder and cream of tartar to separate containers. The acidic substances will change the cabbage water from purple to red. The alkalis will change the water to a bluish colour.

Other dyes

Similar dyes can be made from other food.

- Try blackberries, blackcurrants, carrots, and beetroot.
- Test drops of them in vinegar (acid) and a solution of baking powder (alkali).

Litmus and universal indicator paper

- Pupils can use litmus paper to investigate a range of liquids. Litmus is made from a lichen. There is a red litmus paper and blue litmus paper. The blue goes red in acids. The red variety goes blue in alkalis. Universal indicator paper gives a better range of results.

Science background

An **indicator** is a dye which changes colour in the presence of acids or alkalis.

Water is composed of molecules made from two atoms of hydrogen and one of oxygen. The molecules are sometimes broken down to form hydrogen ions (one hydrogen) and hydroxide ions (one oxygen and one hydrogen).

All acids when dissolved in water form **hydrogen ions**. It is the hydrogen ions which make the indicators turn colour. All alkalis when dissolved in water form **hydroxide ions**. These ions make the indicators show the alkali colours.

The pH scale

Where there are many hydrogen ions the substance has a low pH and is acid. Where the substance has produced many hydroxide ions it has a high pH and is alkali. Both extremes of pH are corrosive.

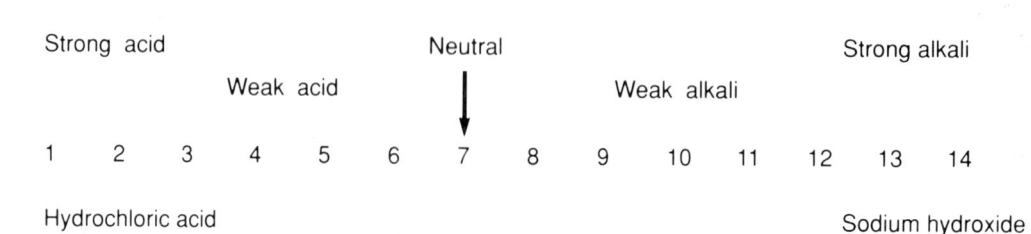

Strong acid | | | | Neutral | | | Strong alkali
Weak acid | | | | | Weak alkali
1 2 3 4 5 6 7 8 9 10 11 12 13 14
Hydrochloric acid | | | | | | Sodium hydroxide

Fig. 38 *The pH scale*

Key Stage 2

MIXTURES

Activities for children

Sieving

- Mix together dried foods such as peas and lentils. Ask the children how the two foods might be separated.
- Some children might suggest using a sieve. They could use bought sieves or make their own from foil dishes or pieces of aluminium foil. Provide suitable tools to make holes of various diameters. Sharp pencils are good because you can vary the diameter of the hole depending on how far the pencil is pushed in.
- Sieve soil using a garden sieve and then display the different grades of soil.

Floaters and sinkers

- Make simple mixtures which cannot be sieved. Ensure one of the solids will float and one will sink. You might use:
  (a) beans and pieces of wax candle
  (b) shavings from a crayon
  (c) paperclips and matchsticks
  (d) pieces of apple and pieces of thin apple peel.

  Ask the children to separate them using water.

Dissolving and filtering

- Obtain some grit salt from the caretaker. Mix in a little extra sand. (NB Don't let the children taste the mixture.) Set out lenses, water, jars and spoons. Add small staples to stimulate magnetic separation of the mixture. The children could record their process using a series of cartoons.

Separating colours

- Put a brown smartie or a blob of ink from a water soluble pen in the middle of a piece of absorbent paper. Carefully place a few drops of water from a pipette onto the sweet or ink blob.

Science background

The only materials which are attracted to magnets are iron, steel, nickel and cobalt. Magnetic separation of a mixture of domestic rubbish is reputed to recover over 90% of steel cans.

Colour separation is known as **chromatography**. The ink of dark felt tip pens and that of food colours is a mixture of pigments. Each pigment moves through the blotting paper at a different rate. Some travel more easily than others and they form the outer ring of colour. You can see the same effect with stains on table cloths for instance where the stain moves out to the edge of the wet area.

USING THE LAND

Activities for children

Building suppliers

- During a quiet period a building supply company might allow you to take the children around the yard to look at the range of materials which are sold.
  NB Only take small very closely supervised groups. A large DIY superstore may be more convenient.
- Talk about the origin of the sand, cement, bricks, plaster, tiles, lavatory bowls, pipes, wire and paint found there.
- Make a collection of different kinds of bricks and walling blocks. What tests can the children devise to investigate the properties of the different materials?
- Collect and display different grades of sand and aggregates. Look at them through a strong lens or microscope. What shape are the grains in the coarser sands and gravels?

Plant nurseries

- Visit a plant nursery to determine what growing mediums plant growers use? Notice that some now use peat-free composts. Ask the children where peat comes from and what are the problems with its continued use.

75

Key Stage 2

- Look closely at peat and peat based composts using a magnifying glass or microscope.
- Sieve the composts. Mix some in water to see the different elements of the compost.
- Examine alternative composts and, in particular, examine Cococompost and vermiculite. Do you have a source of garden compost you could look at?
- Ask the children to design fair tests for the different composts by growing quick growing seeds such as marigolds in them.
- Look at biodegradeable plant pots and test them to see which are most effective. Make your own from paper and newspaper. Which are best?

The impact of farming and housing

- Obtain old maps showing the area near the school. Local museums will help you to locate them. Try to get a sequence showing the area 150, 100 years ago and more recently. Ask the children:
  (a) What changes in the amount of housing can they detect?
  (b) What has been responsible for these changes?
- Try to obtain small scale maps 1 : 25000 ($2\frac{1}{2}''$ to 1 mile) or 1 : 10000 (6″ to 1 mile) of an agricultural area close to the school. Are all the boundaries shown there still intact? If not, what do the children think might have been responsible for their removal? The planning department of the local council might have aerial photographs of the area showing individual trees and hedges which have been removed.

Roads

- Look at old and new maps of your area to find new roads. Look at the amount of land which has been taken up. Have any buildings been demolished to make way for the new roads?

Science background

All building materials except for wood have been extracted from the ground. They include quarried building stone and slate. Roof tiles and bricks are made from fired clay. Cement is made from limestone and clay. Paving slabs and building blocks are usually made from cement, gravel and sand. Plaster is made from gypsum which is quarried largely in the north east of England. Plastics for pipes and wire sheathing is made from oil. Sands and gravels are rarely obtained from beaches as children often think; they are more often the result of river deposits in the fairly recent past.

Peat is formed where vegetation, usually upland mosses or sedges and grasses, accumulates in water-sodden layers. It is only partially decayed and is valued by gardeners as a source of humus. Peat bogs are often valuable wildlife areas. Peat producers argue that it is being created as fast as it is being used. Naturalists argue that some peat bogs, in England especially, are not renewing themselves and should be conserved.

Cococompost is the shredded outer husks of coconuts. Vermiculite is a mineral which has been expanded by heating.

ROCKS

Activities for children

Starting points

The starting point for work with rocks could be

- a walk around the streets looking at rocks used in buildings
- a visit to a museum
- rocks brought in by teacher or children following a holiday
- a visit to an old building eg cathedral
- a topic on coal, oil, buildings or road building
- a visit to an upland area or the coast.

Early investigations with rocks

This work requires a good selection of contrasting rock samples.

- Ask each child to take a rock and describe it to the others in the group.

- Put the rocks into two groups for instance – heavy/not heavy, dark/light. How many criteria can they suggest?
- Draw simple Venn diagrams with some rocks in the overlapping set.
- Play 20 questions with the rocks.
- Physically sort the rocks using a branching tree method.
- Use computer software like Branch and Sort or Noticeboard to record and extend this work.
- Put the rocks into order eg from darkest to lightest, roughest to smoothest, shiniest to dullest.
- Look at manufactured 'rocks' like bricks, blocks, tiles and concrete. Compare them with natural rocks.

The hardness of rocks

- Ask the children to use a lens, fingernail, steel screw, a coin and an iron nail to devise their own hardness tests.

Chemical tests

- Use vinegar to test for lime in the rock. If, after some time, you can see tiny bubbles coming off the rock it is likely that the rock contains lime.

The particles of rock

- Look closely at some hand specimens of rock and observe the particles which make up the rock.
  (a) What small structures are detectable?
  (b) Which rocks show crystals which interlock? These are usually igneous rocks.
  (c) Which rocks have particles that can be rubbed off fairly easily? Are any of the grains rounded like small pebbles? These are usually sedimentary rocks.

Science background

The hardness of rocks is assessed on the **Moh's** ten point scale of hardness. Try scratching with the softest material first: a fingernail. This will scratch very soft rocks like talc (point 1) or gypsum (point 2). A nail is next hardest and a steel file or a screw is harder still.

Rock salt (halite) is sodium chloride in which particles of sand are mixed. It was formed by the drying up of inland seas many millions of years ago. Huge deposits are found in Cheshire.

Igneous rocks are formed from the cooling of molten rocks. This allows the crystals to form in angular shapes and to interlock with one another. Igneous rocks hardly ever contain fossils. Examples include:

(a) *Granite* – a coarse grained, very hard, light coloured rock formed when molten rocks cool very slowly at great depths.
(b) *Basalt* – fine grained, hard, dark rock which cooled fairly rapidly after being ejected from a volcano.

Sedimentary rocks are formed when existing rocks, either igneous or sedimentary, are ground into fragments and deposited as new rock layers. Examples of sedimentary rocks include:

(a) *Chalk* – white, soft, formed from the skeletons of billions of organisms. Chalk is one type of limestone.
(b) *Limestone* – hard, often yellowish rock which was formed in seas partly from the shells of sea creatures. Limestone is mainly calcium carbonate which reacts with vinegar to form bubbles of carbon dioxide. This reaction will take some time to see with the very dilute acids available in school.
(c) *Coal* – the remains of plants which lived in swamps over 200 million years ago.

AIR, WIND AND RAIN

Activities for children

Air is all around

- Take a plastic bag. Try to fold it in four. What makes this difficult? What do you have to do to make it easy?
- Make a sheet of paper move by blowing, flapping a magazine or by blowing air from a squeezy bottle at it.

- Put your finger over a bicycle pump or a syringe. What prevents you from pressing the plungers right the way in?

Measuring wind direction

- Make and use a wind sock. This could be a strip of light paper or a balloon on a string.
- Make a wind vane. Make the tail of the arrow larger than the point. Use a compass to mark the points of the compass.

Measuring wind speed

- Make a simple wind speed measuring device with a piece of card.

Measuring rainfall

- Make a simple rain gauge from a pop bottle cut in half. Record and graph the amount of rain you collect each day.

Science background

The air in the folded plastic bag needs to be squeezed out or allowed to escape in some way if the bag is to be folded easily. The air in the syringe can be compressed but only into about a quarter of its original volume.

Wind direction is always the direction from which the wind is blowing. The wind vane arrow always aligns itself so that it offers the least surface area to the wind. The Beaufort scale is used to measure wind speed.

SENSING THE ENVIRONMENT

Activities for children

Visit

- You could visit the local meteorological station or museum and see which instruments were/are used to sense the environment.

Temperature

- Use thermometers to measure the temperature in different places at school. Include types such as simple thermometers, digital strip thermometers, minimum and maximum thermometers, wet and dry thermometers to measure humidity and soil thermometers.

Wind

- Anemometers can be constructed by the children to measure wind speed.
- Make wind vanes to show the direction from which the wind is blowing.

Atmospheric pressure

- Find a barometer and show how atmospheric pressure is measured.

Rainfall

- Make rainfall collectors to measure the amount of precipitation.
- Use a program like *Weather Studies* obtainable from RESOURCE to record the weather data.
- Make a rain detector.

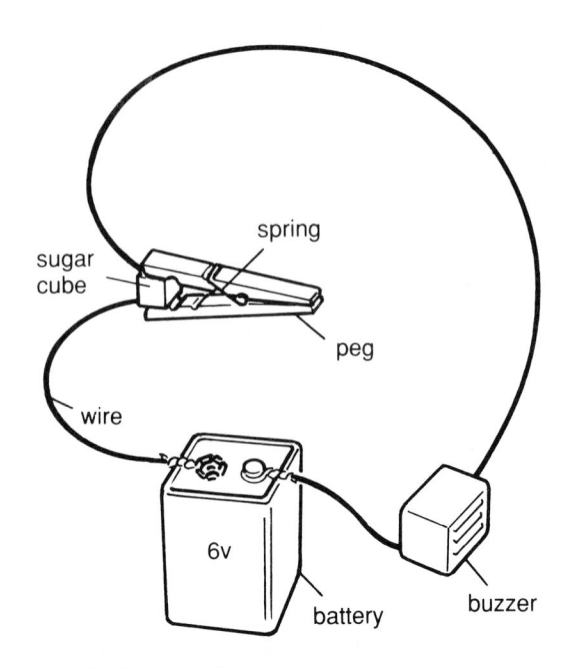

Fig. 39 *Diagram of rain detector*

Detecting light

- Obtain a light dependent resistor (LDR). Wire it into a circuit. The lamp will light when light falls on the LDR. The lamp will go out when the LDR is covered. What uses can the children find for this circuit?

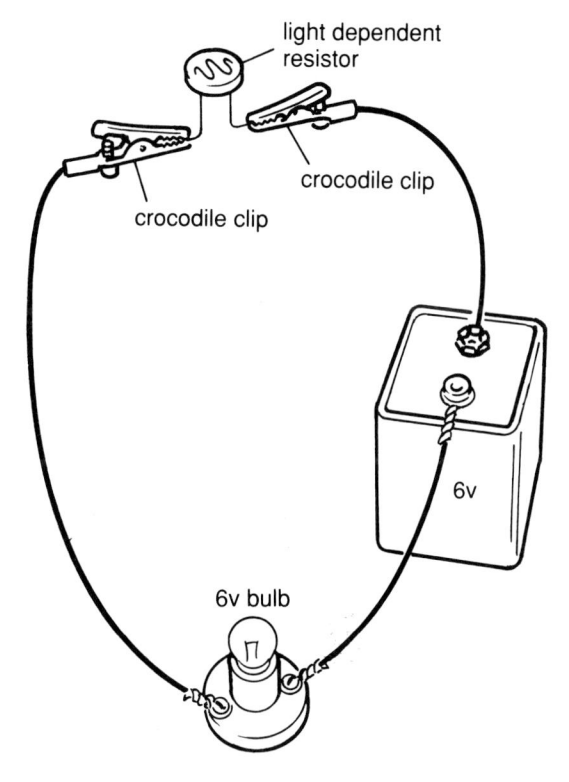

Fig. 40 *Light dependent resistor wired up to battery and lamp*

Using detectors with a computer

- You can use a range of plug-in devices for a computer.

Science background

Some thermometers use the expansion of liquid to measure changes in temperature. Others use electronic devices to do the same job. Particularly useful are the electronic thermometers which have two probes to measure the temperature at two locations simultaneously.

The rain detector relies on the sugar being dissolved by the rain allowing the two wires to meet and complete the circuit.

The resistance to electricity of the light dependent resistor (LDR) depends on the light falling on to it. When there is light the resistance is low and electricity can flow. When it is dark the LDR's resistance to electricity is high. Electronics kits can be bought (eg from Tandy at about £30).

THE WATER CYCLE

Activities for children

Evaporation

- Ask the children what they think will happen to a bowl of water left out in the classroom.
- Ask them to design an experiment to find out:
   (a) in which shape container will water evaporate quickest
   (b) in which place the water will evaporate quickest.

   Make the tests fair.
- Ask the children to list the factors which they think affect the rate of evaporation.

Condensation

- Ask the children what they think causes the water to stream down the insides of windows on cold days. When does the problem seem to be worse?
- Put some ice cubes in a metal container. Add some salt to make the ice go colder. Look at the condensation which forms on the outside of the metal container. Where do the children think it comes from?

In the fridge

- Look in the fridge or freezer.
   (a) What do the children think causes the frost to form?
   (b) What will happen if you get a glass bottle or a tin out of the fridge?
   (c) Will a dish of water evaporate in the fridge?

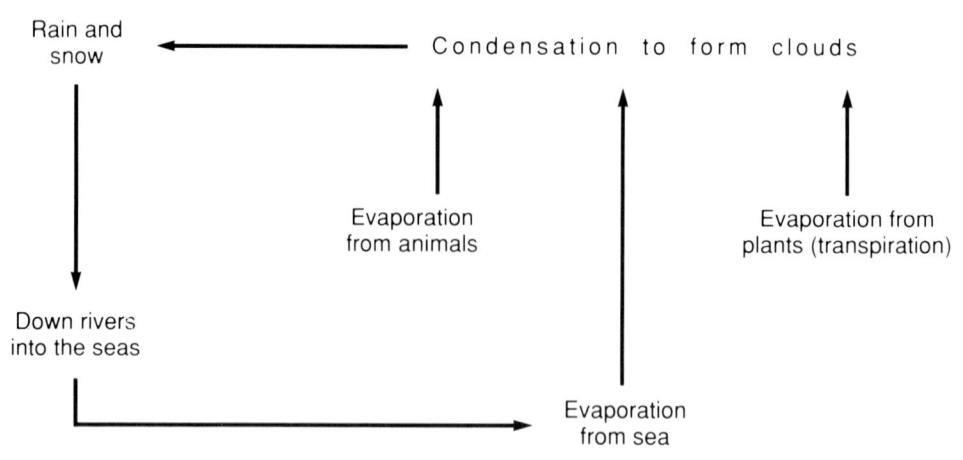

```
                Rain and  ←——————————  Condensation to form clouds
                 snow                           ↑         ↑          ↑
                  │                             │         │          │
                  │                      Evaporation          Evaporation from
                  │                      from animals         plants (transpiration)
                  ↓
             Down rivers
             into the seas
                  │                      Evaporation
                  └─────────────────→    from sea
```

Fig. 41 *Water cycle*

The water cycle

- Make a poster of the diagram above.
- Help the children to relate the large scale ideas which underlie our understanding of how rain occurs to their observations of evaporation and condensation.

Science background

When water **evaporates** the liquid water changes state into an invisible gas called water vapour. The main factors which influence the rate of evaporation are:
(a) the surface area of the the water
(b) the air temperature
(c) the movement of the air
(d) the humidity of the air.

Water vapour can only be seen when it cools sufficiently to **condense** partially into tiny liquid water droplets. It will condense on cold surfaces such as a cold piece of glass or metal.

Clouds, which are masses of partially condensed water vapour, form because the air is cooler at higher altitudes. If these droplets get large enough they will fall as rain.

The atmosphere can include up to 4% water vapour. There is more water vapour in the atmosphere when the air is warm than when it is cold. The amount of water vapour in the atmosphere is measured by **relative humidity**. When the humidity is high, evaporation is slow. When the air is dry and the humidity is low evaporation is very fast.

Table 8 *High and low humidity*

Same temperature	
Low humidity	High humidity
Little water vapour	lots of water vapour
sweat evaporates	no evaporation
cool person	hot sticky person

Frost in a fridge or freezer forms when water vapour in the air comes into contact with very cold surfaces. It then freezes as the temperature is below freezing point.

Water will evaporate very rapidly from food in the dry, cold air of the body of the fridge. It then condenses on the cooling surface of a larder fridge to be drained out and evaporated outside the fridge. In the type of fridge with a built in freezing compartment any water in the air condenses then freezes on the ice compartment.

LANDFORMS

Activities for children

Hills

- Ask the children:
    (a) Where are the hills in your area?
    (b) Which is the highest?
    (c) Do any of them link together to form ridges?
- Look for rock outcrops in your area. Recreation paths are often made with crushed rocks and pebbles found in the locality. In London these are flinty gravel from old river courses.

Valleys

- What do you generally find at the bottom of a valley?
- Follow the rivers of your area on a map.
- Where do all the rivers end up eventually?

Test rocks and make landforms

- Put rock samples of different hardness into a tin. Shake them up with some water.
    (a) Which ones are worn away most quickly?
    (b) How does this relate to the way that hard rocks usually form hills and soft rocks valleys?
- Put soil or coarse sand on a board or in a tray outside. Gently pour on water and examine the resulting landscape.

Visit an upland area

- If it is possible, visit an accessible area like the Peak District where the underlying rocks affect the scenery. Explain the geological history of the area to the children and let them relate this to the scenery.

Science background

All the rocks in the Peak District are of the Carboniferous period. They were laid down just before the coal measures.

Many amenity areas publish simple guides to the geology of the locality.

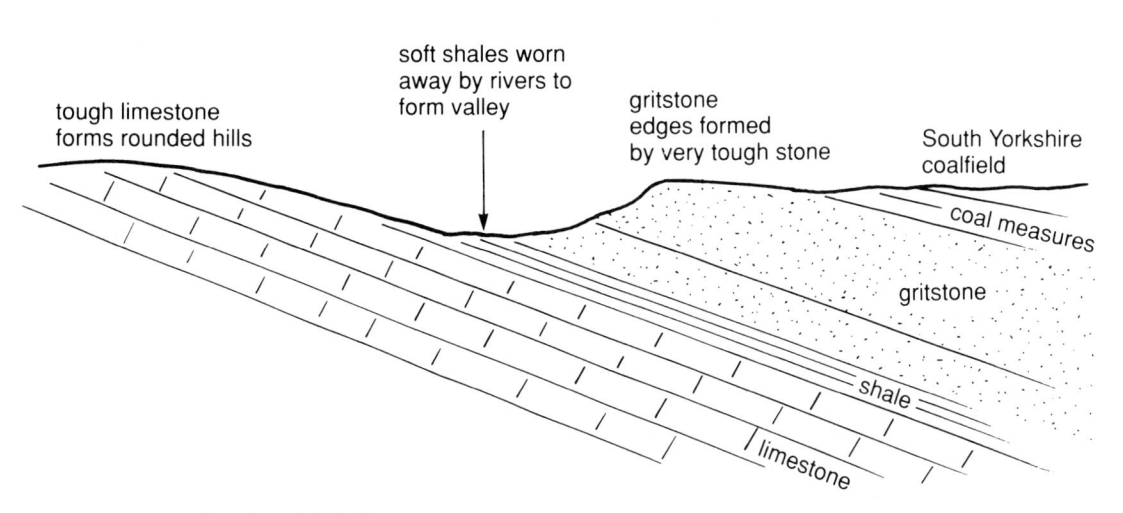

Fig. 42 *Cross-section of Peak District*

Key Stage 2

VOLCANOES AND EARTHQUAKES

Activities for children

Map the volcanoes and earthquakes

- Look at maps of the world which show the positions of earthquakes and volcanoes. These will be seen to be concentrated together around the Pacific rim and the south-east Mediterranean.

Read about eruptions and earthquakes

- Use a variety of secondary sources to find out what happens in an earthquake or volcanic eruption.
- Publish a newspaper which tells the story.

Science background

Earthquakes and volcanoes are concentrated around the edge of the huge **plates** which make up the Earth's crust. These plates are areas of crust which are in constant motion. Where an oceanic plate dips under a continental plate, as in the West Pacific (eg Japan), there are many earthquakes and volcanoes.

Earthquakes occur when one mass of rocks moves relative to another. A crack in the Earth's surface is known as a **fault**. Famous faults include the San Andreas Fault in California. Here the western part of California is moving past the rest of the USA. Where two faults with vertical movement are parallel they form a rift valley. The most spectacular on the planet is the African Rift Valley. This feature is marked by a string of lakes including Lake Nyasa and Lake Tanganyika.

Earthquakes are detected by **seismometers** which give the best evidence about the internal structure of the Earth.

The Earth is made up of layers. The crust and mantle are solid but the core is thought to be liquid.

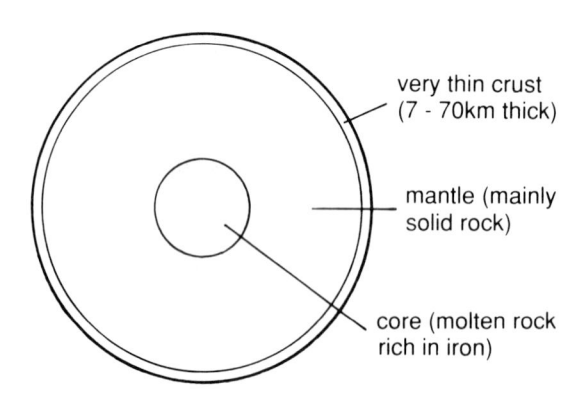

Fig. 44 *Cross-section of Earth*

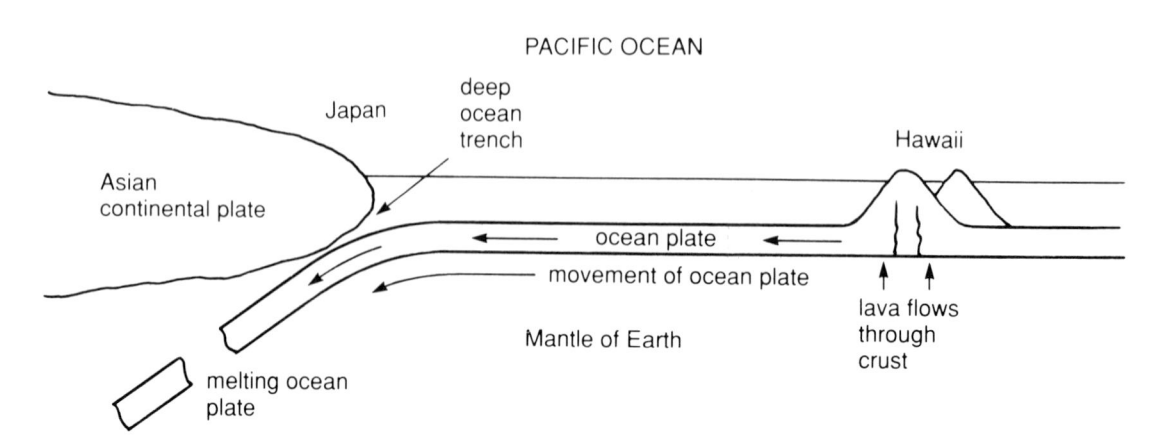

Fig. 43 *Cross-section of sea bed near Japan and Hawaii*

82

It is clear from earthquake waves that the mantle is solid. However, the liquid rock which forms volcanic lava comes from this layer. It is thought that at the very high pressures in the mantle, rocks do not melt completely. However, when there is a release of the pressure the mantle rocks in that area melt and rise up through the crust.

There are many different kinds of volcanoes. Some like those in Iceland and Hawaii pour out liquid basalts while others like Mount St Helens produce huge amounts of ash.

AT 4 Physical processes

Key stage 1

Main scientific idea	Page title	Page
Pushing and pulling can change movements	Pushes and pulls	87
Changes in shape or movement are produced by forces	Forces	88
Factors in floating and sinking	Floating	90
Moving models and toys needs energy	Moving	91
Electricity has many uses in the home. Electricity can be dangerous. Simple electrical circuits can be made with bulbs and batteries. Some materials conduct electricity	Electricity in the home and simple circuits	92
Some materials are attracted by magnets. Magnets repel and attract each other.	Magnets	93
Sound can be made in many ways. Musical instruments produce sound	Making sounds	94
Sound echoes. It can travel through many materials	Sound travels and echoes	95
Sound is made by vibrations	Vibrations	96
Light comes from different sources	Light sources	98
We can distinguish different colours	Colours	98
Light passes through some materials and not others. Some materials absorb light and form shadows	Shadows	99
Light reflects off shiny surfaces	Reflections	100
People are affected by the weather and changes in the weather can be recorded	Weather, seasons and people	100
Temperature is a measure of how hot things are	Hot and cold	102
There are many seasonal changes	The Seasons	103
The Sun appears to move across the sky	The Sun's position	103
The Earth is a sphere in space	Our home planet	104
Why night and day occur	Night and day	105

The programme of study

This states that pupils should be taught:

Electricity

- that many everyday appliances use electricity to construct simple circuits involving batteries, wires, bulbs and buzzers;
- that electrical devices will not work if there is a break in the circuit;

Forces and motion

- to describe the movement of familiar things changing direction;
- that both pushes and pulls are examples of forces;
- that forces can make things speed up, slow down or change direction;
- that forces can change the shapes of objects;

Light and sound

- that light comes from a variety of sources, including the Sun;
- that darkness is the absence of light;
- that there are many kinds of sound and many sources of sound;
- that sounds travel away from sources, getting fainter as they do so;
- that sounds are heard when they enter the ear.

Teaching and learning about physical processes

This attainment target deals with scientific ideas that are linked through the overarching concept of energy but they are likely to be seen as separate by pupils in primary schools.

Teaching and learning about forces

Children have lots of experiences about forces from their play and daily activities. They feel pushes and pulls and see the effects. They exert forces on objects to move them or shape them. At this level they are likely to associate forces with human actions. In primary school we provide further experiences and help children make more sense of them as a basis for scientific understanding and for working with forces in the outside world. So we need to select experiences and help pupils consider explanations for them which will build towards a better grasp of the useful general idea of force. We also want to help them apply their understanding so they are safer and more capable of using forces.

Teaching and learning about electricity and magnetism

Children are surrounded by applications of electricity but may take them for granted. They must be reminded of the dangers associated with mains electricity. All their activities should use standard batteries which are safe, even with water around. If they use a limited range of batteries and bulbs as suggested in the activities in this chapter their work is likely to be more successful and less expensive. By exploring, discussing and applying simple circuits in models children can begin to build their understanding of how electricity flows and its effects. Similarly, play with magnets can lead to their use in models or games. Exploration of electrical circuits or magnets provides a good context for fair testing and lead to more systematic planning of investigations later.

Teaching and learning about light and sound

Sound and light can be explored and enjoyed by young pupils. At the lowest level they will be experiencing specific properties which they can later investigate and begin to understand in terms of more general explanations.

The way that sound is produced and travels can be explored by children as they make music and listen to noises in the environment. They can carry out simple investigations comparing the quality and volume of sound.

Our most important light source is the sun. Children should be warned not to look at strong sources such as the sun, to avoid damaging their eyes. Light radiates out from sources and travels in straight lines. Shadows and reflections are good illustrations of how light travels in straight lines. Young children sometimes confuse shadows with reflections. Shadows can be explored through play at a very simple level and later in investigations which extend understanding and develop skills of measurement and interpretation.

Teaching and learning about heat and fuels

Pupils can begin to appreciate the sources of energy as we introduce them to the fuels used in their school or homes. They can move from comparing how hot or cold things feel to using simple thermometers. Children will already have ideas about heat and also about the Sun, the Moon and the Earth. These can be explored and developed as they investigate shadows over a day, for example.

Cross-curricular links

Topics and settings where forces could be studied include: *Buildings, Playgrounds, Transport, Water, Road safety,* and *Toys.*

Playgrounds, roads, water, buildings and other structures all provide relevant starting points for children's exploration of forces. The scientific investigations in the classroom will often link readily with technological activities. The industrial context, environmental and safety issues provide a natural context for incorporating cross-curricular themes. We can help children become more aware of dangers and better able to avoid accidents. Drama or movement lessons can be used to explore and communicate ideas about movement and forces.

Below is an example of a topic chart on Toys.

Topics where electricity and magnetism could be studied include: *Communications, Games, Homes, Machines, Safety,* and *Toys.*

The investigations of simple circuits might be carried out separately and later applied in models. Alternatively the awareness of how electricity is used and of dangers associated with it might arise in a topic which creates a need for learning about circuits. Children can apply that learning as they consider solutions to problems and make models.

Topics where *sound* or *light* could be studied include: *Safety, Seasons, Senses, Theatre,*

Looking at old toys on museum visit
↓
Comparing with children's toys today
↓
Surveying favourite toys
↓
Toy shop visit — pricing, advertising
↓
Making toys to sell at school fair
↓

Making balancing toys
↓
Making moving toys - driven by elastic, by motors and batteries
↓
Testing our toys - how fast are they?
↓
Investigating what makes things move?
↓
NEXT TOPIC

Fig. 45 *Topic chart for toys*

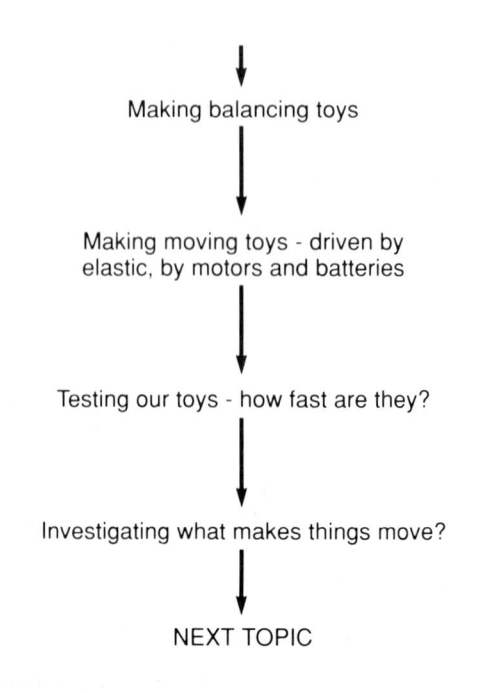

Clothes, Music, Colours, Communications, and *Festivals.*

The importance of light as a symbol can be illustrated during festivals of light. Making lamps for Divali or decorations at Christmas can lead to explorations of how light is produced, what effect it has, how it is reflected and can be coloured. The importance of light in our lives can be explored through art and drama. Assemblies, concerts or puppet theatres are ideal settings for exploring sound and light effects, alongside technological activities and visits.

Resources

Modelling materials and tools are needed for making structures and moving models. Appropriate construction kits for the age group can be used to make some models and also to investigate forces and simple machinery. Collect small vehicles and other toys, planks or guttering for slopes and ramps. Later investigations will need simple measuring equipment such as metre rulers. Floating investigations are helped if the objects can be viewed in a plastic aquarium or sweet jar. Sometimes more room is needed so large plastic guttering, water troughs or even swimming pools are handy then. A variety of objects and materials of different density can be collected.

The musical instruments already used for music making are excellent starting points for talking about sound production. Try to get some from a variety of cultures as well. A comb and thin greaseproof paper or tissue paper are good ways to produce sound and feel the vibration. Collect containers and materials to put in them or stretch across them, sturdy boxes and elastic bands for making simple instruments.

The most important resources for investigating light are good sources of light: torches can be used for many activities but not all will give the strong, sharp beam that some investigations require. Projectors are excellent but ensure children use them safely and correctly. If your classrooms will not black out you need to improvise with large boxes, or black cloth, for some activities. Mirrors should have any sharp edges and corners taped. A good supply of plastic mirrorcard is needed if children make lots of models. Build up a collection of shiny objects, transparent and opaque materials, coloured things and materials. Coloured cellophane and acetate is useful; better quality colour filters are expensive.

If possible have a variety of thermometers, including digital and strip ones. Sturdy, traditional, mounted ones with tubes that are protected can be handled safely and even hung outdoors. Make sure they have a scale which is easily read and covers the appropriate range of temperature. Never use mercury thermometers.

PUSHES AND PULLS

Activities for children

Pushes and pulls

- Put out a collection of toys and objects which are moved by pushing or pulling and ask how each can be moved.
- Push and pull heavier things around the hall in PE.
- Display pictures of heavy loads being pushed, and others being lifted, pulled and dragged. Ask children to collect or sort examples of each.
- Talk about some examples where push and pulls may both be involved – bulldozer, weightlifter.
- Collect and display pupils' words with the pictures. Use arrows or sequences of drawings to show how forces are acting and producing movement.

Games and sports

- When children play games, look at pictures or videos.
- Talk with pupils about what moves, what makes it move, and how the players control the movement:
  (a) when hitting a ball
  (b) when swimming
  (c) when running
  (d) when sliding on ice.

Key Stage 1

- Get them to put arrows or other ways of representing movement and force onto pictures of sport they draw or cut out. Look at comics to see how they represent this.

Move it

- Challenge children to find as many ways as they can to move an object, eg a large bead or air ball, a toy car, a plastic weight. Provide things like string, rubber bands, balloons, straws, that they might use.

Stop it

- Get a battery driven toy vehicle which will turn and climb over obstacles. Then ask pupils to make barriers and find other ways of stopping it.
- Show pictures such as runaway trains, paper blowing away, a football heading for goal, a dog on a lead trying to chase another, and ask 'How can they be stopped?'

Blow it

- Play a game like 'Dead Fishes' where pupils flap magazines to move a tissue paper fish.
- Let the children blow bubbles ouside. On a still day they can try to direct them. On a windy day they can see how the wind pushes.
- Blow ping-pong balls through straws.
- Make small figures to play blow football with.
- Make paper 'sliders' to blow across the desk.

Magnet games

- Use a magnet under a board to move a paper clip.
- Draw a path on a sheet of paper and ask pupils to make a small ball bearing follow the path.
- Show them a magnetic fishing game.
- Push one magnet with another.
- Challenge them to design a game using magnets.

Science background

Movements can be caused by pushing – for instance when we push a pushchair, a swing or piano key. Movements can also be caused by pulling – for instance by pulling a toy along on a string, by pulling up a weed, by pulling our socks on.

Forces are pushes and pulls. Children experience and appreciate forces they can exert or feel. They can associate these with movement. The force may be exerted directly on an object by lifting, flicking, blowing, tugging, restraining, etc or something may be used to apply the force – for instance a bat to hit a ball, a lead to restrain a dog. When we move ourselves we pull our bones with our muscles. At joints the bones move relative to one another and may then move something else; if they push against the ground or pull on a fixed object we move in the opposite direction.

The force exerted by moving air or water can be experienced and used by children. They can feel and use the force of gravity and magnetic force to experience force acting at a distance rather than directly on an object.

Children may understand that forces can start movement and lots of the examples we provide in school will reinforce this.

Strictly speaking a force can produce a change in movement – ie it can start one or speed it up, stop one or slow it down, or alter the direction of a movement.

Children control movements by altering their speed (accelerating) and direction as they do PE, hit balls, roll marbles, play games with spinners or magnets or blow football.

FORCES

Activities for children

How is it moving?

- Display pictures of moving objects. Include pictures of falling, flying, boats with sails, rowing boats, fairground rides, cranes, etc.

- Talk about the sorts of movement and what children think causes them.
- Let them point, mime or draw and help them choose suitable words.

How can we move?

- After playtime, games or PE ask children:
  (a) What sorts of movements can they make?
  (b) How can they change their movements?
  (c) What can they do to speed up or slow down or to change direction?

Changing movements

- Look at pictures or videos of sports and work where movements change, such as
  (a) sledging and skiing, snooker, football
  (b) diggers and bulldozers on a building site.

  Talk about how they move, what stops them, what makes them change speed or direction.
- Children could draw arrows on diagrams, make strip cartoons, use drama or play.

Toy boats

- Help pupils make model sail boats. Collect others which have motors or elastic to drive them. Use guttering or a large water trough.
- Ask children how many ways they can make the boats move. Let them explore their ideas.

Squash and squeeze

- Provide hard and soft materials to squeeze. Ask children what sort of marks they can make.
  (a) What does it feel like when they press and squeeze?
  (b) How strong is each one?
  (c) How hard is it to squash?

Science background

Changes in the movement or shape of an object only occur when there is a force acting on it. The object carries on as it is – either stationary or moving at a steady speed – unless a force makes it increase or decrease in speed or change direction. Although it is easy to see that a force is needed to start something moving our daily experience does not suggest that it will go on moving at the same speed unless another force acts. Moving objects slow down unless more force is applied. This is because unseen frictional forces are acting to oppose the movement.

Children can feel some of these forces in action, for example between moving parts and between the road and wheels as they pedal a bicycle. There is also air resistance as the body moves through the air.

Children can employ a variety of forces to produce changes in movements. For instance to move a toy boat they could:
(a) Push it directly.
(b) Make waves so the water is pushing against the boat.
(c) Blow against its sail, use a boat with an elastic or motor-driven propellor.
(d) Pull it with a string.
(e) Use a toy vehicle or electric motor to pull the string.
(f) Hang a weight from the string and let that fall under the force of gravity.

All the examples above concern forces acting on objects to change their movement. Forces can also alter the size and shape of objects.

What happens when an object is squashed or stretched will depend on the properties of the materials of which the object is made. Those properties in turn depend on other forces within the material.

There are internal forces between molecules which determine many of the properties of the material made up by those molecules. Thus the behaviour of materials when an external force is applied will depend on those internal forces. There are forces of both attraction and repulsion. The balance of those depends on how close the molecules are. Stretching or squashing the material alters this balance. Intermolecular forces resist the external forces causing the stretching and squashing.

Key Stage 1

FLOATING

Activities for children

Water play

Children and adults play with water and we should provide for this beyond the nursery.

- Expect pupils to play when you first give them items to investigate floating. Include objects which float, some which sink, and others that sink as they are filled.
- Introduce surprising ones – large objects that float, small ones that sink, floaters that have holes.

Sorting floaters and sinkers

- Ask children to sort objects into those they think will sink and those they think will float. Provide a suitable collection – for instance plastic and metal spoons and weights, candle, wood, bottle top, stone, marble, bead, golf ball and sponge ball and if possible an air ball that has holes in. Let them test their predictions.
- Display and discuss their findings.

Sinking floaters

- Ask children to find ways of sinking things which floated in their investigation. They may try loading them by sticking things on, filling them with water, tying floaters to sinkers.

Floating sinkers

- Challenge children to make a sinker float – this might be extended to raising a sunken treasure. They may simply lift it or tie it up and then try adding lighter objects, altering its shape or size, reducing its weight. Their attempts will give you insights into why they think things float.

Make a boat

- Set children to make a boat shape with foil or warmed Plasticine. If they have difficulties floating it help them produce a stable shape.

- Build small boats with light wood and dowelling. Try to make them stable and able to carry a load.

At the swimming pool

- If children go swimming ask them what they do to float, how the water helps, why they can swim in water but not in air?
- What does it feel like when they push down on a float, wear armbands, or lift a friend?

At the pond

- Look at a pond or stream. What is floating? Are there any insects or plants right on the surface? What is partly submerged but not sunk to the bottom? What sorts of things are at the bottom?
- Make a frieze showing a vertical section with things at the appropriate levels.

Science background

Children need lots of early experiences to explore the forces involved in floating and sinking. Several factors which may seem to affect floating can eventually be explained by one more general idea. Pupils have to build up slowly toward a higher level of understanding. They may cite factors that have no real bearing. For instance children sometimes think that the depth of water under an object determines how well it floats.

A child may have to try out lots of objects to see if it is really the shape that matters, or whether an object has holes. Sorting out the effect of size and weight will take time and depend on an understanding of those properties. The effect of air inside things may for some time convince a child that this is the crucial factor. In the long term she has to understand how several factors are all affecting whether an object is heavy for its size (ie its density). The concept of density itself will not come quickly or easily, and the idea of relative density compared to that of the water is even more demanding.

Objects which sink come to rest on the bottom of the container. Objects which are suspended in the water or have some part above the surface are floating. Small objects which sink if put in water may sometimes rest on the surface of water. This is because of the surface tension which forms a layer that supports them. Insects like water skaters can be seen on ponds 'walking on water'. Children may or may not regard these as instances of floating. They may also have different views as to whether something that is almost totally immersed but does not sink is to be classed as a floater. Observing the level at which objects floats and recording that in large pictures can bring out these ideas for discussion.

MOVING

Activities for children

Wind-up

- Collect wind-up toys, clocks, etc for pupils to play with. Ask them:
    (a) What they have to do to make them work.
    (b) What happens when they have been wound up?
    (c) Do they go on working for ever?
    (d) When do they stop?
    (e) Why?
    (f) How far will they go?
    (g) How long will they work?

What makes it go?

- Display toys that work in different ways: for instance some which have to be pushed, some which wind up, some which need a battery, some which are pressed down and then spring up. Let children explore them, describe how they work and find others that work in similar ways.
- Group toys or pictures of toys and machines according to their source of energy. Add a few larger scale examples that use other sources, such as pictures of cars, a milk float, a water wheel.

Springs and elastic

- Provide a variety of springs for children to stretch and squash. Compare them and discuss how hard they are to extend and compress.
- With supervision explore what happens when they let go.
- Use them in simple models – for instance inside a cardboard tube to fire a pingpong ball, as a jack-in-the box.

NB Tell them not to point at people and to beware sharp ends.

Bouncing balls

- Collect a variety of balls. Ask the children to predict which will bounce best.
- Ask them to plan a test to compare the balls. If necessary help them to carry out a fair test and to repeat their measurements.

Science background

Very young children learn that things will not go unless they are wound up, or pushed or raised, or their battery 'works'. They can predict and test whether a toy or model will move, how far or for how long. They begin to recognise that something may get its energy from different sources.

The simplest way to explain energy is as that which 'makes things go' (or 'work' or 'happen'). Energy is the capacity to do work. Work is done when a force moves an object. When work is done energy may be stored or released. Energy is transferred but it cannot be destroyed or created.

Energy can exist in several forms – for example:

- as heat energy
- as chemical energy stored in fuels, foods, batteries
- as energy of movement (kinetic energy)
- as energy associated with position (potential energy).

Children can explore the transfer of energy as familiar things move. To lift something we have to work against the force of gravity so the object gains potential energy. A ball is given potential energy when lifted. As it drops this energy of position changes to energy of movement (kinetic energy).

The changes can be reversed as a ball falls and hits the ground and bounces back. If the ball is very **elastic** it will spring back quickly and bounce high – but not as high as it was when first dropped. Some of the energy also changes to sound and heat when the ball hits the ground.

Energy can be stored by squashing, stretching or winding up a spring and by stretching a rubber band or balloon. When a spring is stretched by working against the intermolecular forces it gains potential energy. The spring can be released quickly producing a rapid change to kinetic energy, for instance when a jack-in-the box pops up, or slowly as in a clockwork toy.

Wind-up toys store energy in springs – but you have to work to wind them up.

Machines with a flywheel keep working for a long while because lots of work has to be done to get the heavy flywheel rotating and then the energy stored in it is slowly released. When you push inertia toys you start a similar process – they have an additional bigger, heavier wheel in the centre which is set spinning as the toy is pushed and goes on spinning after you stop pushing.

Many children's toys nowadays work from electric energy, usually supplied by a battery where it has been stored as chemical energy.

ELECTRICITY IN THE HOME AND SIMPLE CIRCUITS

Activities for children

What uses electricity?

- Cut out pictures from magazines showing things which use either mains electricity or batteries.
- Ask the children to draw pictures of the electrical things they used yesterday eg television, radio, table lamp, toy car, talking doll, watch, clock. Sort them into two groups: those which use mains electricity and those which use batteries. Talk about those which can be dangerous.
- Make a poster or picture showing electrical hazards in the home.

Simple circuits

- Working in pairs, light a bulb using one cell and two pieces of wire about 20 cm long. Give the children unlimited time for this and only intervene if they are really stuck. The pleasure of final success is considerable. A single cell cannot harm or be damaged under normal circumstances. There are several ways of lighting the bulb and two are shown here.

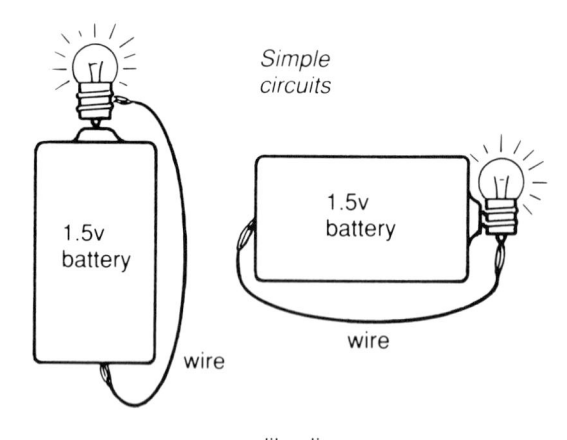

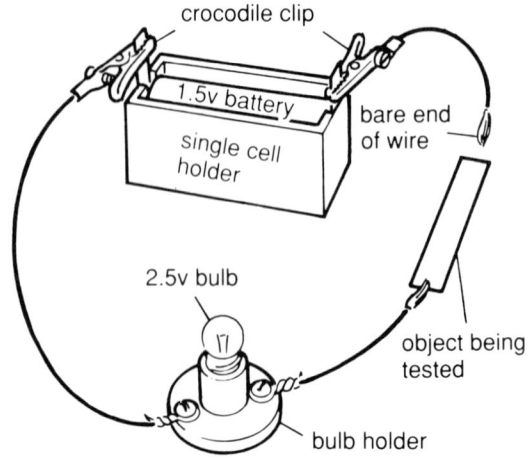

Fig. 46 *Various electrical circuits*

- How many ways can the children think of?
- Draw the successful methods.

Key Stage 1

Use holders for convenience

- Use a bulb holder and a battery holder.
- Use wires with crocodile clips already fixed on the ends.

Conductors

- Use a simple circuit to test which materials conduct electricity.

Science background

An electrical cell produces electricity as a result of a chemical reaction. In schools we usually use 1.5 volt (V) cells. A combination of two or more 1.5 V cells makes a battery. People commonly refer to single cells as batteries. If at all possible obtain single cell holders. The holders which hold two or more cells are difficult to use and difficult for young children to understand. Use the large size 'D' cells. They are more economical than the small 'AA' size.

For the activities on this page use single size 'D' 1.5 V cells (batteries). Use 1.5 V, 2.5 V or 3.5 V bulbs. The 1.5 V bulbs will glow brightly but they are not as robust as the 2.5 V. The 3.5 V bulbs will glow rather feebly.

What is electricity?

Electricity can be thought of as a flow of electrons from the negative end of a cell to the positive. Electrons are tiny particles. They are the outermost parts of an atom. Electricity will only flow where there is a complete pathway. This is known as a circuit. In diagrams of circuits electricity is often shown by arrows flowing from the positive end to the negative end of a cell. This convention was established before electrons were known to flow.

To make the bulb glow electricity must pass through the filament of the bulb. There must be a connection to the silver nipple at the bottom of the bulb and the brass screw. The electricity will pass between these connections and through the filament. (See the figure above.)

The filament of the bulb is a very thin wire. Electricity cannot pass through it easily so the filament glows and produces light. Filaments are usually made of the metal tungsten.

The plastic coating of the wire you use must be stripped off to show the metal core. Electricity passes through this metal core. It cannot pass through the plastic.

All metals conduct electricity. Wood, plastic, paper, fabric and most other materials do not conduct electricity.

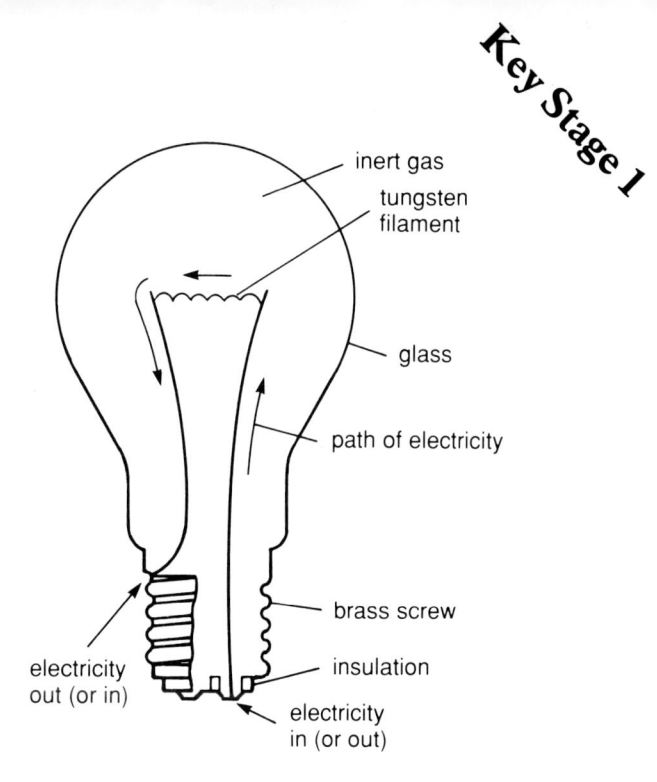

Fig. 47 *Cross-section of light bulb*

MAGNETS

Activities for children

Magnets in all shapes and sizes

- Play with a collection of different kinds of magnets and metal and non-metal objects.

Magnetic interest

- Set up an interest table which includes different kinds of magnets and things which are attracted to magnets and those which are not.

Young children will focus on the object whilst older children will be able to recognise that it is the material from which the object is made which matters.

Which part of the magnet is strongest?

- Ask the children to investigate whether a magnet is strongest at the ends or the middle.
  (a) How will you test this?
  (b) Is it true for all types of magnets?

Attraction and repulsion

- Play with two magnets and make them attract and repel each other. Can the children predict if the ends will attract or repel just by looking?

Magnetic compass

- Float a bar magnet on a dish in a bowl of water.
  (a) In which direction does the north pole point? (Don't forget to make sure all other magnets are kept away from the compass.)
  (b) What happens when you bring a magnet close?

Use a magnetic compass

- Play with a bought magnetic compass. Let the children see that it points in the same general direction wherever they are in the school. It might for example always point roughly in the direction of the main road.
- Bring one end of a magnet close. Talk about what happens. What do the children think will happen when the other end is brought close? Try it.

Compare the strength

- Challenge the children to find ways to test the strength of three magnets. Can they make the test fair?

Make a magnet

- Make a needle or a pin magnetic by stroking it with *one* pole of the magnet in *one* direction.

(Stick the pin in a cork to avoid pricked fingers.)
  (a) Will your pin now pick up small iron and steel objects?
  (b) How long does it stay magnetic?

Science background

The Earth's magnetic field acts as though there was a bar magnet at the centre. The **north pole** of a magnet is attracted to magnetic north.

Magnetic force is concentrated at the ends of a magnet. These are the poles. Unlike poles attract. Like poles repel. Most magnets are painted with the north pole red and the south pole blue. Some magnets have a mark on the north pole.

In magnetic materials (iron, nickel, cobalt) each molecule acts like a magnet. Normally they are randomly arranged so their effects cancel each out.

When a material is **magnetized** each of the molecules is brought into line. This combines all their magnetic force. Stroking a pin or needle with a magnet turns the pin or needle into a magnet. If a magnet is broken two magnets are made.

When in storage magnets may lose their power. To avoid this, **keepers** of soft iron are used to create a closed loop of magnetism. Do not allow the children to drop or tap magnets. This jolting will shake the molecules back into their disorganized arrangement and reduce the magnetic strength.

MAKING SOUNDS

Activities for children

Listen

- Sit and listen quietly in the classroom. What sounds can you hear?
- Go for a sound walk. What sounds do you like? Which sounds are unpleasant?

Sort the sound

- Ask the children to suggest ways in which the sounds could be sorted. They might suggest:
  (a) sounds we make, sounds made by machines, sounds made by animals
  (b) banging, scratching, rubbing, loud-speaker, blowing.

Explore musical instruments

- Let the children explore the sounds made by a variety of musical instruments.
- Encourage them to talk about what each sounds like and the way in which they are made.
- Ask the children how they would group the instruments. They might choose those you hit, those you blow and those you pluck.

Make simple shakers

- Make simple musical shakers. Use a variety of containers and fill them with a variety of materials.
- Explore the effect of using large beans, split peas, lentils or semolina.
- What effects can you make using different containers?

Recorded sounds

- Make recordings of different sounds. Talk about what they might be.
- Take the tape recorder on a local visit. Record any interesting or unusual sounds.

Science background

Sound is present almost all the time in most urban environments. Sounds are produced by causing air to move in some way. Blowing or talking moves the air directly. Other methods involve making another material vibrate by scraping, scratching, hitting or banging. In loudspeakers electrical energy causes a cone of paper to vibrate which in turn vibrates the air next to it.

SOUND TRAVELS AND ECHOES

Activities for children

Listening

- Cover your ears with your hands. Why can't you hear as well?

Channel the sound

- Put two funnels in a length of hosepipe. Use them as a speaking tube.
- Make a hearing trumpet.
  NB No sharp points. Tell the children not to put things in their ears.
  (a) Does this help you to hear faint sounds?
  (b) Which animals have big ears? How does this help them?
  (c) Does cupping your hand round your ear help you to hear things?

Sound travels through solids

- Put your head to the table when someone taps the other end.
- Investigate what happens to the sound when there is something soft between ear and table.

String telephones

- Make a string telephone using two yoghurt pots. Investigate:
  (a) Which type of pot or cup makes the best receiver.
  (b) Which type of string makes the best line.
  (c) Whether it matters if the string is slack.
  (d) What happens if two lines cross and touch.

Echoes

- Stand about 20 metres from a large wall or in a subway. Listen to the echoes from the wall. Which is the best place to make echoes?

Science background

A speaking tube prevents the sound vibrations from spreading out. A hearing trumpet collects sound from a greater area and concentrates it. Prey animals like rabbits have large ears to locate and concentrate faint sounds. Most sounds which we hear travel through the air. Hard materials like wood conduct sound very well indeed. Soft materials like fabric absorb the sound energy. String is soft but transmits the sound well so long as it is held tight.

Sound travels relatively slowly (350 m per second). When it hits a solid object it can be absorbed or reflected. Soft surfaces will tend to absorb the sound. Hard surfaces will tend to reflect it. Objects with many surfaces at different angles will tend to scatter the sound whereas a hard flat surface may reflect the sound as an echo. Bats and dolphins use sound echoes to 'see' objects.

VIBRATIONS

Activities for children

Twanging a ruler

- Twang a ruler or another flexible object on the table. Look at the way it vibrates.

Twanging an elastic band

- Watch the way in which an elastic band vibrates after it has been plucked. Attach it to a strong cardboard box. When it is twanged feel the box vibrate. Notice that the sound is increased.

Explorations with a tuning fork

- Strike the tuning fork on a relatively soft object like a piece of cork.
    (a) Listen to the sound produced.
    (b) Watch it vibrate.
    (c) Touch it on your skin and face to feel the vibrations.
    (d) Touch the surface of a bowl of water with the vibrating tuning fork. (See below.)

Fig. 48 *Tuning fork in water showing vibrations*

Draw sound travelling

- Ask children to draw how they think sound travels from the vibrating source to their ear.
- Draw a sequence of pictures for display with captions similar to these shown below.

Sound is made by vibrating objects (e.g. a bell or a guitar string)

Sound travels through the air

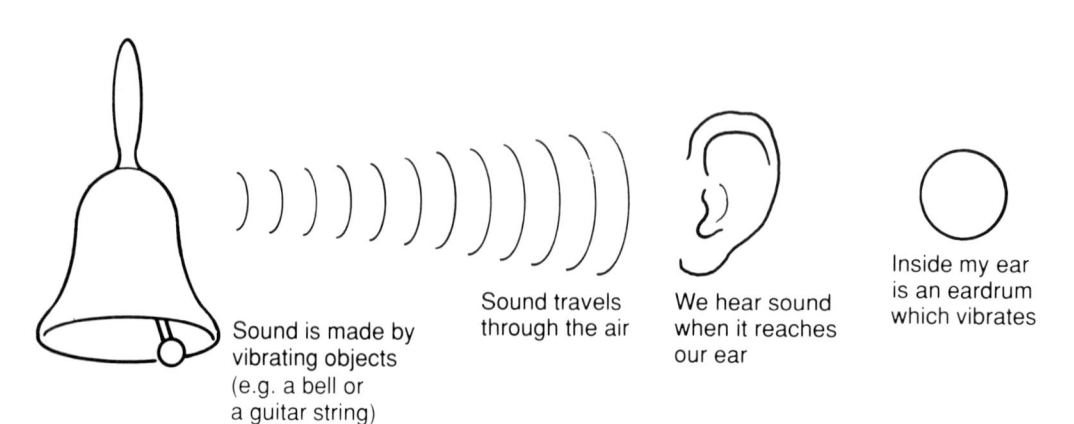

We hear sound when it reaches our ear

Inside my ear is an eardrum which vibrates

Fig. 49 *Picture sequence of how sound reaches the ear*

Key Stage 1

Science background

Sounds are transmitted through **vibrations**. These vibrations can pass through solids, liquids and gases. Sound travels through air as pulses of compressed air and pulses of rarefied (less compressed) air.

Imagine a drum skin vibrating after being hit. This happens very rapidly and is detected as a vibration. These sound waves travel out in all directions from the source of the sound rather like the ripples on a pond. The popular image of sound waves is shown below, and stems from comics and the electronic representation of sound waves by **oscilloscopes**. The crest of the oscilloscope wave shows the compression of the sound wave and the trough shows the rarefaction caused by the sound wave.

A **slinky spring** which is sold as a toy demonstrates the way in which sound waves travel. Hold the spring extended on a smooth floor. Send a pulse from one end and see how the compression travels to the other end of the spring.

In solids the same process of compression and rarefaction goes on but as the **molecules** in a solid are more firmly bound the sound energy is transmitted more rapidly and with less loss.

Sound cannot travel in a **vacuum** (where there is no air). In space, where there is a a near perfect vacuum, sounds cannot be transmitted. Instead astronauts communicate using radios. The publicity for one horror film was scientifically accurate when it said 'They can't hear you scream in space.'

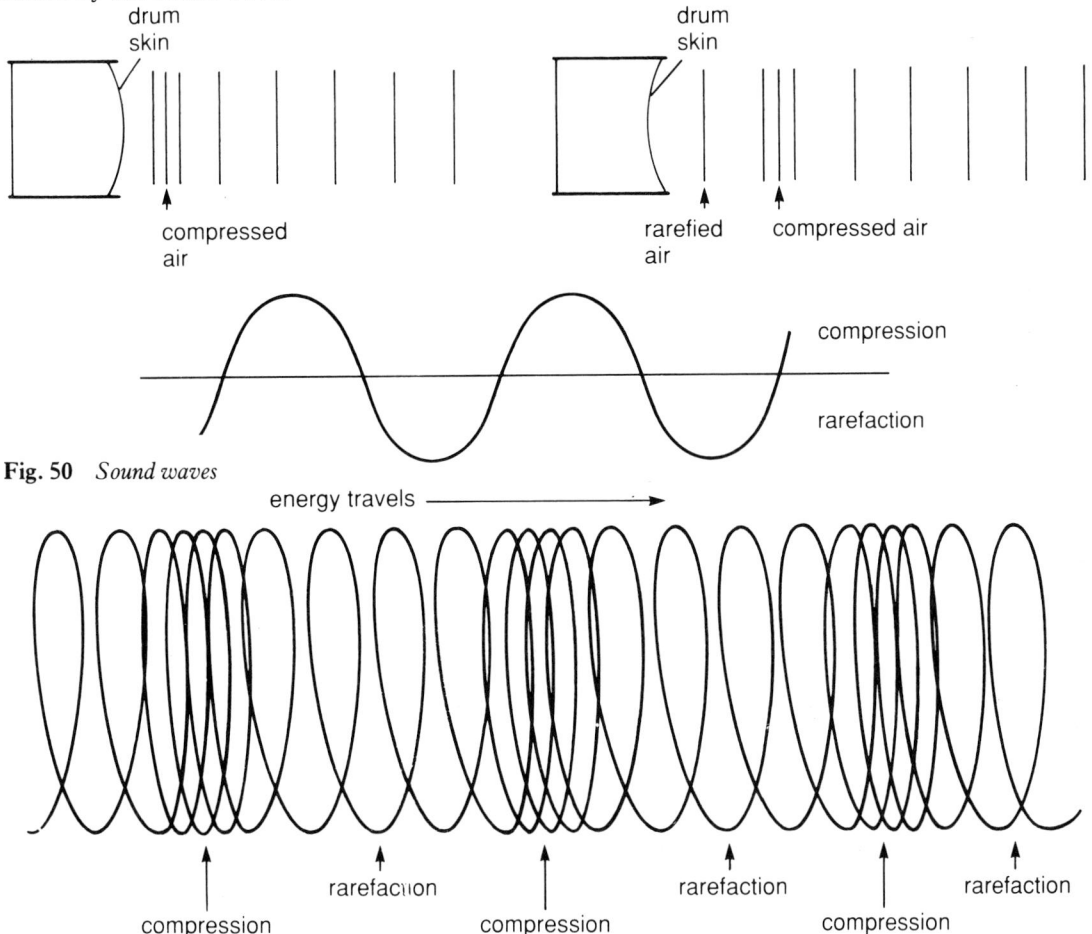

Fig. 50 *Sound waves*

Fig. 51 *A slinky spring showing how sound waves travel*

97

Key Stage 1

LIGHT SOURCES

Activities for children

Spot the light

- Look at pictures of rooms with windows and artificial light sources. Ask where the light comes from. Get children to point or draw circles round the sources of light. Use day and night examples.

What makes light?

- Collect colour magazines and catalogues with illustrations of lots of different lamps, torches, and some less obvious sources of light such as televisions. Children can cut them out, make collages, or sort into sets of do/do not emit light.

Will it light up the dark?

- Tell stories about the dark and talk about what helps you see at night.
- Ask who has a nightlight at bedtime.
- At dusk or on a foggy day look at headlamps or streetlamps.
- Look at pictures of spotlights in a theatre or a sports ground.

Songs and rhymes and festivals

- Sing songs and rhymes like 'Twinkle, twinkle little star'.
- Display or make candles and lamps during seasonal festivals of light.
- Make collages or draw pictures of fireworks and bonfires, candles and decorations.

Science background

Children need to realise that the light they use comes from somewhere and to appreciate that there are a variety of sources of light. The sunlight which illuminates their world by day is only a tiny part of the light which radiates out from the sun. Other stars also emit light but we only notice this when there is not a lot of background light from the sun or artificial lights. Children may not realise the stars are distant bodies giving out light but they will associate them with twinkling light, bright points in a dark background, and terms like 'shine'. They will have experience of artificial sources such as lamps and torches, fluorescent lights, TV and computer screens. Draw their attention to other things which emit some light – such as candles, fireworks, fires and cookers. Some may have toys which glow. Others might have heard of glow-worms.

NB Teach them to avoid touching hot objects and looking directly at intense sources of light, especially the sun.

COLOURS

Activities for children

Playing with colour

- Collect paint colour cards, decorator's books and materials.
- Make a paint shop play area. Supply different coloured fabrics or wallpaper and let children choose those they like to decorate the play corner or a model house.

Colour displays

- Use the familiar classroom colour displays to introduce the main colours of the spectrum.
- Display examples from nature where colour is used to make things stand out, such as birds or flowers.

Colour helps us

- Show clothing that uses bright colours. Ask why we wear different colours. Compare clothing and armbands designed to show up because of their bright colour.
- Look at street signs and advertisements to see what colours they use.
- Make pictures or models of traffic lights.

Which shows up best?

- Investigate which colours show up best:
  (a) Find how far away different coloured skittles can be seen.
  (b) Stick coloured paper inside a large box and find out which colour is easiest to see.

Can you see the difference?

- Show pictures of animal camouflage.
- Ask children to make a collage in which an animal can hide by being camouflaged.
- Challenge them to colour a box so it can be hidden outside (or in the classroom). Test to see which box is hardest to see.

Science background

What we call white light is made up of a range of colours (**the spectrum**). Coloured objects absorb some light and reflect only a part of the spectrum. The colours we see depend on the parts of the spectrum the objects reflect. Thus objects we see as red have absorbed all the light except the red part of the spectrum.

The spectrum ranges from red through orange, yellow, green, blue, indigo and violet (but the last ones are hard to distinguish). People can detect lots of shades. Some people cannot distinguish some colours – we say they are 'colour blind'.

SHADOWS

Activities for children

Catch my shadow

- On a sunny day play shadow games outdoors.
  (a) Chase shadows and try standing on them.
  (b) How small can children make their shadow?
  (c) Can they make their shadow climb a wall?
  (d) Can they hide their shadow?

Light and shade

- What objects are casting the shadows? Look for sharp and fuzzy shadows.
- Draw pictures which show sun and shadows:
  (a) Try pencil or black crayon on white paper.
  (b) Chalks on black paper.
  (c) Cut out black paper to stick on white card.

Hands

- Use a projector or other good light source to cast shadows of hands on a screen. Let children play at making shadow shapes. Ask them to find how to make their shapes bigger or smaller, higher or lower.

Silhouettes

- Pin up a large piece of white paper. Provide a safe, strong light source. Ask children to make a clear shadow of someone's head on the paper and draw round it.
- Make a set of silhouettes to display.

Shadow puppets

- Use cut out figures to cast shadows. Let children explore what happens with the light in different positions and then try the figures in different positions. Set them to make a small shadow theatre using a large box (white paper at one end, otherwise dark) and card figures on sticks.

Which make shadows?

- Give children a torch and a range of materials – some transparent like acetate, some opaque. Investigate which materials will cast shadows and which will let the light through.

Science background

Light passes through some materials but is stopped by others. Materials which absorb lots of light are **opaque**. Those which let light through are **translucent**. If we can see clearly through them we call them **transparent**. On the other side of an opaque object there is a shadow where the light does not fall. The size and position of this shadow will depend on the size and shape of the object and of the light source. This is a good illustration of how light travels in straight lines.

REFLECTIONS

Activities for children

Is it shiny?

- Display a collection of shiny objects. Include some flat, some round, some smooth and some with uneven surfaces. Give children time to explore and talk about what they see. Introduce a torch.

Reflections

- Hang a large mirror in the classroom and give children smaller mirrors. Talk about what they can see, and where they appear to be.

Mirror games

- Provide cards with arrows to show reversal. Hold cards with half a picture against a mirror to make complete pictures. Find which letters of the alphabet look the same in a mirror. Reflect the light from a torch so a spot of light hits a target or follows a path.

Two mirrors

- Put two mirrors together, edge to edge. Look in them and move one slowly so the angle between them changes. How many reflections of themselves can children see?
- Put an object in between the mirrors and see how many **images** of the object there are with the mirrors at different angles.

Kaleidoscopes

- Let pupils make simple kaleidoscopes by taping two mirrors together at 60° and sticking another mirror or a piece of black card on the third side. Put a few tiny coloured beads or sequins inside and seal one end. Look through the other end.

Science background

Light is reflected from some surfaces. Shiny surfaces reflect lots of light. If the surface is rough the light is scattered unevenly. Light reflects evenly from a smooth surface. If we change the angle at which the light strikes a mirror then it is reflected off at this different angle.

WEATHER, SEASONS AND PEOPLE

Activities for children

What weather do you like?

- Ask the children to draw pictures showing their favourite weather. Do they always like it hot and sunny?
- Ask why farmers and gardeners like rainy weather.

Weather stories

- Tell the children stories with a weather theme such as *The sun and the wind*, *In which Piglet is entirely surrounded by water*, *Postman Pat's foggy day/rainy day*.

Weather sayings

- What do the children think these weather sayings mean?
  (a) 'Red sky at night shepherd's delight.'
  (b) 'Rain before seven dry by eleven.'

Clouds

- Look at the clouds and ask:
  (a) What are the clouds like today?
  (b) What colour are they?
  (c) Do the children think it will rain?
  (d) Where do they think rain comes from?

(e) Are the clouds between us and the sun and moon? How do the children know?

Forecasting the weather

- At the beginning of the day ask the children what they think the weather will be like at lunchtime. Do they think it will be a wet playtime today?

Windy weather game

- Collect a variety of objects such as pop bottles, balls, balloons, skittles, plastic bags, paper. Ask the children which objects would blow away most easily on a windy day. Let them suggest ways to test this.

Record the weather

- During a period of changeable weather, fold an A3 sheet of paper into four. Draw what the weather was like yesterday. Draw what it is like today. Do drawings on the next two days.

Make a chart

- Make a simple daily chart showing the weather, like the one below. Tick the things you notice each day:

	Mon	Tues	Wed	Thurs	Fri	Sat	Sun
Clouds	✓						
Wind	✓	✓					
Sun			✓				
Rain	✓						
Hail							
Snow							
Fog							

- Wet playtimes: Add information to your chart about the number of playtimes missed because of the weather.

Science background

In Britain there is a constantly changing pattern of weather. This is because the island is in the path of **depressions** which occur when warm, wet air from the Caribbean Sea and Atlantic Ocean meets the cold air from the polar regions. The warm wet air condenses where it comes into contact with the cold air and rain is formed. Wind is associated with depressions as the temperature and pressure differences between the two air masses gives energy to the air.

Many of the familiar weather sayings are true simply because the weather is so changeable. If it is raining at seven o'clock it is likely that a change will have taken place within five hours. 'Red sky at night' is often true because much of the rain comes from the West. If there is cloudless sky to the West, the Sun's rays will still reach us long after the Sun has set. The red light from the Sun is bent towards us by the atmosphere so we see a red sky.

Cumulus clouds are white and fluffy and are usually a sign of good weather. *Cumulonimbus* clouds are the huge piles of white and grey clouds which rise up to great heights with heavy tops. These often indicate thunder and storms.

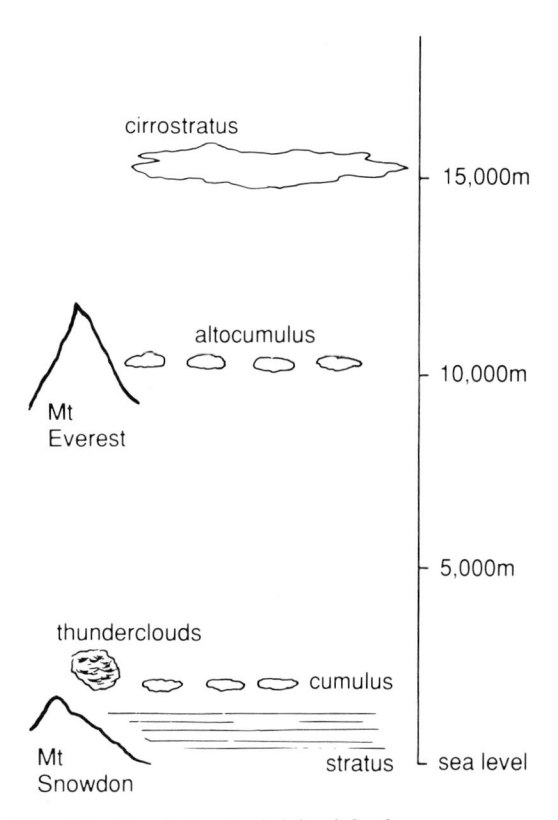

Fig. 52 *Graph showing height of clouds*

Key Stage 1

HOT AND COLD

Activities for children

NB Emphasise safety in all heat activities.

Hotter and colder

- Ask pupils to think of things which are hotter than themselves. What things are colder? Begin with objects in the classroom and then look outside. List the things they think of or use pictures to prompt ideas: eg swimming bath, ice creams, icicles, icebergs, desert scene, warm drink, bonfire. Sequence the pictures from hottest to coldest.

Warming up

- On cold days explore ways of keeping warm, for example
    (a) standing by a radiator (transferring heat from a warmer object)
    (b) exercising (producing more heat in our body)
    (c) wrapping up in lots of clothes (insulating).

Temperature

- Use a sturdy, clear thermometer with a simple scale. Ensure pupils know how to use it.
    (a) Measure the temperature of some icy water.
    (b) Measure the temperature of some warm water.
    (c) Measure the temperature of some water from the tap.
- Ask the children to mix warm and cold water and estimate the temperature by feeling with their fingers before measuring. Try different mixtures.
- Let the children measure the temperature in different places around the room.

Cooling

- Fill a hot water bottle and screw the top on tight.
    (a) Give pupils a thermometer with which they can measure the surface temperature of the bottle easily and safely.
    (b) Do this at regular intervals.
    (c) Record the changing temperature in a table.
    (d) Challenge pupils to find the best way to keep it warm.

Science background

Temperature is a measure of how hot something is. Heat will move from a hotter to a colder place until they are at the same temperature. Heat can therefore be considered as a form of energy on the move. Children feel heat energy that comes from the Sun and other sources such as fires.

Heat can move in three ways:

(1) By convection when a liquid or gas carries heat with it.
(2) By conduction when heat is transferred through a material.
(3) By radiation when heat energy travels without needing a medium to carry it. Heat radiates as waves at the infra-red end of the spectrum.

The movement of heat can be reduced by insulation. Some materials such as metals conduct heat well. Others like cloth do not – they are insulators. They can be used to slow down the rate at which something like a hot water bottle cools to the same temperature as its surroundings.

The distinction between heat and temperature is not obvious. A small drop of water spilled from a boiling kettle is at a high temperature but has little heat. On the other hand there is much more heat in a bathful of water at a much lower temperature. More energy is needed to heat up the water for a warm bath than to boil a kettle for a cup of tea.

Different sorts of thermometers are becoming more familiar:

- simple strip ones that read a limited range
- digital ones which display numbers
- more traditional tubes of glass with or without a mounting
- probes which can be used to sense the

temperature and read on the spot or through a computer.

The commonest scale is the Celsius one (°C) which has the melting point of ice at 0 °C and the boiling point of water at 100 °C. Celsius and Centigrade are identical scales but the name Celsius is preferred. The Fahrenheit scale is still quoted on weather forecasts but the numbers are less easy to use – except for those of us who grew up with them! The absolute scale of temperature is measured in °Kelvin; absolute zero is 0 °K which is −273 °C.

Our body temperature is maintained at 37 °C. If we lose too much heat our body temperature drops (**hypothermia**). This can be the result of exposure in cold or wet conditions or lack of food to supply energy. The body only functions within a narrow range of temperature. Information about the temperature of the surroundings comes to our brain along nerves from heat receptors in the skin. These respond to changes in temperature and we are better at detecting changes than estimating what the temperature is.

THE SEASONS

Activities for children

Look at trees

- What differences do children notice between the trees in winter and summer? List them.
- In the spring look at the emerging leaves and blossom. Which tree comes into leaf first? Which tree flowers first? Bring in a twig (eg horse chestnut) to come into leaf in the warmth of the classroom.
- In the summer make leaf prints and drawings of the trees and leaves.
- In autumn collect the fruit and seeds from the trees.
- List other differences between the seasons.

Grow bulbs

- In the autumn plant daffodils and hyacinths. Keep the compost or bulb fibre moist, cold and dark. Every month look at the bulbs to see their progress.

Nature diary

- Keep a brief nature diary of the things the children see in one place throughout the year. A part of the local park or wasteland might be suitable.

Science background

Changes in the warmth and amount of light from the Sun affects many plants and animals. For example, deciduous trees lose their leaves as a response to:
(a) the low temperatures which might damage their delicate tissues
(b) the low light levels at which leaves cannot work efficiently as food producers
(c) the loss of water through the large surface area of the leaves which cannot be made up from the roots if the ground is frozen.

Bulbs develop their roots during the cold dark winter. Their shoots develop only after a strong root system has been established. The leaves will use the spring sunshine to make food to replenish the stock in the bulb.

The axis on which the Earth spins is tilted so that the northern part of the world enjoys summer when it is tilted towards the Sun and winter when it is tilted away.

THE SUN'S POSITION

Activities for children

NB Remind the children not to look directly at the Sun. They should shade their eyes when noting the Sun's position.

Where is the Sun?

- Choose a time when it is likely to be sunny all day and a place in the school playground from where you can see the Sun all day.

Key Stage 1

(a) Go out at 9 am. Ask the class to note the position of the Sun.
(b) Do the same at the start of each playtime.
(c) Talk about the way in which the Sun appears to move.
(d) Record the Sun's apparent movement on a wallchart.

A shadow clock

- Lay a large sheet of paper on the ground outside. Stand a skittle or a weighted plastic bottle or a stick in a weighted pot to act as a shadow stick. If you can only work inside stand a pencil in some Plasticine on the window ledge.
  (a) Draw round the shadow made by the object every hour or so. Ask the children what makes the shadow. Note the change in the shadow's length and its position.
  (b) Talk to the children about why they think the shadow changes position and length during the day.
  (c) Keep the paper on which you drew the shadows. This can be compared with one done six months later.

Science background

The reason for not looking directly at the Sun is that the lens at the front of our eyes concentrates the Sun's light and heat onto the delicate retina at the back of the eye much in the same way that a magnifying glass can concentrate sunlight to burn paper.

The Sun appears to move across the sky because the Earth turns on its axis. However, since we are all turning with the Earth we cannot feel this movement. An analogy is to imagine that you are on a train standing at a station. If the train next to yours appears to move, there is no way of telling whether it is your train or the one next to you that has moved. If you can see beyond the train (or the Sun) and see that other more distant, probably stationary objects have also moved, then you can be sure that you have moved and not the other train (or the Sun).

OUR HOME PLANET

Activities for children

Look at a globe

- What do the blue areas of the globe represent?
- What are the brown and green areas?
- Find the country where we live.
- Do any of the children in the class or their parents come from other countries? Find these countries also.

Fly around the world

- Trace imaginary or real flights around the world starting from the nearest airport. Do you need to turn around when you want to come home?

A deep hole

- Where would you come out if you dug a hole right through the earth?
- If you lived at the North Pole where would you come out?
- What deep holes do the children know about? Have any of these come out the other side?
- What would the children expect to find at the centre of the Earth? (Fact or fancy).

Go up and out

- Where would you get to if you went straight up into the sky? The Moon? The Sun?
- What would you go through to reach them?
- Have people ever visited the Moon?
- Have they ever stood on the Sun?
- Talk about pictures of the Earth taken from space.

A space station

- Talk about what people would need to take with them if they wanted to live in space. Where would they get water, food and clothes?

Key Stage 1

Science background

Even the deepest holes which have been drilled have failed to penetrate the Earth's crust. In scale, the Earth's crust is thinner than an eggshell. Digging through the earth would of course be impossible because of the great pressures, the very high temperatures and the molten core. The fact that it is impossible should not stop the children from talking about it!

When you go straight up you leave the Earth's atmosphere behind and enter space. Space is a nearly perfect vacuum so there is no air. There is no water or food. If people went to the Moon they would need to take everything with them. The Earth is an oasis of life in an otherwise, as far as we know, lifeless solar system.

NIGHT AND DAY

Activities for children

Day and night

- Talk about the differences the children notice between day and night.
    (a) What can they see in the sky at night?
    (b) What can they see in the sky by day?
- Look at pictures of the same scene by day and by night.

Use a globe

- In a darkened classroom or a large cupboard shine a torch at a small globe.
    (a) What does the torch represent?
    (b) How much of the globe is in the torchlight?
    (c) When the Sun lights up our side of the Earth what sort of things do you do?
    (d) What do you think the children who live on the other side of the Earth are doing when it is dark?

The turning Earth

- Fix a tiny figure or a small piece of card on the globe using a removable material. Turn the globe anticlockwise as you continue to shine the torch. Ask the children:
    (a) When is it time for the figure to get up?
    (b) When is it the middle of the day?
    (c) When is it bed time?
- Ask the children to find out:
    (a) How many times the Earth turns in one day.
    (b) How many times it turns in a week.

Science background

The Sun is the source of all our energy including all our light, apart from the light we get from other stars. Moonlight is light from the Sun reflected from the Moon's surface.

The Earth turns from east to west. This makes the Sun appear to rise in the east and set in the west. When you look down at the North Pole the Earth turns anticlockwise.

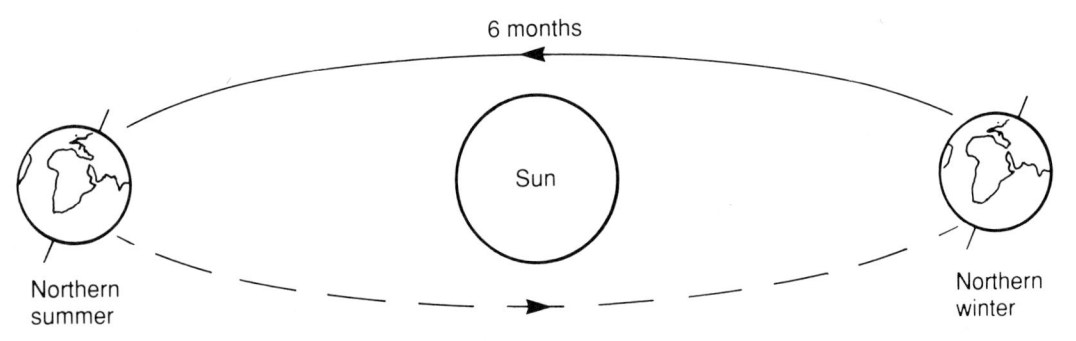

Fig. 53 *Sun and Earth*

Key stage 2

Main scientific idea	Page title	Page
Floating depends on the relative density of the object and the water it is in	Upthrust	110
The effects of forces depend on their size and direction	Size of forces	111
Gravity pulls. Weight is a force	Gravity and weight	113
Gravity and air resistance act on falling objects	Forces on the move	114
Forces can be in balance. Structures	Balanced forces	115
Forces and movement can be measured. Friction is a force	Speed and friction	117
Energy can be stored. It is transferred in moving machines	Energy for movement	118
Conductors allow electricity to flow and insulators prevent the flow. The flow of electricity can be varied	Conductors, insulators and resistors	120
Switches are breaks in a circuit	Switches	121
Electricity can make a magnet	Electromagnets	122
Components can be arranged in series or parallel	Series and parallel circuits and circuit diagrams	123
We use a range of electronic devices	Everyday electronics	126
Electronics can be used to control	Switches, logic and control	127
The frequency of vibrations affects the pitch of sounds	Pitch	128
The amplitude of vibrations determine the loudness of a sound	Louder and softer	130
Sound takes time to travel	Speed of sound	131
We see things because light from them enters our eyes	Seeing	131
Light travels in straight lines	Straight light	132
Mirrors reflect light in a predictable way to form images	Mirrors and reflected light	132
The direction and colour of light may be changed when it passes through some transparent objects and materials	Colours and bending light	134
Changes of state involve heat	Heat and temperature	136
Fuels are energy sources	Fuel	137
The Sun's inclination alters during the year. The Sun is a star	The Sun and other stars	139
The Moon orbits the Earth and reflects the Sun's light. Its appearance changes during the month	The Moon	141
The solar system is a group of planets orbiting the Sun. The spaces between the planets are vast	The solar system	143

Key Stage 2

The programme of study

This states that pupils should be taught:

Electricity

- that a complete circuit, including a battery or power supply, is needed to make electrical devices work;
- how switches can be used to control electrical devices;
- ways of varying the current in a circuit to make bulbs brighter or dimmer;
- how to represent series circuits by drawings and diagrams, and how to construct series circuits on the basis of drawings and diagrams;

Forces and motion

- that there are forces of attraction and repulsion between magnets, and forces of attraction between magnets and magnetic materials;
- that objects have weight because of the gravitational attraction between them and the Earth;
- about friction, including air resistance, as a force which slows moving objects;
- that when springs and elastic bands are stretched they exert a force on whatever is stretching them;
- that when springs are compressed they exert a force on whatever is compressing them;
- that forces act in particular directions;
- that forces acting on an object can balance and that when this happens an object at rest stays still;
- that unbalanced forces can make things speed up, slow down or change direction;

Light and sound

- that light travels from a source;
- that light cannot pass through some materials, and that this leads to the formation of shadows;
- that light is reflected from surfaces;
- that we see light sources because light from them enters our eyes;
- that sounds are made when objects vibrate but that vibrations are not always directly visible;
- that the pitch and loudness of sounds produced by some vibrating objects can be changed;
- that vibrations from sound sources can travel through a variety of materials to the ear;

The Earth and beyond

- that the Sun, Earth and Moon are approximately spherical;
- that the position of the Sun appears to change during the day, and how shadows change as this happens;
- that the Earth spins around its own axis, and how day and night are related to this spin;
- that the Earth orbits the Sun once each year, and that the Moon takes approximately 28 days to orbit the Earth.

Teaching and learning about physical processes

Forces

The scientific concept of force is highly abstract and may be difficult for many children to understand. The programme of study emphasises the ideas about balanced and unbalanced forces. When the forces acting on an object are balanced it is either stationary or moving at a constant speed. The first part of this idea is fairly easy to grasp but the idea that an object can be moving yet still have balanced forces acting on it is highly abstract and very difficult for most children to understand.

The everyday usage of terms such as energy, force, weight, mass and friction is often incompatible with the standard scientific ideas. Wherever possible children should be encouraged to use the appropriate scientific term.

Electricity and magnetism

Whenever they study electricity pupils should be reminded of the dangers associated with mains electricity. An understanding of the way electricity flows in a circuit is essential before children can begin to understand more complex ideas like parallel circuits. Children can often construct circuits correctly and make the bulb light but unless teachers explore their ideas with them children may not actually understand much about electrical flow. Many hold the view that electricity flows down both wires and meets at the bulb. Other children feel that electricity only flows in one of the wires and gets used up in the bulb.

Light and sound

Many children also have unscientific ideas about how we see and hear. For instance they may believe that their eyes send out something to the object. This idea is reinforced by comics which show rays beaming out from superheroes' eyes! Everyday language suggests that seeing is an active process rather than the reception of light – we 'look at' things to see them. The scientific view is that we see an object because some light from a source is reflected from it and then enters our eyes.

The idea that light radiates out from sources and travels in straight lines is not obvious. Children may think of light as simply surrounding them or filling the room. This may be supported by everyday phrases such as 'the room was bathed with light' and the experience that light seems to be everywhere as soon as we turn a switch. The enormous speed of light (around 300 million metres per second in space) accounts for the apparent instantaneous effects. Sound travels much more slowly and needs a medium to carry the vibrations. It cannot pass through space but light can.

Energy resources

Children can use and extend their skills of planning and investigation as they explore ideas about heat and energy. For example if they observe ice cubes melting they can be helped to turn their observations about the changes into testable questions and plan fair tests. If they are able to work at a higher level they can be asked to identify the variables they think may affect the change of state (for instance, as wax melts and vapourises in a burning candle) and plan controlled investigations to test their hypotheses.

In the course of such investigations we can not only promote the children's skills but also develop their understanding of how energy can be stored, of the changes and products associated with burning fuels, and that fuels which we use as sources of energy are likely to run out.

Earth in space

There are opportunities for direct observation and interpretation of results when studying the Earth in space. However it is particularly useful for engaging pupils in another aspect of scientific activity, namely evaluating theories and evidence.

Not many people instinctively think of the Sun's progress across the sky as being the result of the Earth turning on its axis. Similarly, for all everyday purposes we think of the Earth as being flat and only rarely do we think of the Earth as a globe. As part of our teaching strategies about the Earth in space we can turn these apparently problematical points to our advantage. Children can be asked to debate whether the Earth really is flat. What is the evidence on either side? What evidence do we have for supposing that the Earth goes round the Sun and not the other way round?

Children will find that there are many parallels between their own ideas and the historical development of ideas about the Earth's place in the solar system. Teachers and children may find it comforting to know that many of the finest minds in past times had very similar non-scientific views about the Earth.

As with other areas of science there is much to be gained from asking children to draw their ideas. For instance the apparently simple idea about which way is down can produce at least two radically different pictures of the global position.

This area of work, in key stage 2 especially, relies very heavily on children seeing the relationship between objects in three dimensions. To achieve this children must be able to manipulate models and explain their spatial relationship both by talking and in drawings.

Cross-curricular links

Topics and settings where forces could be studied include: *Transport, Flight, Bridges, Road safety, Sport,* and *Movement*.

Visits to a building site, a bridge, a garage, a canal or port, an adventure playground, or a fairground can be a stimulus to investigations of forces. The scientific investigations in the classroom will often link readily with technological activities, industry, the environment and safety issues. IT can be used, for instance to control models. Drama is a useful way to communicate ideas about movement and forces.

Topics where electricity, sound or light could be studied include: *Roads, Senses, Broadcasting, Theatre, Advertising,* and *Communications*.

The importance of sound or light in our lives can be explored through a study of the media, communications industries, advertising, art and drama. Alongside increasingly systematic scientific investigations of their properties other aspects of science can be developed if appropriate – energy resources for instance. Health education, environmental education and industrial awareness can be promoted. Issues can be explored in debates and role play.

Resources

Modelling materials and tools are needed for making structures and moving models. Construction kits can be used to make models and investigate forces. Legotechnic and many others have useful cards and teachers' notes to suggest activities and give background information. Collect small vehicles and other toys, planks or guttering for slopes and ramps. Later investigations will need measuring equipment such as a stopclock or digital watch, spring balance, and a top pan balance if possible. A good range of weights will help. Stands or supports and weight hangers are useful but can be improvised if necessary.

Floating investigations will require objects of different densities, spring balances, and a plastic aquarium or sweet jar. Materials for modelling and loading boats and somewhere they can float and move along will be useful.

Different sorts of instruments are valuable to explore the production and properties of sound. Recorders show how pitch can be varied by changing the column of air, a guitar illustrates factors which affect pitch in strings. A tuning fork can be used in a number of investigations. Sources of sound such as buzzers or bleepers, a tape recorder, and a soundmeter are all useful but many investigations of sound can be done with basic materials such as a range of elastic bands, strong boxes, rulers, bottles and straws. One of the best pieces of equipment for learning about sound is the humble string telephone.

Torches can be used for many light activites but not all give the strong, sharp beam that projectors will. A blackout will be needed for some activities. Mirrors should have any sharp edges and corners taped. A good supply of plastic mirrorcard is needed if children make lots of models. Hand lenses are an important item for lots of science investigations. Other lenses and prisms are expensive to buy but you may get old spectacles or tops of decanters free. Translucent coloured materials such as cellophane and acetate are useful. Better quality colour filters are expensive. Without such filters and identical light sources (eg stage spotlights and filters) you will not mix light to get pure white. Nor will spinners of coloured card look perfectly white. Illustrations in books sometimes imply that it is easy to mix pure white light or produce a perfect spectrum in the classroom.

Buy only one size of battery and matching battery holders. Large size batteries such as size 'D' or HP2 or SP2 are robust and economical. Buy single cell holders which can easily be linked together positive to negative to make higher voltages. Rechargeable batteries should not be used for these activities. If they are short circuited they become very hot and can cause nasty burns. Use bulbs which have a voltage higher than, or the same as, the total voltage of the batteries in the circuit. Wire cutters, small screwdrivers and crocodile clips can be stored in small open topped containers. Buy or make up short lengths of wire with crocodile clips attached. Store by clipping the crocodile clips side by side on a piece of hardboard. Remind teachers and children not to take the screws out of bulb holders. They are very difficult to refit and will get mislaid.

If possible have a variety of thermometers, including digital ones and strip thermometers as well as the more traditional tubes. These should not be mercury-filled and need to be sturdy and cover the appropriate range of temperature. Hand-hot water is the safest source of heat but you will need other sources as the investigations become more developed. Candles are useful and children can learn safe working through careful introduction of these. Many schools can use the cookers and fridges they have for heating and cooling. More detailed guidance on safe and suitable equipment is available from LEAs and the ASE booklet *Be Safe*.

A mounted globe is an essential prerequisite to work on the Earth in space. You may well find that the most satisfactory results are obtained with relatively small models about the size of a large melon. These have the advantage that they are easy for children to handle and also the beam of a large torch is able to illuminate a whole hemisphere. Large globes need very large light sources. If children wish to stargaze, a pair of binoculars is valuable. There are lots of slides and pictures of planets and stars, including superb ones taken by NASA. Contact the nearest planetarium or astronomical society for lists and addresses and expertise. Software such as that produced by RESOURCE is also available to explore the stars and ideas about them.

UPTHRUST

Activities for children

Feel the push

- Use a big piece of polystyrene or inflated balloon and a large container of water. Ask pupils what they feel as they push down slowly on the polystyrene.

Stretching bands

- Hang an object like a stone from a piece of elastic or rubber band or a spring. See how far it stretches.
- Watch the elastic as the object enters the water. See how far it stretches when the stone is immersed.

Weighing in water

- Weigh an object in air using a spring balance. Ask pupils to predict what it will weigh in water.
- Lower the object gently into water and read the weight on the spring balance. Try this with some things which sink and some which float.
- Add lots of salt to the water and weigh them again.

Displacement

- Lower a stone carefully into a clear measuring jug of water. Measure how much water is displaced by seeing how much the level rises.
- Repeat with different objects including small dense sinkers and large floaters.

Science background

When an object is placed in water it **displaces** some of the water. This is true both for objects which sink and those which float. As the object displaces the water, it is pushed up or supported by the water – a fact which is true for floaters and sinkers. This 'push up' is called buoyancy or upthrust. The amount of upthrust is the same as the weight of water which is displaced by the object and holds for both sinkers and floaters.

An object which floats in water experiences an upthrust which is equal to its total weight. A floater is effectively weightless. As it is lowered into water on a spring balance the scale shows its weight apparently reducing till it is zero. If it is suspended from a piece of elastic the elastic shortens till it is no longer stretched by the object. The pull down of the object's weight is counteracted by the push up of the upthrust from water. The resultant force is zero.

Table 9 *Loss of weight in water*

Object	Weight in air	Weight in water
Stone	125g	90g

An object which sinks in water appears to lose some weight. The weight lost by a sinker is equal to the weight of water which the sinker displaces. The upthrust opposes the downward pull of gravity on the object but there is still a resultant force down which stretches elastic a little or shows as a reduced weight on the spring balance.

Things are likely to sink if they are heavy for their size, and may float if they are light for their size. Children may come to this qualitative appreciation before they can deal with the precise terms and units for a definition of density. Whether an object floats or sinks in water depends on whether it is as heavy as an equal volume of water. It is not the weight or size of an object that determines if it floats but its density relative to the density of water. Small objects sink if they are denser than water. Large objects float if they are less dense than water.

Density is the mass of one cubic centimetre of a material or object.

$$\text{Density} = \frac{\text{Mass}}{\text{Volume}}$$

- The density of water is 1 gram per cubic centimetre (1 g/cm^3).
- Things which float in water have a density less than 1 g/cm^3.
- Things which sink in water have a density more than 1 g/cm^3.

Ships float even if they are made of a dense material like steel because they are hollow. The air inside them is very light. The total density of the hollow steel and air is less than 1 g/cm^3. A ship displaces a weight of water equal to its own weight. The weight of a ship is referred to as its displacement. As the boat is loaded the ship sinks lower so displacing a greater weight of water.

A denser liquid exerts a greater upthrust because the same volume of displaced liquid weighs more. So it is easier to float in salt water. Liquids of different densities which do not mix will float at different levels so oil, water, etc can be seen as separate bands with the least dense at the top.

SIZE OF FORCES

Activities for children

Rolling

- Roll toy vehicles down a ramp and see how far they go after they run off it. Ask children to make them go as far and straight as they can.
- Ask them to carry out fair tests to find out what happens if the ramp is made steeper.
- Investigate the effect of loading the vehicle (a large stable vehicle which runs smoothly when loaded is needed for this).

Crashes

- Investigate the effect of crashing a toy vehicle by building a model wall at the foot of the ramp, running two vehicles down opposing ramps, putting some foam or Plasticine on the front of a vehicle and running it into a brick.
- Investigate the effects of loading the vehicle or making it go faster.

Spinning

- Make spinners from card discs and wood dowelling, or use large spinning tops.
- Try longer and shorter pieces of dowelling (or pencils), bigger and smaller discs, spinning faster and slower.
- Add a paper clip or piece of Blu-tak at different points and spin.

- Put a second clip or piece in different positions.

Pressure

- Make a soft slab of Plasticine. Rest a weight on it. Compare the marks made by the same weight resting directly on it and pressing on it via a sharp object.
- Ask pupils to devise a way to measure how the mark varies as the surface area touching the Plasticine is changed.

Science background

The effects of a force will depend on its size and direction. Forces vary in their size and they can be measured. The unit used to measure a force is the newton (N).

- The force needed to peel a banana is about 1 N.
- The force of gravity pulling on a 1 kilogram mass is about 10 N.
- The force used when kicking a football is about 100 N.
- The force on a ball being struck by a snooker cue is around 150 N.
- The force of a car engine is of the order of 1000 N.

A force acts in a particular direction. The direction can be represented on a diagram by an arrow which starts at the point where the force acts. If more than one force acts in the same direction then they can be added to calculate the resultant total force. If two forces act in opposite directions they can be subtracted to calculate the resultant force. If forces act at angles to one another the size and direction of the resultant force can be worked out or shown on a diagram.

Children can begin to explore the size of forces and their directions in familiar movements, for instance on swings or roundabouts. The idea of a **centripetal force** which acts toward the centre can be experienced by swinging an object round on a string when the pull in the string can be felt.

It is harder to start, alter or stop the movement of a big mass than a little one. A large heavy adult on a swing or a sledge is more difficult to get going, less easy to divert, and hurts more if they run into you than a small light child. The faster the sledge or buggy the more it hurts when it hits you! **Momentum** is the product of mass and velocity. Big slow objects like a supertanker and small fast objects like a bullet can have a large momentum.

force of gravity

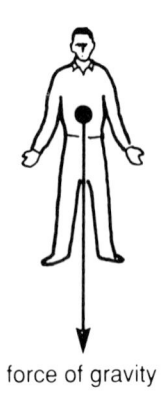

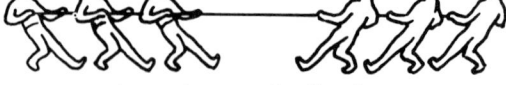

forces in opposite directions

force of gravity on load

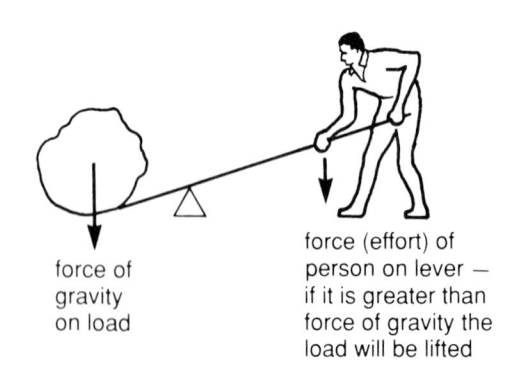

force (effort) of person on lever — if it is greater than force of gravity the load will be lifted

Fig. 54 *Diagrams showing gravity and force*

When a force acts on a surface there is an equal and opposite force pushing back. This force of reaction can be experienced if we press on a surface, run into something, or crash a vehicle. The effects of the forces of action and reaction may be different because they are acting on different objects. If you drop a tomato on the floor the forces are equal but they have different effects on the floor and the tomato. If you push against the side of a swimming pool the side stays there but you float away.

A force has a greater effect on a surface if we reduce the surface through which it acts. Thus stilleto heels make deeper marks than flat shoes worn by the same person. The weight is the same but the pressure from the stilleto is greater. Pressure is force per unit area.

GRAVITY AND WEIGHT

Activities for children

Hang it

- Use hanging weights or make a simple holder from a margarine pot. Measure the length of the spring with different loads. Use the spring to find the weight of objects.
  NB Securely fix a spring and suspend masses from it. Make sure they cannot damage toes or the floor.

How much force?

- Use a spring balance marked in newtons (N) to measure the weight of objects.
- Use the balance to lift and pull heavy objects up slopes and along surfaces. Record the force. Emphasise that in each case the reading is a measure of the force pulling on the end of the spring.
- Use the spring balance to weigh objects.

How fast do they fall?

- Drop two balls of different weights. Ask pupils to predict if one will land first. Ask them to do fair tests to find out.

- Try other pairs of objects which are fairly dense and are not affected by air resistance.

Falling

- Drop objects onto a surface where they can safely land and make a mark – for instance a piece of expanded polystyrene or Plasticine in a tray.
- Drop them from different heights and compare the marks they make.
  NB In all dropping activites check for safety – for instance if pupils need to climb on anything or are dropping hard objects.

Science background

Children discover at a very early age that things fall down. They may learn to associate this with the term gravity. However their ideas about gravity may be quite different from the scientist's view. We are unlikely to help them develop that view by simply giving them a definition or attaching the label gravity to some activities. We need to help them build up their understanding of how gravity is a force that we experience on Earth as a downward pull.

Gravity is a force of attraction (a pull in other words) between bodies. A large body such as the Earth exerts a large force of attraction. The pull gets less as you go further away but does not stop suddenly as you leave the atmosphere. The Moon pulls, but less than the Earth because it is smaller. The pull of gravity acts through space or through solids, liquids or gases.

When we measure the weight of something we are measuring the pull of the Earth's gravity on it. This is not the same as the mass of the object. The mass, or amount of stuff, will be the same wherever the object is. It will weigh less on the Moon than on Earth because the moon pulls less than the Earth.

The standard scientific unit for measuring gravity and other forces is the **newton** (N). The kilogram is the unit used to measure mass. On Earth the weight of one kilogram is about 10 N. We can measure the weight of an object using a spring balance marked in newtons. The Earth's gravity pulls the object down and stretches the spring. The more mass the object has the further it stretches the spring.

We can also measure the weight by compressing a spring in a spring weighing scale. When we use a pair of scales to balance an object against kilogram masses we are comparing two masses rather than measuring the weight of each.

If we took the scales to the Moon they would still give us the same result when we compared the two masses. The spring balance would however read about a sixth of what it showed on Earth.

The weight of an object will make no difference to how fast it falls. However this may be denied by pupils as it contradicts common-sense expectations. Testing this may be complicated by air resistance if the objects they drop are made of different materials or differ in shape or size. As things fall they accelerate so if they are dropped further they are travelling faster when they hit the ground. They will have a greater momentum and exert a greater force when they land.

FORCES ON THE MOVE

Activities for children

Paper drop

- Drop two identical pieces of paper in the same way from a height of about 1m. Do the activity several times. Record results in a simple table. Draw simple diagrams showing the force of gravity pulling the paper down and air resistance operating in the opposite direction.
- Change the way in which one of the pieces of paper is dropped. Predict which will hit the ground first. Ask the children to explain what they see.
- Crumple one of the pieces of paper or fold it to reduce its air resistance. Compare it with a whole sheet dropped flat. Draw diagrams showing the forces on the pieces of paper in each of these activities.

Feather drop

- Drop a fluffy feather and look at the way it falls. Kapok, thistledown or similar very light fluffy stuff will fall in much the same way as a feather. Emphasize the observation that all these objects seem to drop at a constant rate.
- Draw diagrams showing the forces which act on the feather.

Parachute drop

- Make parachutes from light sheets such as plastic from carrier bags or tissue paper. Investigate what happens when you vary:
  (a) the size of canopy
  (b) the size of the hanging weight
  (c) the material the canopy is made from.
- Draw diagrams of the forces acting on the parachute at different stages in its descent. Relate this to the way in which the feather falls.

Science background

In the first investigations which used identical pieces of paper the force pulling down was gravity. Since both pieces of paper had the same mass the force of gravity on both was identical. This is true even when the paper is crumpled up or folded. The force of gravity on the paper can be shown with arrows of the same length pointing downwards.

The force which slowed the pieces of paper was air resistance. This varied depending on the surface area of the paper as it fell through the air. So, a flat open piece has a much greater air resistance than a piece which is crumpled or falls edge on. The force of air resistance can be shown by arrows pointing upwards. Long arrows show a larger air resistance than short arrows.

When looking at the feather or parachute notice that they are stationary when in the hand. They speed up for the first part of their fall and then fall at a constant speed.

Throughout their fall the force of gravity on the feather or parachute stays the same. The air resistance on an object increases with speed. An

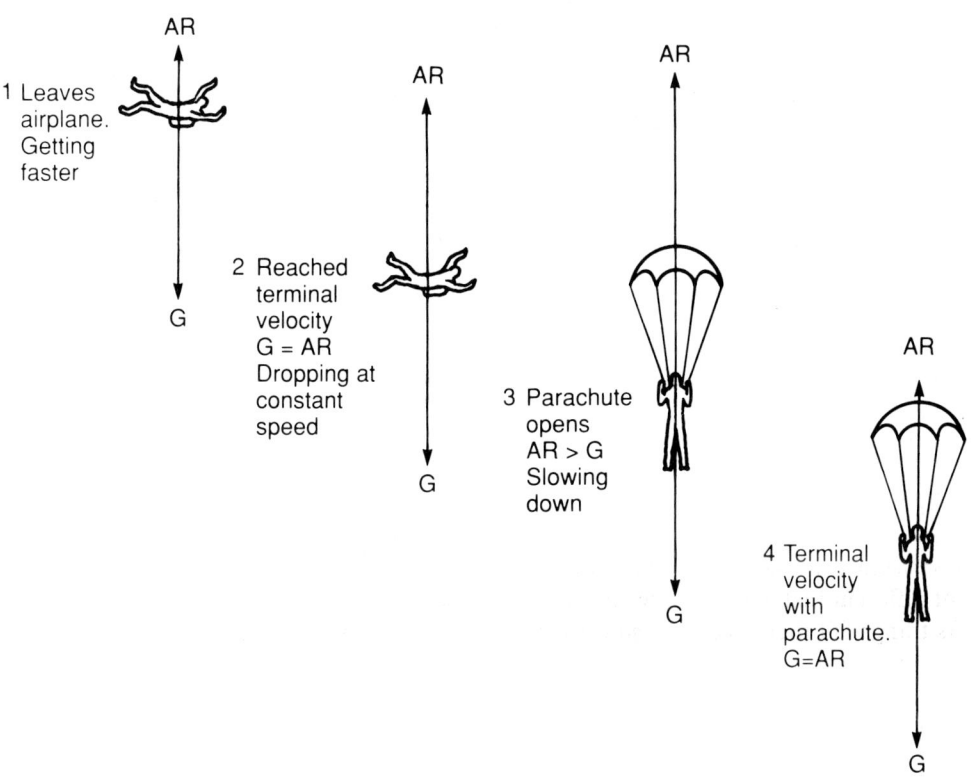

Fig. 55 *Diagrams showing the forces acting on a free-fall parachutist at different stages during the descent*

object falling quickly has much more air resistance on it than when falling slowly.

When the feather or the parachute is speeding up the force of gravity is stronger than the air resistance. The arrow for gravity is bigger than that for air resistance.

When they are falling at a constant rate (neither speeding up nor slowing down) then the forces of gravity and air resistance are equal. At first this seems to suggest that the feather or parachute would be hovering. However, remember that the feather was already moving before the forces became equal.

BALANCED FORCES

Activities for children

Equalisers

- Use an equaliser or long rule with small weights. Keep a fixed weight at one end and balance it with different weights in different positions on the other side. Help pupils see patterns in their results by making a table of distances and weights.

Balancing toys

- Show pupils some balancing toys such as balancing birds, tightrope walkers, wobbly figures. Ask them to make simple ones using materials such as card, wire, cork, wooden dowelling, Plasticine and paper clips.

Bridges

- Build girders of various shapes with folded card. Compare the loads they will carry.
- Make simple beam bridges to cross a fixed gap. Test and improve them. Make girder bridges by joining card strips or pieces of wood or use rolled up newspaper to make big ones.
- More elaborate models can be built, including suspension bridges using fine wire or strong thread, and cantilever bridges.

(a) Beam bridge

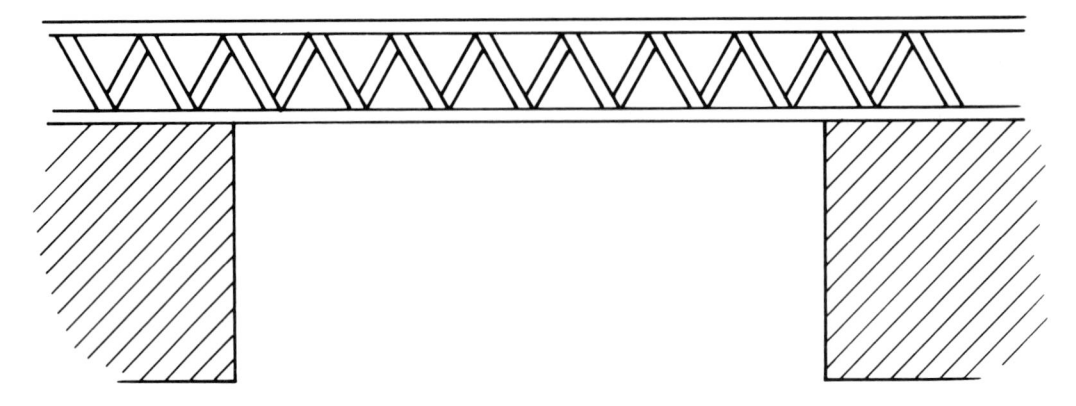

(b) Suspension bridge

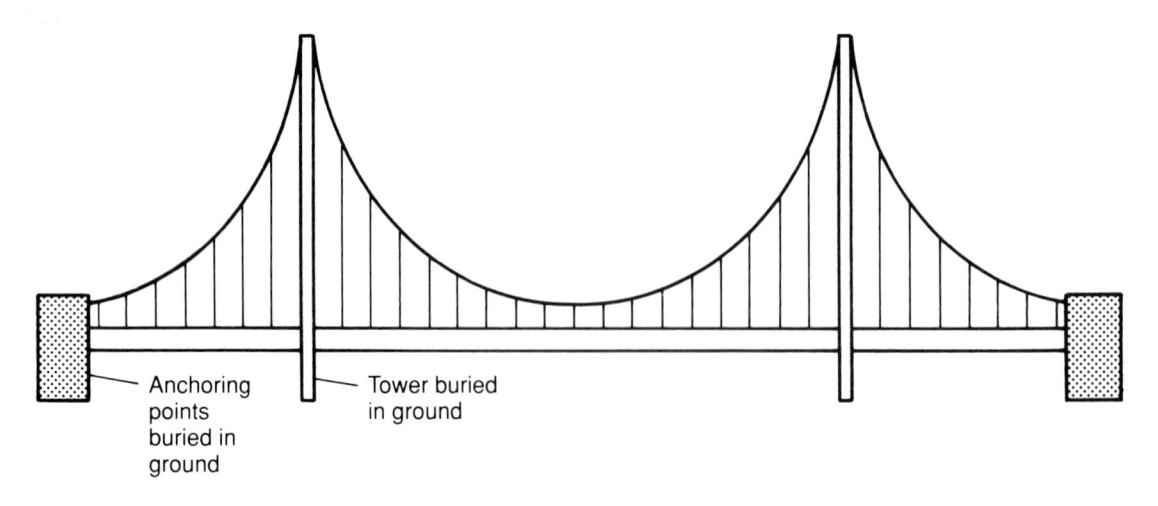

Anchoring points buried in ground

Tower buried in ground

Fig. 56a & b *Beam bridge (a) and suspension bridge (b)*

Build a shelter

- Challenge pupils to build a structure in which they can sit using only newspaper. Rolled tubes of paper can be joined in various shapes, such as a tipi or a frame tent. As they work draw attention to the need to balance forces so the structure is strong and stable.

Science background

If two or more forces act they may balance one another out. If they do not then there is a resultant force which may cause a movement. For example two opposite and equal pulls on a rope in a tug of war produce no movement. If one side pulls harder than another they move.

Two equal pulls down on opposite ends of a beam or equaliser will produce no movement. We can balance the pulls by hanging equal masses at equal distances from the central pivot or by hanging unequal masses at different distances. Moving the mass further from the pivot increases the leverage: a small mass a long way from the centre will balance a larger one nearer the centre.

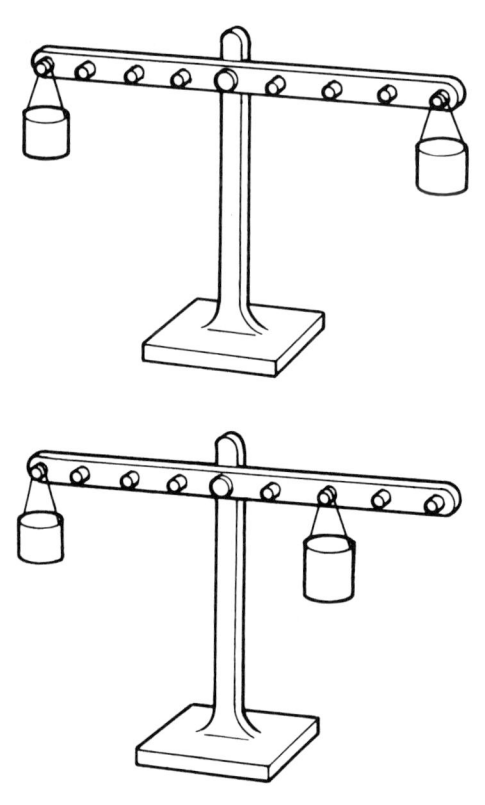

Fig. 57 *Equal weights – equal distance. Different weights – different distance*

A seesaw will go down at one end if someone pulls on it or climbs on it. If there is another rider of the same weight at the other end they can move the seesaw by pushing on the ground. To balance two children of unequal weight on a seesaw one has to sit nearer to the pivot in the middle.

Balancing toys are designed so that their weight is low down. This means they have a low balancing point (**the centre of gravity**). If pushed or pulled they will tend to return to their original position.

If materials are arranged so they resist forces we call the arrangement a structure. A dandelion stem is a natural structure in just the same way as a bridge is a structure made by people. Our skeleton is a structure that resists forces and so is the building in which we live. A sheet of newspaper which will not normally stay stiff can be rolled into a tube which will support many times its own weight. This is a simple structure. If a small force is applied to a tube of newspaper it will bend. Once the force is taken away the tube will return to its normal shape. If a larger force is applied the structure will fail and the tube will crease.

When structures collapse (move) forces are acting on them. Wind pushing against a structure such as a tree or a building has to be resisted by the structure. Many forces may be balanced in structures such as buildings. They are mostly the result of gravity pulling on the parts of the structure. The way those forces act and are resisted can be seen most clearly in structures like bridges and cranes where there is a visible framework or where struts and buttresses have been added to stop a building falling down.

SPEED AND FRICTION

Activities for children

Rolling

- Roll model vehicles or skateboards down a slope. Ask pupils to carry out controlled tests of how they run on different surfaces. They could measure the distance travelled along a piece of carpet placed at the foot of the slope, then a piece of vinyl, polystyrene, and other material.

Sliding shoes

- Ask pupils which shoes or trainers they think grip best. Let them devise tests to compare some. They might measure the force needed to pull them along, find how steep a slope has to be before they slide, and compare each shoe on different surfaces as well.

Slippy

- Slide or pull a load across polished wood, ice in a tray, greasy or oily wood.
  (a) Which is slipperiest?
  (b) How can children make surfaces more or less slippery?
  (c) How can they measure the slipperiness?

Speedy

- How fast can the children run? Get them to time themselves over a short fixed distance. Discuss the difficulties of accurate timing. Use a stopwatch or stopclock if possible. Provide a long tape measure as well.
- Ask them how they could measure their speed without a stopwatch.

A bicycle

- Bicycles can be used to explore many ideas on forces. Friction can be investigated by testing the stopping distance on different surfaces, checking the brakes, derusting and oiling moving parts.
- The transfer of movement, and use of levers and gears can be explored.

Science background

Friction is the name given to forces which oppose the relative movement of two surfaces. They can be thought of as holding forces which act along the surfaces. They are most obvious when something is moved along a rough surface. We can feel the force resisting movement if we are pushing or pulling against it – for instance dragging a sledge across rough ground. We can measure the forces needed to pull something across different surfaces.

Frictional forces do not just act between solids. As an object moves through liquids or gases there can be friction. So the movement of a boat pulled through water and a rocket falling through the atmosphere are both opposed by friction.

One effect of friction can be to wear surfaces and heat them. This is not always the case but it is in many of the examples children meet – for instance rubbing their hands together, sandpapering, riding a rusty bicycle. We often wish to reduce friction so that things move more easily, and there is less wear – for instance we oil moving surfaces. Sometimes we want to increase friction to slow down or stop movement – for instance in braking.

Movements have direction and speed. Velocity is the term scientists use to include speed and direction. Speed is a measure of distance covered in a certain time. We can measure the speed of something by timing how long it takes to travel a fixed distance or how far it travels in a fixed time. The standard unit for speed is metres per second (m/s).

If the speed changes as something gets faster or slower it is said to accelerate. The rate of change of speed is the rate of acceleration. If we are passengers in something that speeds up or slows down rapidly we can feel the force.

ENERGY FOR MOVEMENT

Activities for children

Models that move

- Make working models, for instance cranes. Fix a pulley to an axle and drive it with a battery-powered electric motor.

Elastic driven

- Make simple models driven by elastic bands. Small moving ones can be made from cotton reels. Investigate the relationship between number of winds and the distance travelled.
- With suitable supervision children can make models of old siege catapults and test their performance, firing paper or Plasticine missiles.

Wind power

- Make simple model windmills and test different shapes and sizes of sail.

Key Stage 2

- More elaborate models can incorporate pulleys or gears to transfer movement and change its direction.

Water power

- The transfer of energy from moving water can be shown by pouring water from a height onto a plastic waterwheel toy.
- Model water wheels can be made using plastic and wood. Compare the effect of water falling directly from a tap onto the wheel with water running into it along guttering.

Science background

Energy is not always available where and when we need it so we use various ways of transferring it, storing it, and releasing it in a controlled way.

Windmills were used to convert the energy from the moving air into movement of grindstones. In modern wind turbines the rotors driven by the wind turn a generator to produce electricity.

As water falls on a water wheel energy is transferred to the wheel and is then, via gears or belts or levers, used to drive machinery or a grindstone. The energy from the moving water is transferred even more efficiently as it moves the blades in a modern turbine which drives an electrical generator.

Classroom models can use several ways of transferring energy: eg a belt drive.

Fig. 58 *Belt drive*

Gears which engage with one another can form a train along which movement energy is carried. If gears have teeth at different angles the movement 'turns a corner'.

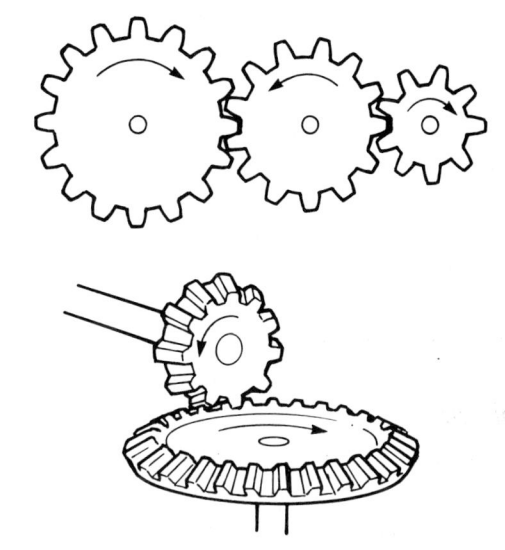

Fig. 59 *Gears with teeth*

Rotation can be turned into backwards and forwards movement, or vice versa using cranks and levers.

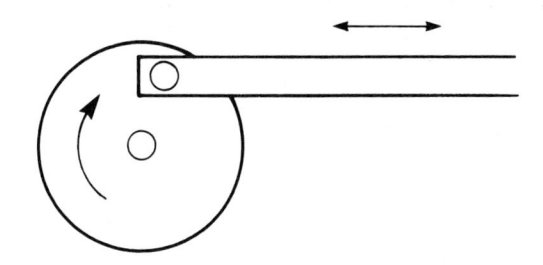

Fig. 60 *Crank*

The energy stored in stretched elastic may be transferred suddenly to a missile in a catapult. By slowing the rate of release we can use it to drive wheels or a cotton reel 'crawler'.

Key Stage 2

Investigating how the amount of movement is related to the amount of energy we put into the elastic band is a good introduction to the idea that energy can be measured.

The storage of energy in the chemicals in the battery makes it convenient to keep and transfer when we need it. Children can begin to see links between stored elastic energy and chemical energy if they use both. They will encounter rechargeable batteries and begin to see the parallels with other examples of storage of electrical energy and chemical energy.

CONDUCTORS, INSULATORS AND RESISTORS

Activities for children

Varying the resistance

- (a) Cut a pencil in half lengthways.
  NB Take great care when doing this. Have one prepared for the children to use.
- (b) Test whether the pencil lead is a conductor or an insulator.
- (c) Does the length of pencil lead the electricity has to travel through make any difference to what you see?

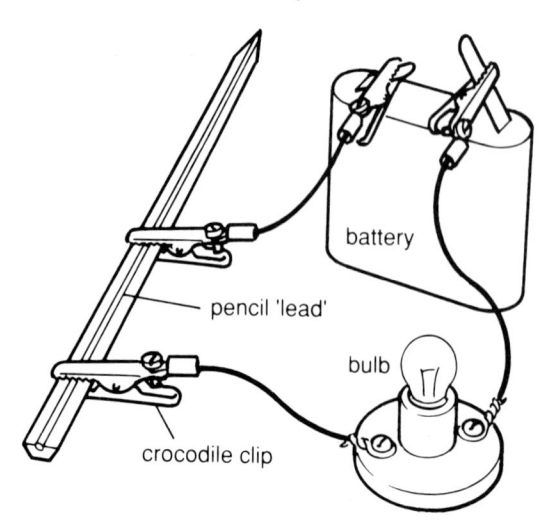

Fig. 61a, b, c *Pencil lead conductor (a), Variable resistor (b), Semi conductor (c)*

Use a variable resistor

- Buy a variable resistor from a suppliers and connect it as illustrated. Note what happens to the brightness of the bulb when you turn the control knob.

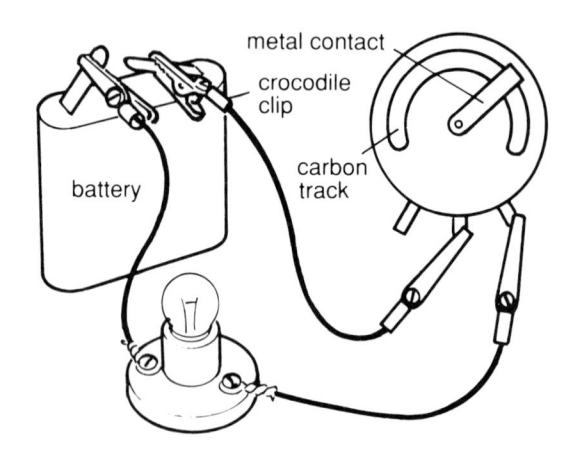

Semi-conductors

- Make simple circuits which include electronic components such as resistors, light-dependent resistors, diodes and light-emitting diodes.

A simple circuit which includes a 100 ohm resistor with brown, black, brown bands painted on it is illustrated below.

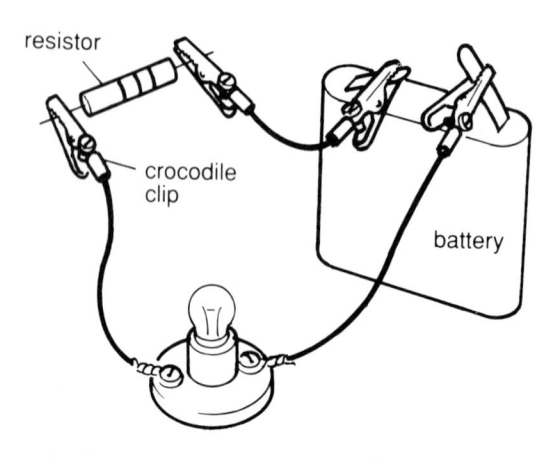

The resistance of a light dependent resistor drops when light falls on it.

Science background

Good **conductors** allow electricity to pass through easily. Metals are good conductors of electricity. Good **insulators** completely prevent the flow of electricity. Plastics are good insulators. Materials which resist the flow of electricity allow some electricity to flow through them.

Good conductors have many free **electrons**. These electrons can flow round a circuit carrying the electrical charge. In insulators the electrons are bound very strongly so cannot flow round a circuit.

The filament of a torch bulb is a good example of a resistor. In this case the wire is so thin that electricity finds it difficult to flow. The wires running from the battery are much thicker so allow electricity to flow easily without heating the wire. Many domestic electrical fires are caused by people using wires which are too thin for the amount of electricity flowing through them.

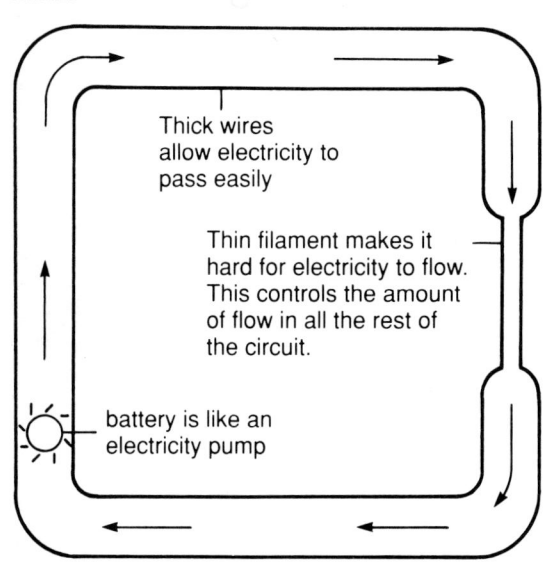

Fig. 62 *Electricity passing through wire and filament*

Current is the flow of electricity from one place to another. **Voltage** is a measure of the pressure of the electrical flow. The voltage of batteries and bulbs must be matched if they are to work properly. For example, a 6 V battery will blow the filament of a 3 V bulb because it overheats. The same battery will cause a 12 V bulb to glow very dimly.

Some materials, like carbon are resistors. This is shown by the way the carbon in the pencil resisted the electricity. The longer the rod of carbon through which the electricity had to pass, the greater the resistance, and the dimmer the bulb.

Carbon is used in many commercial variable resistors. There is a carbon track with two connections. One wire needs to be connected to the centre connection and the other to one of the outer connections.

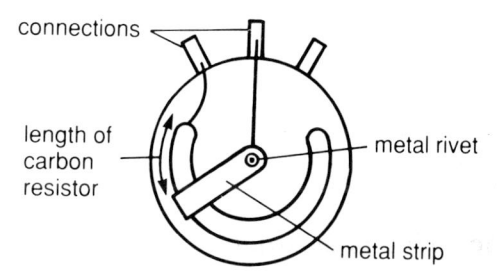

Fig. 63 *Carbon resistor*

Resistance is measured in ohms (Ω). The thin shiny resistors which are used in many electronic circuits are made of compressed carbon and the amount of resistance is colour coded. Their resistance can be from less than one ohm (1 Ω) to millions of ohms.

Short circuits happen when electricity flows through a good conductor such as a wire and there is no resistor in the circuit. There must normally be a resistor such as a bulb or motor in circuits otherwise the wire will get hot and the battery will run down quickly. Normal dry cells have some internal resistance which slows this process. Rechargeable batteries have little internal resistance so they give out all their stored electricity very quickly.

SWITCHES

Activities for children

Home made switches

- Make a circuit with two wires with bare ends. Touch them together to make the light flash.

- Wrap the two bare ends around drawing pins. Push the pins into a scrap of wood. Use a paper clip to connect the two pins. Alternatively use a piece of foil to make the connection.

Morse code signaller

- Use two switches to send morse code messages.

Reed switches

- Wire a circuit which includes a reed switch. Bring a magnet close to the switch. Listen carefully as the two pieces of metal inside the glass tube click together.

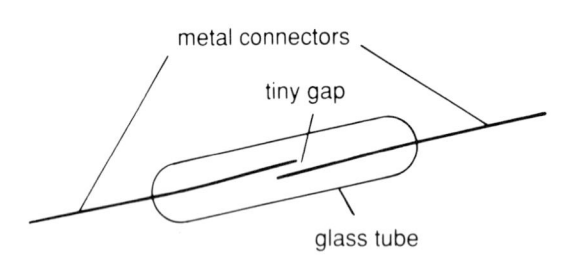

Fig. 64 *Reed switch*

Tilt switches

- Tilt switches can be used to detect movement and the position of objects. They consist of mercury sealed in a tube. Make a simpler version using a plastic tube and a ball of foil.

Pressure switches

- Sandwich a thin piece of foam with a hole in the middle between two pieces of foil. Wire a lamp and battery to the two pieces of foil. The lamp will come on when the sheets of foil are pressed together.
- Can the children make a burglar alarm using any of these switches?

Science background

A switch is a device which can make or break a circuit. Normally switches are mechanical but **transistors**, which are semiconductor devices, can be used as switches.

A **relay** is a type of switch where a small electrical current operates an electromagnet which in turn operates another switch controlling a large current. A good example of a relay is the ignition of a car. The wire to the ignition key is thin and would resist the large current needed to operate the starter motor.

ELECTROMAGNETS

Activities for children

All currents produce magnetism

- Set up a simple circuit with a switch. Place a small magnetic compass under the wire. What happens to the compass when the circuit is closed?

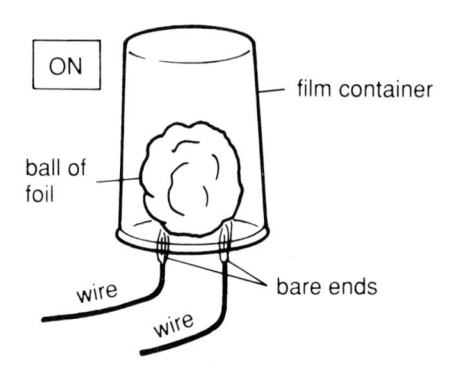

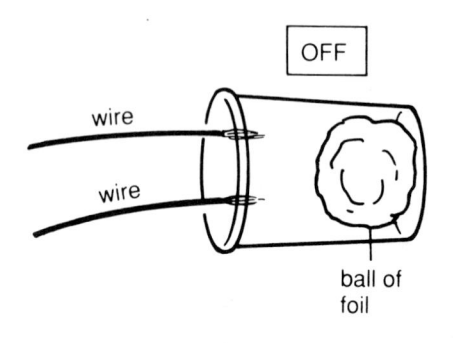

Fig. 65 *Tilt switch*

The above activity works best without a bulb in the circuit. However, do not leave this type of circuit on for more than a few seconds as it is a short circuit and the wire will become hot, wasting the battery very quickly.

Electromagnet

- Coil a long piece of wire around a large nail and connect it to a switch and a cell. Use it to pick up paperclips and staples.
- Can the children make a more powerful electromagnet?
- What ways do they suggest to test the strength of their electromagnets?

   NB Disconnect when not in use.

Motors

- Connect a motor into a circuit. Ask the children if they can make it:
   (a) Go faster and slower.
   (b) Go in reverse.
- Look inside a scrap motor. Touch the semi-circular metal pieces with a screwdriver. What are they? What do you think happens to the copper windings in the motor when electricity is passed through them?

Science background

When a current flows through a wire a magnetic field is produced around it. If the current is reduced by putting a resistor like a bulb into the circuit then the electromagnetic effect is reduced.

Electromagnetism can be enhanced by coiling wires around a soft iron core such as a large nail. The position of north and south poles depends on the direction of the current. The poles can be reversed by reversing the current. Connecting a larger battery or winding more wire around the nail increases the strength of the electromagnet.

- Electromagnets are very useful.
- Relays are electromagnetic switches.
- Buzzers, bells, speakers, earpieces are all operated by electromagnets.

Motors have coils of wire which become electromagnets when electricity is passed through them. The coil is attracted to the surrounding circular magnet.

SERIES AND PARALLEL CIRCUITS AND CIRCUIT DIAGRAMS

Activities for children

Series circuits

- Make a circuit with two bulbs as illustrated. If one bulb glows more brightly than the other ask the children to test whether it is the position of the bulb or the bulb itself which causes this effect.

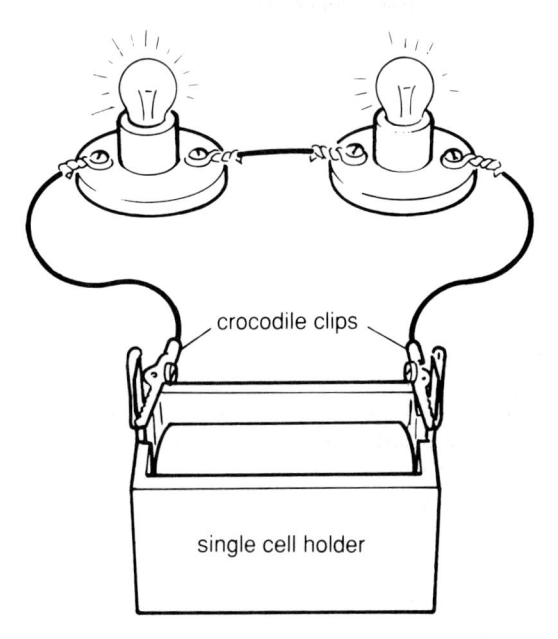

Fig. 66(a), (b), (c), (d), (e) *Series circuit (a) series circuit diagram (b) parallel circuit (c) parallel circuit diagram (d) light-emitting diode in a series circuit (e)*

- Make the same circuit using identical bulbs. What do they notice?
- Ask the children to predict what will happen when one bulb is unscrewed.
- Investigate how many bulbs can be put in series and still glow.

The circuit diagram for this circuit is shown below.

series

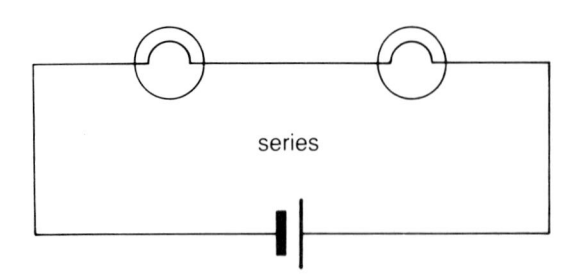

Parallel circuits

- Make a circuit with two identical bulbs as illustrated. Follow the path of the electricity from the positive end of the cell back to the negative end of the cell in each case. Notice that the current splits in the parallel circuit.

- Ask the children to predict what will happen when one bulb is unscrewed.
- Investigate how many bulbs you can wire in parallel off on cell.

The circuit diagram for this circuit is shown below.

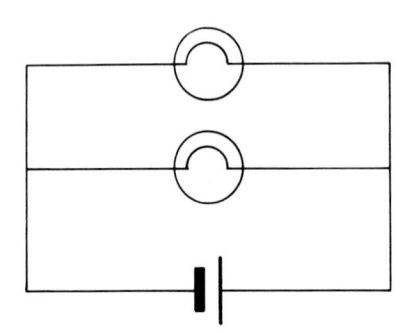

Light-emitting diode

- Set up a circuit with the light-emitting diode (LED) in series with a bulb and two cells. (Diodes only allow electricity to flow in one direction so if it does not glow reverse the connections.) The bulb will not glow with the diode in the circuit. What can you say about the amount of current needed to make the LED glow compared with that needed to make the bulb glow?

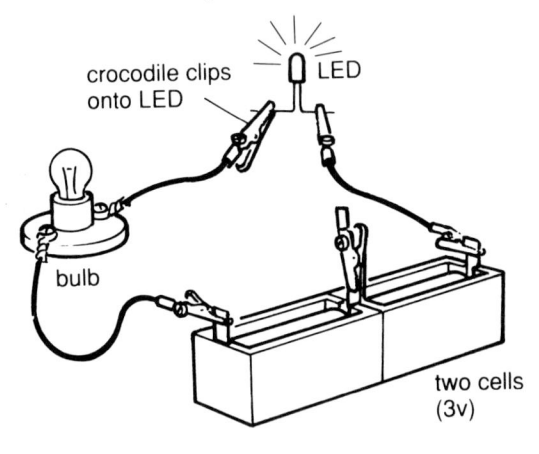

crocodile clips onto LED
LED
bulb
two cells (3v)

Science background

When the components of a circuit are arranged in **series** the electricity passes through each component in turn. The **resistance** of each component is added to work out the total resistance of the circuit. In a series circuit identical bulbs will glow equally regardless of their position in the circuit. Many children will think that the bulb closest to the cell will get more electricity. This is not so. If the bulbs are not identical, one may glow more brightly than the other.

A parallel circuit is arranged so that the electricity can follow several pathways. If you follow the path of the electricity you will notice that each component is linked directly to the cell with no other components in that part of the circuit. One bulb can be disconnected without affecting the other.

The light-emitting diode (LED) should have a bulb or a small resistor in the circuit. If there is no resistor then the LED may blow. The LED needs only a small current to light so it is very economical. Even when the bulb is not glowing there is electricity passing through the filament. You can show this by unscrewing the bulb. This will cause the LED to go out.

The symbol for a battery is:

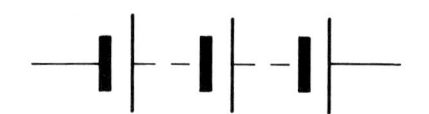

The symbol for a cell is:

The symbol for a wire is:

crossed

joined

The symbol for a switch is:

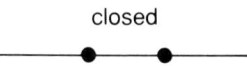

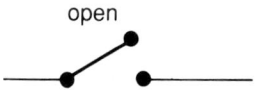

closed

open

The symbol for a bulb is:

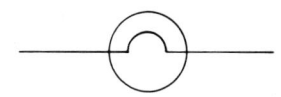

The symbol for a variable resistor is:

The symbol for a resistor is:

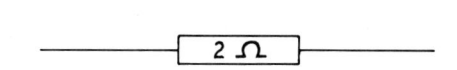

The symbol for a diode is:

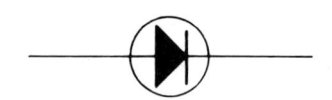

The symbol for a light emitting diode is:

Fig. 67 *Electrical symbols*

Key Stage 2

EVERYDAY ELECTRONICS

Activities for children

Visit

- Talk with the shop manager of the local electrical shop about the sorts of devices which are on sale.
- Distinguish between electrical and electronic devices.
- Obtain a catalogue. How many of the devices are owned by people in the class?
- Keep a class log showing how often the children use electronic devices.

Grouping

- Ask the children to classify electronic devices according to their function. For example, they could group together all those which: count; clean; take still photographs; record moving images; receive images; receive sound; play games; write or print; record sound; and tell the time.
- Play 20 questions with the unknown object an electronic device.

Examine

- Programmable sewing and knitting machines are good devices to examine in detail. In the present climate both are gender-specific and studying them may play some small part in showing that electronic items are used by both girls and boys.
- Examine a scrap electronic device and make a careful drawing of the components. Take it apart and test it with a test circuit. The volume control will operate like a dimmer. What effect do the different resistors have?

NB Use only battery operated devices and emphasise that children should never do this at home.

Science background

An electrical device is operated by simple manual switches. Electronic devices use a range of sensors which often have some automatic control. A simple spin-drier is electrical whereas a modern washing machine is electronic – the washing machine has sensors for amount of water and temperature. The sequence of operations of a washing machine depends on a programming device.

The first electronic components were valves. These were glass bulbs which had a vacuum inside them. They were delicate and expensive to make. Transistors were invented in 1949. **Integrated circuits** (**silicon chips**) contain a great many miniature **transistors**. A number of electronic components are illustrated.

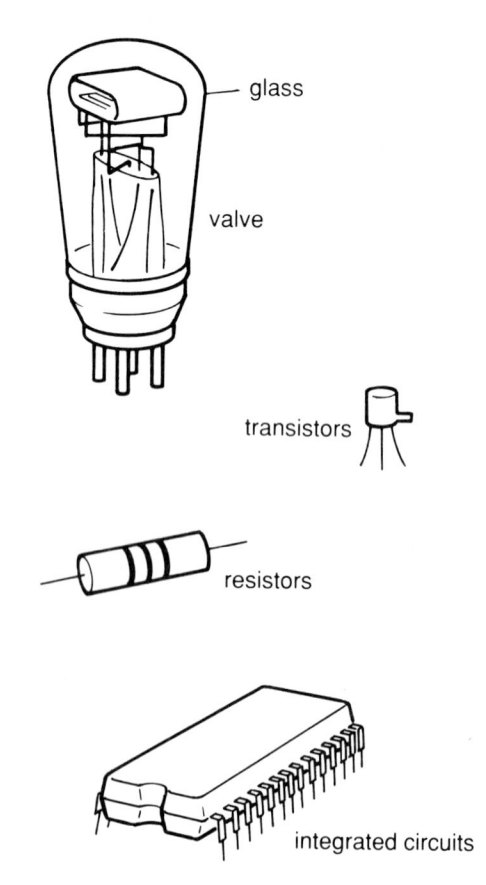

Fig. 68 *Electronic devices – valve, transistor, resistor and integrated circuits*

Integrated circuits contain huge numbers of miniature components in a tiny space. They are enormously complicated and vastly expensive to design, but once they are in mass-production they can be manufactured very cheaply indeed.

Key Stage 2

SWITCHES, LOGIC AND CONTROL

Activities for children

Logical switches

Use any type of switch for these investigations. Homemade switches shown on page 121 will do.

- **Circuit 1**

  Set up the simplest circuit. Label the switch A. Record in table form what happens to the bulb.

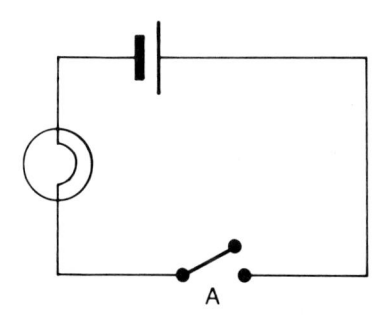

Fig. 69a *Simple switch*

Switch A	Lamp
off	off
on	on

- **Circuit 2**

  Set up a circuit as illustrated. Label one switch A and the other B.
  (a) What happens when you close one switch?
  (b) What happens when you close both switches?

  Again, record your observations in table form.

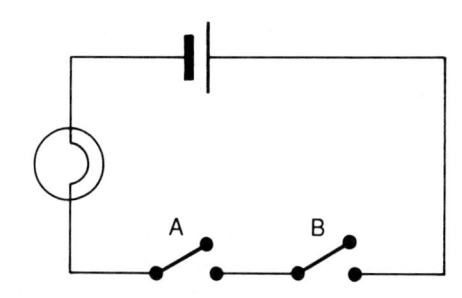

Fig. 69b *AND gate*

Switch		Lamp
A	B	
off	off	off
on	off	off
on	on	on
off	on	off

You could either allow the children to complete a partly filled in table themselves or show the group how to fill it in from scratch.

- **Circuit 3**

  Set up a circuit as illustrated. Label one switch A and one B. What happens when you close and open the switches? Record your observations in table form.

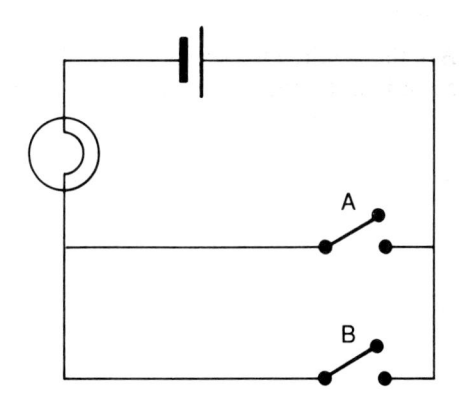

Fig. 69c *OR gate*

Switch		Lamp
A	B	
off	off	off
on	off	on
on	on	on
off	on	on

- **Circuit 4**
  (a) Use a NOT logic chip on a ready made board. Wire it up as suggested by the supplier. A good NOT switch (or inverter) is suggested in the Tandy 200 in one electronic project lab.
  (b) A simple alternative which illustrates the principle of a NOT gate is to make a parallel circuit where one of the routes is a short circuit.

127

The bulb lights normally until the switch is pressed on. When this happens the electricity flows down the short circuit and the bulb no longer lights. Contrast this with what would happen with an ordinary circuit when a switch was pressed.

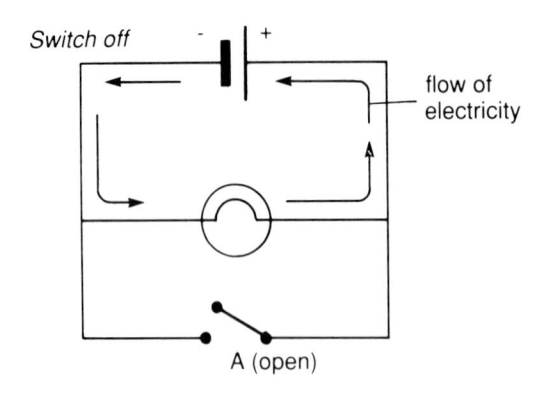

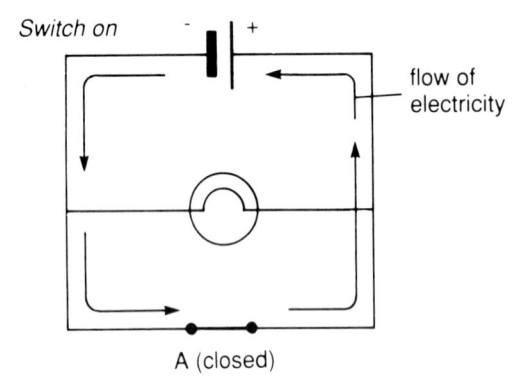

Fig. 69d *NOT gate*

The table for a NOT switch is given below.

Switch	Lamp
on	off
off	on

Computer switches

You can use computer control packages available from various suppliers eg RESOURCE to control a range of devices. Read NCET (1989) *Primary Technology: The Place of Computer Control* for more ideas.

Science background

Each of the four tables in this section are referred to as **truth tables**. They are an important aspect of the logic which is used to design the operation of computers. The switches themselves are sometimes referred to as **logic gates**.

Circuit 1 introduces the idea of a truth table.
Circuit 2 is an illustration of an AND logic gate. This is so called because switch A and switch B need to be on to light the lamp.
Circuit 3 is an illustration of an OR logic gate. Either switch A or switch B could operate the lamp.

The three circuits above work when the switch is closed and the circuit is complete.

Circuit 4 is a NOT switch and it works the other way round. If there is an input to the NOT switch then it will turn off the circuit. The circuit illustrated above is a crude representation of a NOT circuit. A better way of showing a NOT gate is to use an electronics kit or to talk to your local secondary school who will have access to the correct components.

PITCH

Activities for children

Bottle collection

- Collect bottles, plant pots and tins (NB with no sharp edges) and tap them with a light wooden stick.
  (a) Arrange them in order from the one which makes the highest pitched sound to that which makes the lowest.
  (b) Do they sound better if you hang them from a piece of string?

Bottle notes

- Collect four identical bottles. Do they all make the same note when you tap them?

(a) Investigate what happens when you pour water into the bottles.
(b) Can you play a tune?
(c) Use eight bottles to make a musical scale.
(d) Tune it using a piano or recorder.

- Investigate what happens when you blow across the tops of the bottles filled with different quantities of water. Ask the children to predict which bottle they think will make the highest note and which will make the lowest. Test their prediction.

Xylophone

- Make a xylophone from pieces of wood sawn into different lengths.
  (a) Investigate different ways of mounting the wooden pieces so that they vibrate easily.
  (b) Make a scale by tuning your xylophone with the white notes on a piano. Cut or file some wood off to raise the pitch.

Tune a guitar

- Try to tune a guitar.
- Ask the children to list the variables involved in producing the different notes.

Vibrating air in tubes

- Cut paper straws as shown. Will the short straws or the long straws make the highest note?

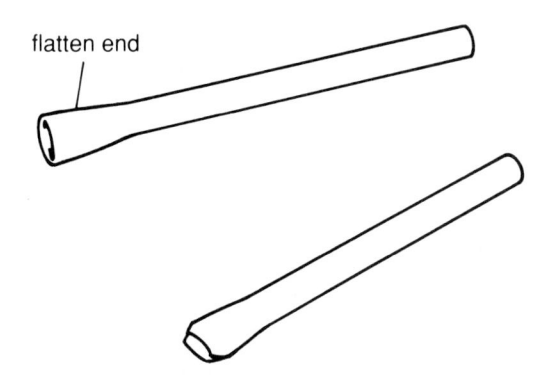

Fig. 70 *Paper straws*

- Investigate the notes obtained by blowing into a range of musical instruments.
  (a) What is the main factor affecting the pitch of the note?
  (b) Can the children use their experience with blowing across the tops of bottles and the changing length of the straws to help explain this?

Vibrating ruler

- Make noises by twanging a ruler. Notice that it vibrates. It makes low notes when there is a lot of ruler vibrating. You can see that the vibrations are relatively slow when the note is low.
- When the ruler is short the note it produces is higher. The vibrations are too rapid to be seen easily.

Science background

Sound is produced by vibrations. When the vibrations are very rapid the pitch of the sound is perceived to be high. When the sound is produced by few vibrations per second the pitch is low.

Hertz (Hz) is the international unit of frequency. One Hertz is equal to one vibration per second. The human ear can detect vibration frequencies between 20 and 20,000 Hz. This is the range of vibrations we know as sound. **Ultrasound** is sound composed of vibrations above 20,000 Hz. They are used to internally scan the human body. **Infrasound** is composed of vibrations below 20 Hz. They have no practical use at present.

The pitch of the note produced by vibrating objects such as a bottle or clay plant pot depends largely on the size of the object. For instance, a large bell will have a lower pitch than a small bell. When a bottle is nearly full of water the pitch of the note obtained by tapping the bottle is low because of the large amount of glass and water vibrating. When you blow across the top of the bottle the pitch of the note is high because there is a short column of air being vibrated. This is like the recorder or flute when none of the holes are covered. The column of air being vibrated is short and so the pitch is high.

The pitch of the sound of a plucked string is determined by three variables:

(a) the length of the string
(b) the density (weight of a given length) of the string
(c) the tension of the string.

LOUDER AND SOFTER

Activities for children

Deaden the sound of a bell

- Set up a battery operated electric bell.
    (a) Look at the way it vibrates.
    (b) Touch the vibrating bell very lightly.
    (c) Feel the vibrations.
    (d) Hold the bell firmly.
    (e) See that the noise is less now that the bell's movement is reduced.

Watching a ruler

- Make sounds by twanging a ruler.
    (a) Ask the children to make quieter and louder sounds.
    (b) Notice that when you twang the ruler hard it moves a great deal and the sound is loud.
    (c) When you twang it lightly the ruler only moves a little and the sound is soft.

Making sounds softer

- Investigate the different ways you can deaden the sound of a battery operated radio or a loud ticking clock.

Making sounds louder

- Tap a tuning fork. Investigate ways to amplify the sound it produces. You might try to put it on a box or a tin. Place grains of rice on the surface of the tin and look at the way they vibrate. As the sound dies away notice how the grains vibrate less.

Science background

The loudness or volume of a sound depends on the amount of energy in the sound wave. The greater the size of the vibrations (their **amplitude**) the greater the energy. (See below.)

A ruler which moves a very short distance after being gently twanged has a small amplitude of movement and so moves less air than the same ruler twanged hard. The volume of sound is measured in **decibels** (dB).

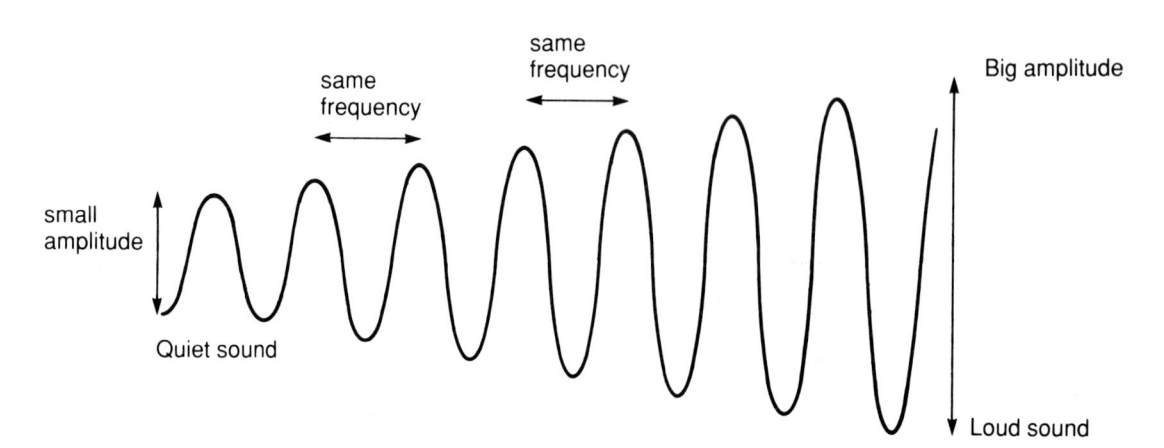

Fig. 71 *Amplitude of sound*

SPEED OF SOUND

Activities for children

Sound is slower than light

- If there is a thunderstorm talk about the way the thunder follows the lightning.
- If you have a golf course nearby stand in a safe place to watch distant golfers tee off. The sound will reach you after you see the golfer drive the ball.
- Ask a child to stand in the distance at least 100 metres away. Get them to make a clearly visible action that has a loud accompanying sound eg: banging together white blocks of wood. The sound will be heard after the action is seen.

Echoes

- Stand near to a high wall. Make loud, sharp sounds by hitting two blocks of wood together. Do you notice any echo?
- Do the same again but this time stand about 50 metres from the wall? You should notice the echo.

Find the speed of sound

- Challenge the children to time the echo.
- Ask them to make a new sound each time they hear the echo of the last sound. Practise this. When they have got a good rhythm the children can find the time taken for the sound to go to the wall and back ten times and divide this by the distance (50 m × 2 × 10).

Calculate the time and distance

- Tell the children the speed of sound. Get them to calculate things like the time it would take for them to hear a loud explosion in a nearby town.
- The noise of the eruption of the volcano Krakatoa was heard at least 1000 km away. How long would it have taken the sound to travel that far?

Science background

Sound travels at the speed of approximately 350 metres per second. It travels faster in warm air than it does in cold air. Light travels at the speed of 299,000,000 metres per second. Lightning is the flash of light caused by an electrical spark jumping between clouds or between a cloud and the ground. Thunder is the noise made by the spark. Echoes are the reflection of sound waves from a solid surface.

SEEING

Activities for children

How do you see?

- Get children to list things they can see which are not actually light sources.
- Ask them to draw and describe how they think they see something on their list.
- Discuss where the light comes from when they can see things.

Shine a light

- Make a viewing hole in the top of a big box and a hole in the side to shine a torch through. View an object in the box with the torch on.
- Ask the children why they think they cannot see the object when the torch is off and the light hole is covered.
- Ask children to draw diagrams showing the path of the light when they see the object.

Eyes

- Ask children to look at each other's eyes or their own in a mirror and draw large pictures or make collages to show the parts: eyelids, eyelashes, white, iris, pupil.
  NB Teach children about protection of eyes.

More or less light?

- Working in a shady spot pairs of children can take turns to shine a torch into their partner's

Key Stage 2

131

eye, turn it off and watch the pupil of their eye change in size.

Science background

Light radiating out from sources may strike objects and be scattered off them to our eyes. If we direct a narrow beam of light we can control what the light strikes. We only see objects if light from them enters our eyes through a hole in the front called the pupil.

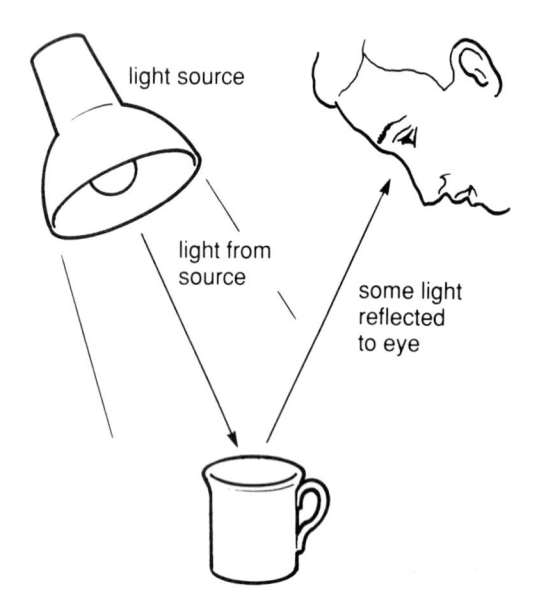

Fig. 72 *How we see objects*

The iris makes the pupil larger when there is less light, and smaller when there is more. The pupil looks black, the surrounding iris is coloured and around that the eye looks white (with some blood vessels).

STRAIGHT LIGHT

Activities for children

Light goes straight through holes

- Make a small hole in the centre of three pieces of card. Stand the cards in line in front of a projector or strong torch. Adjust them so the light will pass through all the holes. Stretch a piece of string through the holes.

Shadows

- Use a projector or strong torch to shine a beam of light onto a screen. Stand a toy figure in front of the screen. Ask children to investigate the shadow when they:
  (a) move the figure toward the light
  (b) move it sideways.
- Switch off the light, move the figure and ask them to predict where the shadow will fall. Make multiple shadows using two torches.

Science background

A narrow beam of light travelling through a series of holes is a demonstration of how light travels in straight lines.

Physicists use the term ray to refer to the direction of the path light takes and draw arrows to represent rays. Detailed ray diagrams are probably best left to secondary school. Children can observe how beams or rays of light travel in a straight line when sun shines through gaps in clouds, when a projector is on in a dark room, when light passes through dust or fog, and if they see floodlights at sports grounds or spotlights in theatres.

The idea that light travels in a straight line can be used to explain the position and size of shadows. If light strikes an opaque object a shadow will be cast on the side away from the light source. If we move the object or the light source we change the angle at which the light strikes the object and so the shadow moves.

MIRRORS AND REFLECTED LIGHT

Activities for children

What can we do with mirrors?

- Let children use mirrors to:
  (a) see around corners
  (b) look over their shoulders

Key Stage 2

(c) see above or below obstacles.
- Make periscopes from tubes or long boxes. Cut 45° slits to hold small mirrors. Make holes opposite the mirrors.

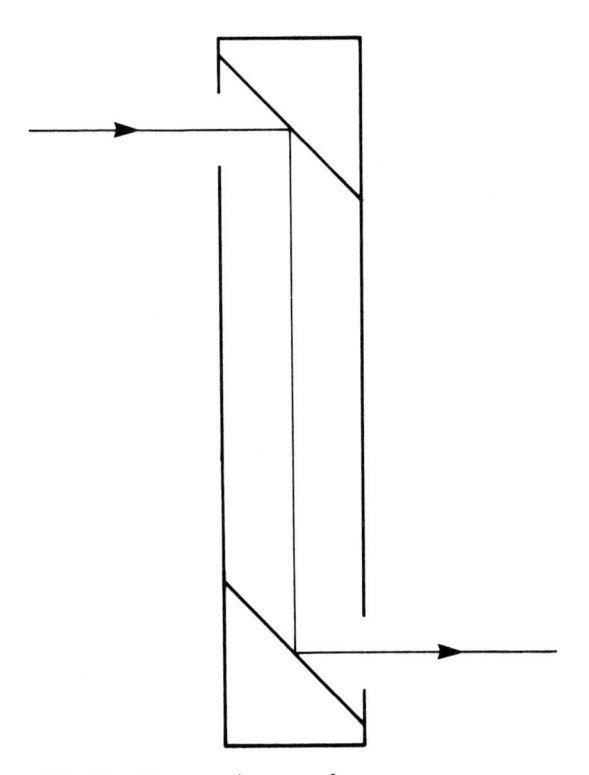

Fig. 73 *How a periscope works*

Bouncing light

- Shine a narrow beam of light from different angles onto the same spot on a mirror. Ask pupils to predict where the beam will be reflected each time.
- Use string or black paper and chalk to trace the path of the light beam. Compare the angle at which it strikes and leaves the mirror.

Pepper's ghost

- Stand a sheet of clear perspex securely on a flat surface. Put a jar of water a little way behind it. Light a candle the same distance in front of the perspex. Look at the perspex. The candle should look as if it is burning in the jar of water. This principle was used in theatres long ago to create the impression of a ghost.

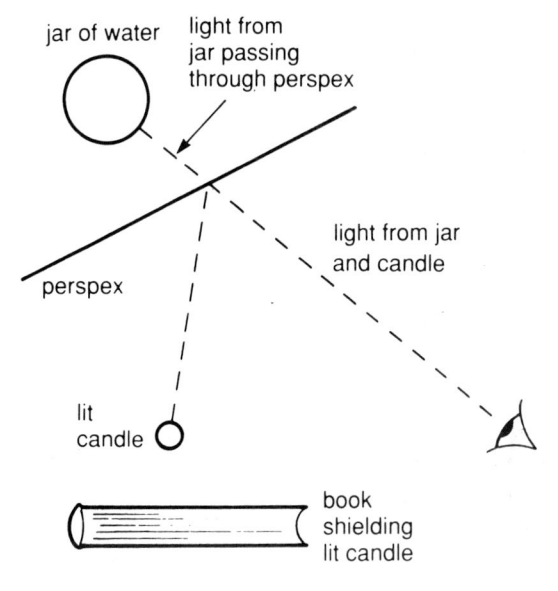

Fig. 74 *Pepper's ghost*

Object and image

- Stand a toy figure in front of an upright mirror on a large sheet of paper.
    (a) Ask pupils to point to where its reflection (the image of the figure) appears to be. Mark the paper to show where the figure and its image are.
    (b) Ask pupils to draw lines showing where they think the light travels.
    (c) Measure the shortest distance from the figure to the mirror, and from the image to the mirror.
    (d) Do this with the figure in different positions.

Curved mirrors

- Let children explore their reflections in concave and convex mirrors. Compare them in the front and back of a shiny spoon. If necessary prompt with questions such as:
    (a) Do you look bigger or smaller?

133

(b) Do you look the right way up or not?
(c) Do you look clear or blurred or bent?
(d) What happens as you get nearer or farther away?

Science background

Plane mirrors are smooth shiny flat surfaces which reflect light regularly. Because light travels in straight lines it bounces off at the same angle at which it hit the mirror.

Light reflected from one mirror will be reflected again from another mirror if they are at appropriate angles. We use this to direct light from an object into our eyes through a periscope.

The light reflected to our eyes by a mirror looks as if it had come from a point behind the mirror. We see an image at that point. The image will be as far behind the mirror as the source was in front of it.

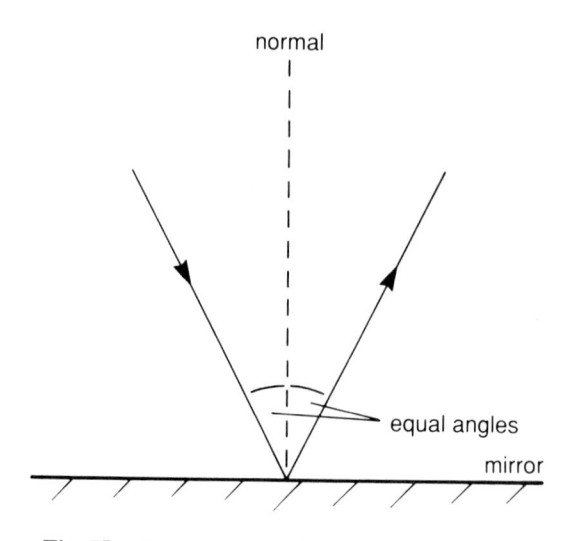

Fig. 75 *How a mirror works*

A curved mirror can be thought of as made of lots of little plane mirrors, all at slightly different angles. They will make the light bounce back at different angles from each point on their surface. Therefore they can make the light spread out, or bring it together, depending on whether they curve inwards (concave) or outwards (convex).

COLOURS AND BENDING LIGHT

Activities for children

Coloured spinners

- Make card circles with a pencil through a hole at the centre. Colour sections red, green and blue. Spin them and see what colour they look.
- Try different colours.
- Use bright crayons, paint or sticky coloured paper.

Adding coloured lights

- Get three identical torches which make sharp beams of light. Put a red filter over one, green on the second torch and blue on the third. Shine two of the coloured torches onto the same spot.
- Try different pairs of colours and then all three.
- Draw or tabulate the results.
- Use the torches to make coloured effects in a model theatre.

Subtracting colours

- Make card spectacles with red acetate instead of lenses. Make some green and some blue ones. Investigate what different coloured objects look like when viewed through each colour. Make a table of results.
- Look through two colours at once. Try three.

Bending light

- Let children look through glass jars (empty and filled with water), drops of water, spectacles.
- Compare fatter and thinner lenses. Measure how much things are magnified by looking at a ruler or lined paper.
- Find where the lenses are in a microscope and binoculars.

Key Stage 2

Splitting light

- Make a spectrum. The best way is with a prism held in sunlight. The overhead projector can produce good effects.

Violet light is bent most by the prism. Red light is bent least

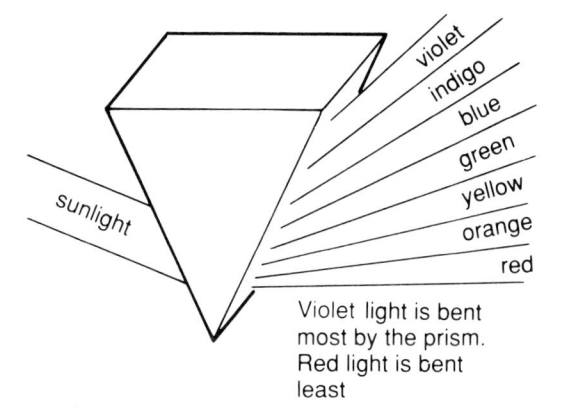

Fig. 76 *Splitting sunlight*

Science background

Light travels at slightly different speeds in air, water and glass, so it bends when it passes from one to another, for instance from air to glass. This bending (**refraction**) may make things look different. We use glass lenses to make things look bigger or nearer. The shape of the glass affects how much the light is bent. Fatter lenses magnify more than thinner ones. A prism also bends light as it enters and as it leaves the glass.

We call sunlight white light. It can be split up into different colours, for example as it passes through glass or drops of water, because the different colours bend by different amounts. The different colours of light are produced by different **wavelengths** of light.

Light waves are just part of the spectrum of electromagnetic waves, which includes very high energy short waves such as X-rays and Gamma rays at one end and radio waves at the other.

Visible light is the electromagnetic radiation which the eye detects. Blues and violets are toward the ultra violet end of the spectrum and red toward the infra red end. Ultra violet light tans and burns skin. Infra-red radiation is produced by hot objects.

Coloured light can be mixed. Shining two or more colours together onto a white surface is called mixing by addition. As we shine more colours we add more light. The primary colours of light are red, green and blue.

- Red and green light produce yellow.
- Blue and green produce cyan.
- Blue and red produce magenta.
- Red, green and blue light mixed in equal quantities produce white light.

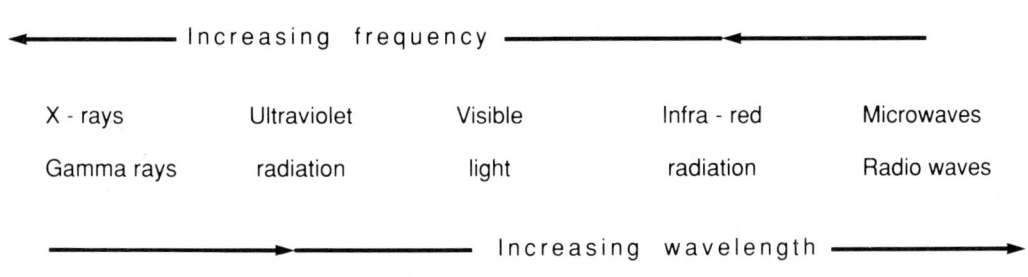

◄──────── Increasing frequency ────────◄

| X - rays | Ultraviolet | Visible | Infra - red | Microwaves |
| Gamma rays | radiation | light | radiation | Radio waves |

──────── Increasing wavelength ────────►

Fig. 77 *Electromagnetic radiation*

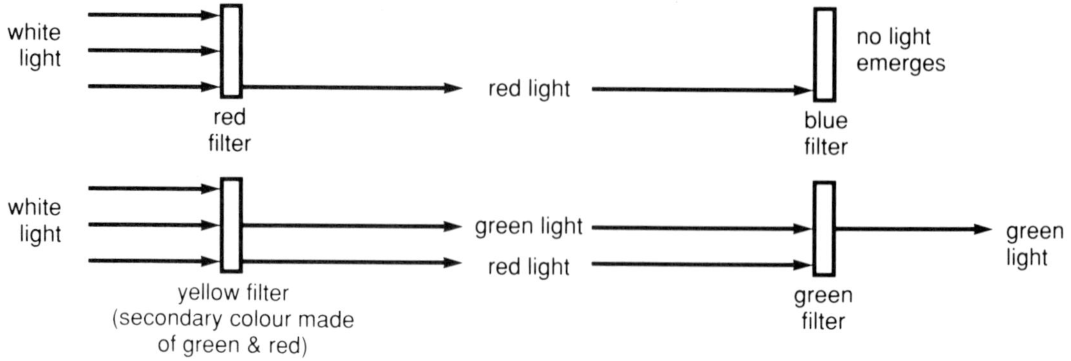

Fig. 78 *Mixing colour by subtraction*

If white light is passed through a coloured filter this absorbs all wavelengths of light except those of that colour. There is less light and we call this mixing colour by subtraction.

Mixing paint is essentially mixing by subtraction because the different pigments absorb light other than light of their colour. The primary colours of paints are different (red, blue and yellow) because paints are impure. Children usually learn about mixing paints before they mix light.

When coloured discs are spun fast the eye cannot distinguish the light from the separate coloured sections so the different colours are added together. They will not produce pure white but the effects are striking.

HEAT AND TEMPERATURE

Activities for children

Candles

NB With all heat activities teachers should ensure safe working. The main risks are from loose clothing and hair, lots of paper, crowding and movement.

- Give pairs of pupils a candle in a secure holder. Do not light candles until the pupils are prepared. Ask them to describe, draw and explain what happens to the wax, the wick and the flame. Where do they think the wax goes? How does it change? What happens at the wick and just above it?

Freezing and melting

- Make ice cubes or ice lollies. Let some melt. Challenge pupils to see how long they can keep one from melting.
- Measure the temperature of melting crushed ice. (A probe with a digital read out is ideal for this as children can see the temperature without removing the thermometer).
- Put other liquids in small identical containers and place them in a freezer to see which freeze. Try milk, cooking oil, salty water. Investigate the temperature they melt at.

Cooling

NB Supply stable cans or jars, thermometers, water which is hot but safe to touch.

- Ask children to carry out a fair test of different materials to see which is the best insulator. They should graph the temperature as the water in each container cools.

Science background

When a new candle is lit the heat from the flame of a match ignites the wick. As this burns it gives out heat which melts some wax; the molten wax evaporates to become vapour which can burn when it is hot enough. In a candle that has been used before there is wax on the wick already and this melts so the candle lights more quickly. The heat from the burning wax vapour melts more wax. This liquid wax travels up the wick and evaporates in turn. This process sustains itself and if the candle burns evenly most of the solid wax candle will change to liquid then to vapour which will burn to form carbon dioxide and water. Usually some liquid runs down the candle, cools and solidifies again.

Heat energy supplied to a substance increases its internal energy. This will produce a rise in its temperature. If the substance is a solid at its melting point there will be no increase in temperature until it has melted. This is because the change from one state to another requires heat energy to break the bonds between molecules. The same has to happen when a liquid changes to a gas.

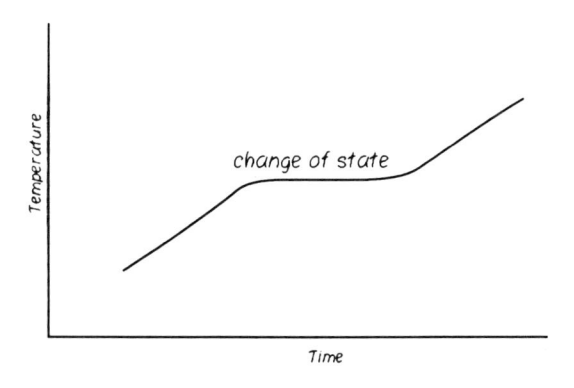

Fig. 79 *Graph showing the change of the state of a substance across temperature and time*

Freezing is the reverse of melting. A thermometer should read 0 °C in freezing water and melting ice. If water is colder than the surroundings to start with it will warm up. Ice will take much longer to warm up as heat energy is needed to melt it first. Hot water will cool down until it reaches the same temperature as its surroundings. Children may expect that water will go on cooling down below the room temperature, even to zero, and it is worth asking them to predict what will happen. Alternatively they may think insulation can keep the water at a higher temperature for ever without supplying more heat and their explanations might give valuable insights into how they think about heat. The rate at which heat energy moves from the hot water to the cooler surroundings is faster when there is a big difference in their temperatures so the graph of temperature against time will curve as this rate slows.

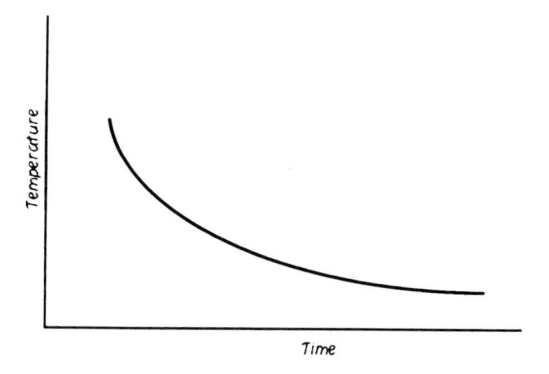

Fig. 80 *Temperature/time graph of a cooling object*

As a gas is heated the molecules gain more energy and are further apart. So hot air is also less dense than cold air. Hot air therefore will rise and cold air sink. Such movements of air, or of liquids, which are being heated carry heat by convection. **Convection currents** may be noticed in the liquid wax round the wick of a burning candle and in the air above it.

The scientific explanation of all these changes is based on the theory that matter is made up of atoms and molecules which may be joined together and which may vibrate or move. As heat energy is absorbed the movement of the molecules may increase (a rise in molecular kinetic energy).

FUEL

Activities for children

What do we use?

- Pupils could survey what sources of energy are used in school, at home, locally.
  (a) How is the school heated and lit?
  (b) What fuel is used for cooking in their homes?
  (c) What drives the transport they use?

Key Stage 2

Where does our energy come from?

- Draw flowcharts to show where the energy came from to light and heat the school, cook meals, and move the bus. Trace the flowcharts back to the source (in most it will be energy stored in fuels from sunlight falling on plants long ago). Arrows from that to the present applications can emphasise the flow of energy and can be compared with food chains.

What should we use?

- Organise a debate about the advantages and drawbacks of different sorts of energy sources, eg
  (a) Cooking and heating with gas v electricity.
  (b) What fuel is safe and handy when camping?
  (c) Coal-fired or nuclear power stations.
  (d) Fossil fuels or renewable sources?

Save it

- Make posters showing how energy needs can be reduced: travel less, insulate, shut doors, keep rooms at a cooler rate, use 'low energy' bulbs and appliances, switch them off.
- Look at the electricity/gas meter going round. Then calculate the electricity or gas bill.
- Try other ways to trap energy – make a simple solar panel from large plastic tubing fixed on a frame covered in black.

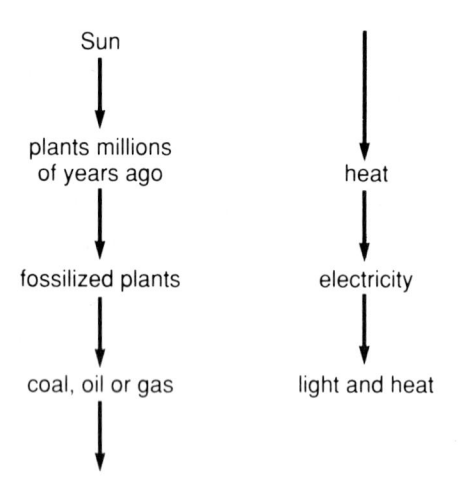

Fig. 81 *Flow chart – where energy comes from for heat and light*

Fossil fuels

- Display samples of coal, peat, oil, and pictures (NB not samples) of petrol and diesel and other inflammable fuels such as camping gas.
- Give pupils reference materials to research the origins of fossil fuels.

How is it produced?

- Books, videos, charts, software and visitors can all be used to find out more about how a particular industry processes the fuel and produces energy in the form it is needed.
- Visits can be arranged to power stations.

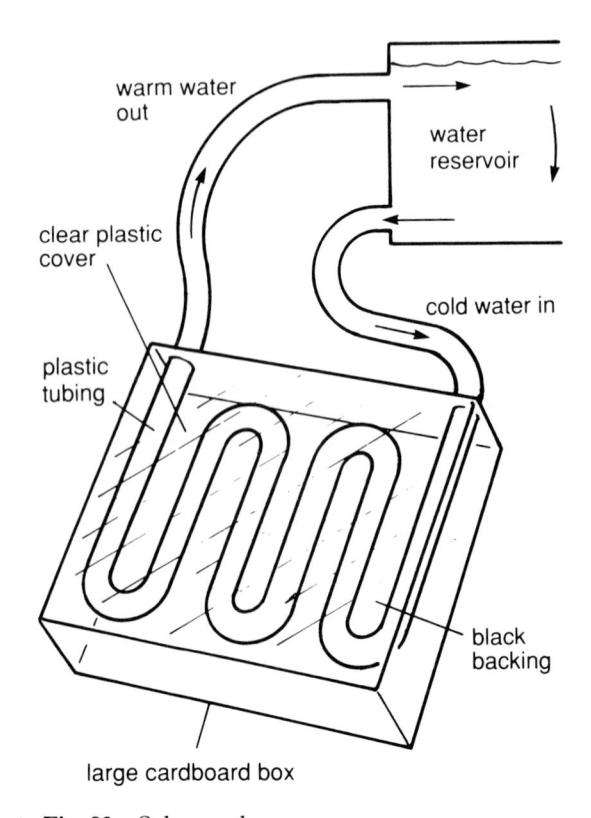

Fig. 82 *Solar panel*

Science background

Oil, gas, coal, and other less familiar fuels like peat, are referred to as fossil fuels. They are derived from plants which trapped energy from sunlight. In the case of oil this happened about 200 million years ago; for gas and coal it was even earlier.

Fossil fuels are used directly or processed to make other fuels such as petrol as well as many materials (eg plastics are made from oil). Fossil fuels are burnt to release energy as heat which is converted to electrical energy in power stations. The transport and transfer of energy from those sources is a major industry which pupils may take for granted.

The different fossil fuels have different advantages, drawbacks and costs. Some combination of those with renewable energy sources will probably provide energy for homes and industry in the world which pupils will inhabit.

As adults, today's children will need to consider the role of nuclear power which has potentially devastating side effects but can produce enormous amounts of energy from small amounts of material. This is done by splitting the nuclei (nuclear fission) of uranium atoms. If this fission is not controlled a chain reaction leads to an explosion. In a nuclear power station the process is controlled and the heat energy released is converted to electrical energy. In the sun, energy is released by nuclear fusion as hydrogen nuclei join to form helium nuclei.

The power industries provide many books and charts, slides and films and some software which can be useful secondary sources. Visits to power stations can be stimulating and bring home to children the scale of power generation and the safety hazards. Information may be too detailed and partial so teachers will need to set it in context.

THE SUN AND OTHER STARS

Activities for children

Big numbers

- Try to imagine a million things.
    (a) How long would it take to count a million pound coins one by one?
    (b) How tall would the pile of coins be?
    (c) How long would it take to walk a million steps?
    (d) How many small beads will fit in a beaker?
    (e) How many beakers would you need to take a million beads?

The night sky

- On a clear night ask the children to look out at the night sky in the early evening. Ask them to spot any group of stars. Locate the stars in relation to a landmark such as a tree or a chimney. What do they think they will see when they look at their stars again in an hour? Why do they think this?

The Pole Star

- Find North.
- Look for the Plough.
- Find the Pole Star (North Star). The other stars appear to revolve around the Pole Star. What ideas do the children have to explain this? (See overleaf.)

Nearby planets

- At certain times of the year the very bright star which you see in the west just after sunset is in fact the planet Venus. Watch Venus set in much the same way as the Sun sets a short time earlier.

Science background

The **Sun** is a small star in the **galaxy** called the **Milky Way**. The Sun might be small for a star but it is still about a million times the size of the

Key Stage 2

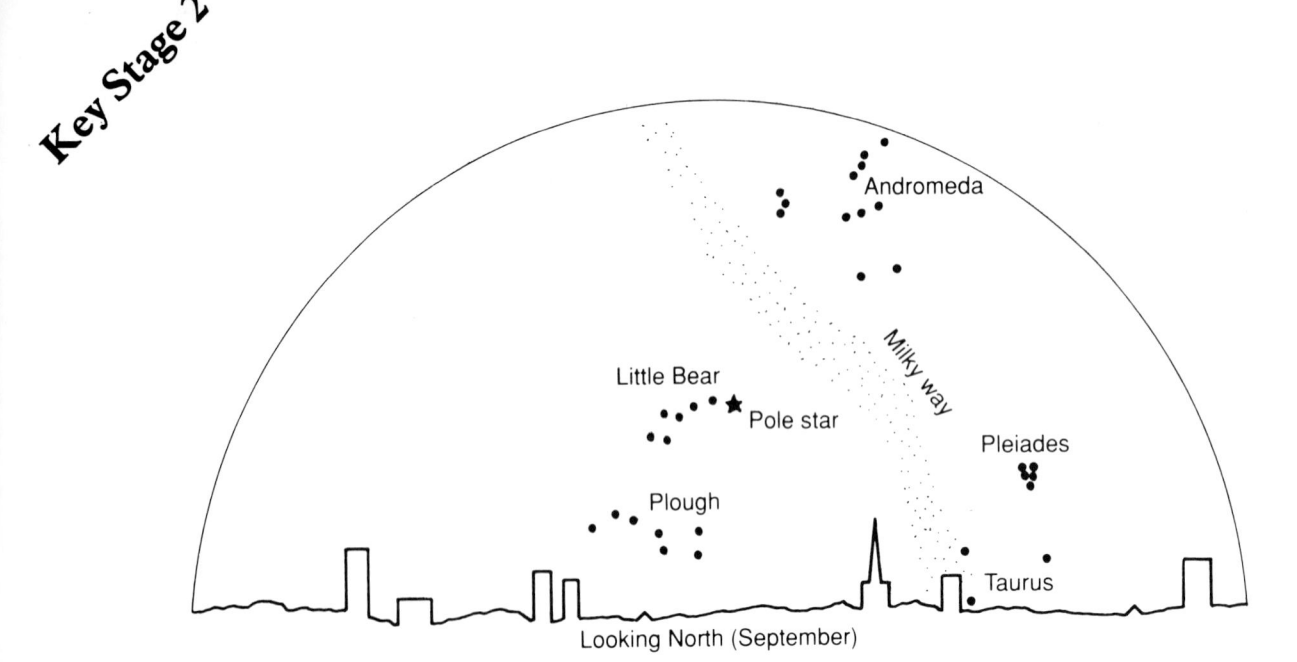

Fig. 83 *The sky at night*

Earth. The Sun is 149,000,000 km away. The light from the Sun takes over 8 minutes to reach the Earth. The next closest star is Sirius (the Dog Star) which is so far away that its light travelling at 300,000 km per second takes $8\frac{1}{2}$ years to reach us. A **light year** is the distance that light travels in a year. The Milky Way is approximately 100,000 light years across and contains billions of other stars.

You can see Venus just after sunset in the west because it is orbiting close to the Sun.

The stars appear to move during the night due to the rotation of the Earth. Like the Sun and the Moon they appear to rise in the East and set in the West. The **Pole Star** doesn't appear to move because it is in line with the Earth's axis.

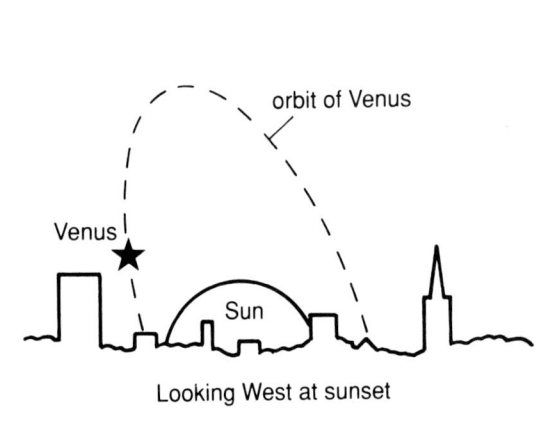

Fig. 84 *Venus at sunset*

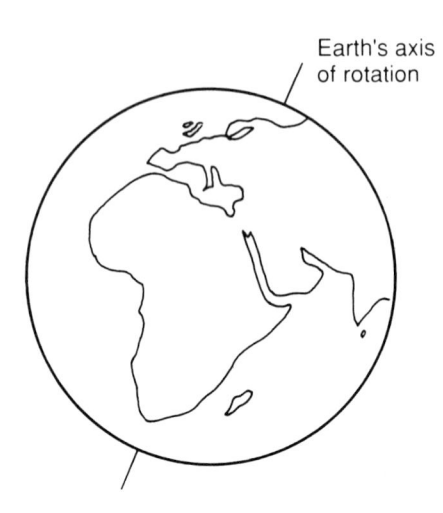

Fig. 85 *The Pole star in relation to the Earth*

The Sun is about 4600 million years old. It has a life expectancy of another 5000 million years. It is a ball of mainly hydrogen and helium gas. At its centre hydrogen atoms are crushed together in the process of **nuclear fusion** to create helium. This process results in the release of great quantities of energy.

The temperature at the core of the Sun is 15 million degrees celsius. At its surface it is only 6000 °C with sunspots being slightly cooler.

Life and death of stars

Stars are formed from clouds of gas and dust called nebulae.
(a) The dust shrinks in on itself due to the pull of gravity. Nuclear fusion begins once the density and temperature are high enough.
(b) Once established the star shines steadily as a main sequence star. The Sun is at this stage.
(c) At the point when the hydrogen has been used up the star expands as a Red Giant.
(d) The giant star collapses in on itself once all its fuel is converted into helium.
(e) Very large stars may become black holes.
(f) Black holes may explode as novae. One such was witnessed a few years ago. The previous one visible from the Earth was seen in 1054.

THE MOON

Activities for children

The phases of the Moon

- Make observations of the phases of the Moon.
- Ask the children to devise a simple chart to record the changing appearance of the Moon over a 28 day period.

Investigate the phases

- Fix a fairly large white ball on a stick. Make sure it is not too heavy. Let the children work in threes or pairs after watching their teacher demonstrate the idea.
  (a) Stand with your back to a strong source of light (eg strong torch or OHP). Hold the ball so you can see the whole of the illuminated side of the ball. This is like a Full Moon.
  (b) Stand so you cannot see any of the illuminated side of the Moon. This is the New Moon.
  (c) Stand so that half the lit up side can be seen. This is a Half Moon.
  (d) Rotate the ball round the observer's head in an anticlockwise direction (when viewed from above). Ask the observer to record the way in which the illuminated side of the Moon changes.

Draw the Moon's surface

- Ask the children to draw the surface features of the Moon. This can be done with naked eyes or even better if binoculars are available.

Science background

The Moon does not produce its own light, it simply reflects the Sun's rays. It rotates around the Earth every 28 days and turns on its own axis every 28 days so that the same side is always turned to the Earth. This means that the children should not see any changes apart from the illumination.

The phases of the Moon are caused by the way in which it reflects the Sun's light. When the Moon is between the Sun and the Earth we cannot see the light it reflects. When it is opposite the Sun we can see the whole face of the Moon. (See overleaf.)

- The New Moon is when the whole of the dark side is facing us.
- The Crescent Moon is when you can see a sliver of the Moon.
- A Gibbous Moon is larger than a half Moon.
- The Full Moon is when the whole of the illuminated side of the Moon is facing the Earth.

The Moon does not have an atmosphere. There have been periods when the Moon was geologically active and there are large areas of basalt flows on the Moon which were at one time thought to be seas. These basalt flows occurred

Key Stage 2

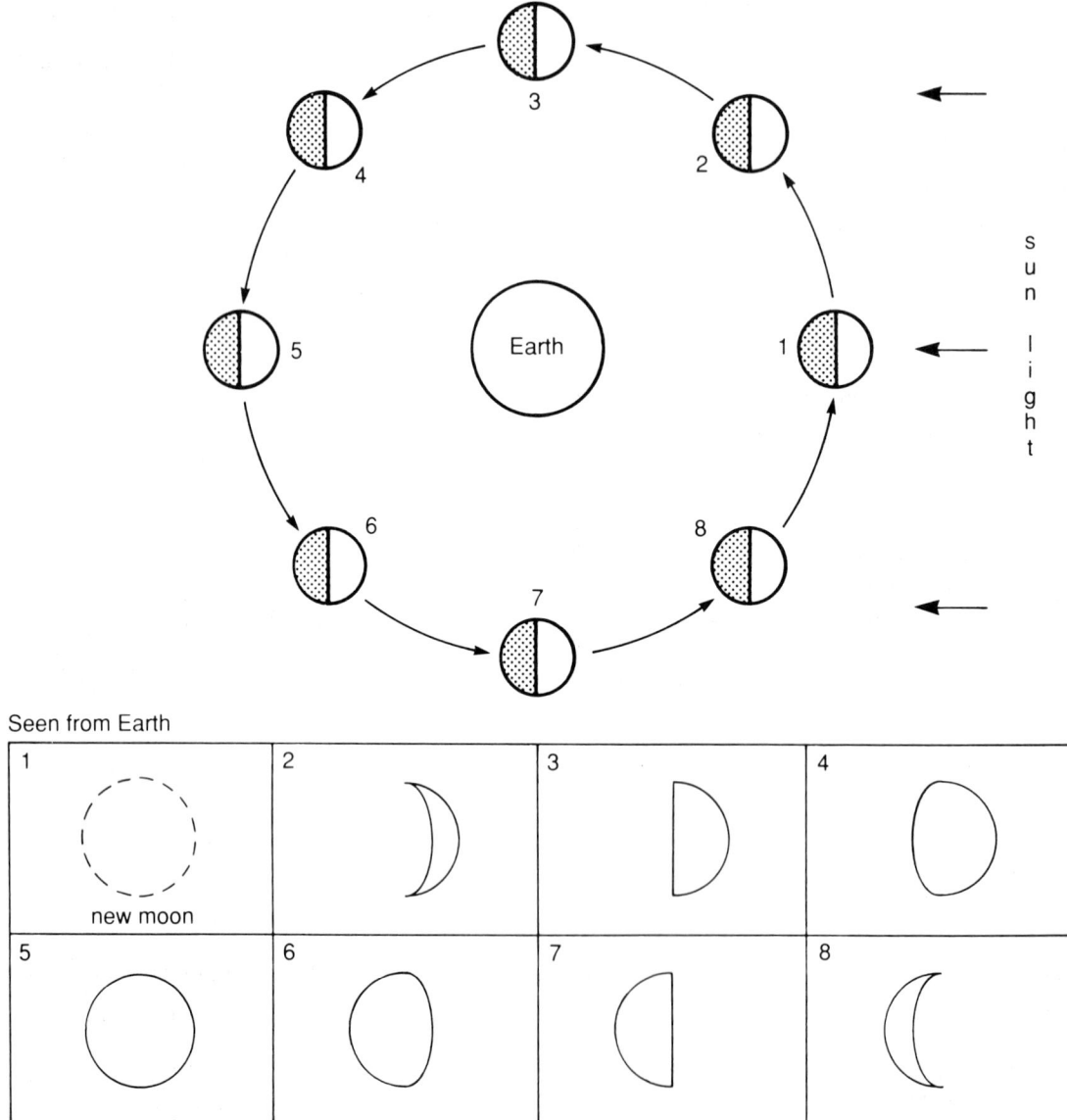

Seen from Earth

1	2	3	4
new moon			
5	6	7	8

Fig. 86 *The phases of the Moon*

relatively recently in the Moon's history. The massive craters on the Moon are the result of meteor collision and the fact that the 'seas' are relatively free of craters shows that meteors were once much more common than now.

The tides in the Earth's oceans and seas are caused by the attraction of the Moon and Sun with the Moon's influence dominant because it is much closer. When the Sun and the Moon line up the tides are particularly pronounced as spring tides. When the Sun and Moon are at right angles the tidal movement is relatively small and neap tides are the result. There are two neap and two spring tides each month.

Key Stage 2

THE SOLAR SYSTEM

Activities for children

The scale of the solar system

- Make a scale model of the solar system. Use circles of card or peas and seeds to represent the planets. The children will quickly realise that most of the solar system is empty space.

The seasons

- Use a small mounted globe to show the children that the Earth always tilts one way. Represent the Sun with a powerful wide beam of torchlight. Keep the light and the globe at the same level during the demonstration. Shine the light at the globe. As the globe orbits the Sun, one hemisphere (half sphere) is nearer the Sun than the other. The hemisphere closest to the Sun enjoys summer. The hemisphere furthest from the Sun endures winter. After six months the positions are reversed and the other hemisphere is closer to the Sun.

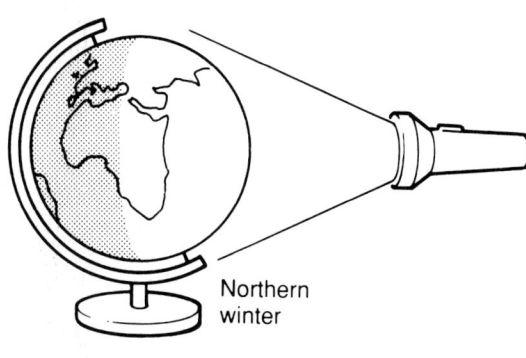

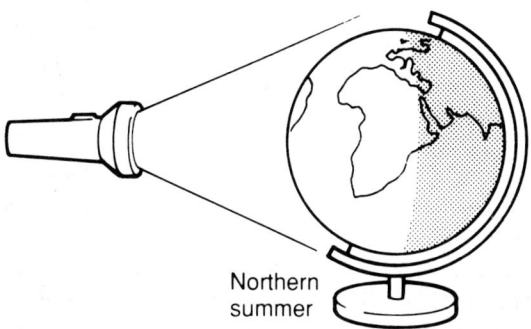

Fig. 87 *Torch and globe to show northern winter summer*

Day length

- Stick a tiny figure on Britain on a globe of the Earth.
  (a) Are the shadows longest when the northern hemisphere is nearest or furthest from the Sun?
  (b) Is the figure in the Sunlight for longer in the model's summer or winter.
  (c) Compare the length of winter and summer daylight in Madrid and Manchester.

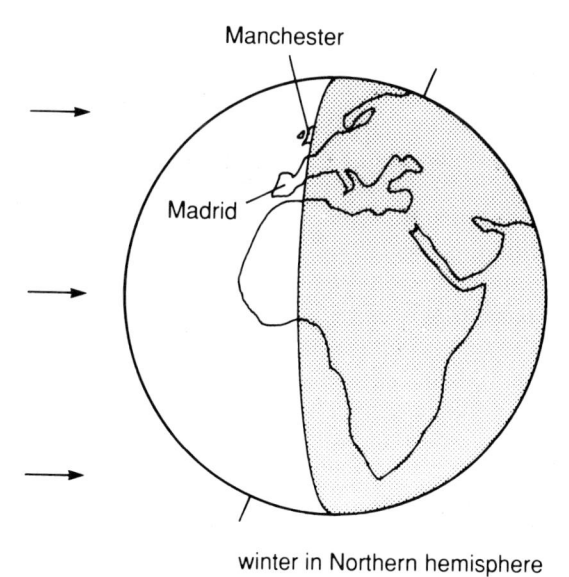

Fig. 88 *Globe showing Madrid, Manchester and the sun's rays*

Science background

Use a large ball such as a beach ball (approx 30 cm diameter) to represent the Sun. The table overleaf shows what scale the planets would be.

The Earth's orbit round the Sun is an oval or ellipse. As the Earth orbits the Sun it is turning on its axis. This produces day and night. The way the Earth is tilted on its axis leads to the differences in the seasons.

When the northern hemisphere is tilted away from the Sun it receives less heat and light

143

Relative proportions of the planets to the sun in a scale model using a 30cm diameter ball for the sun.

	Size of model	Scale distance from the Sun
Mercury	1 mm	12 m
Venus	2 mm	22 m
Earth	3 mm	30 m
Mars	1½ mm	46 m
Jupiter	30 mm	170 m
Saturn	25 mm	300 m
Uranus	10 mm	600 m
Neptune	10 mm	900 m
Pluto	1 mm	1250 m

energy. This is shown most extremely at the North Pole. Notice that the Sun shines all day on the northern polar regions in summer and not at all in the winter when the northern hemisphere is tilted away from the Sun.

The seasons are marked by the **solstices** when the Sun appears to stop setting further north each evening in midsummer and stops setting futher south each evening in midwinter. These days are the longest and shortest respectively. On the day of the summer solstice the Sun is overhead at noon at the tropic of Cancer. At the winter solstice the Sun is overhead at noon at the Tropic of Capricorn. This is how the tropics are defined.

The **equinox** is the day when the length of day and night are equal. This occurs in autumn and spring. On the days of the equinox the Sun is directly overhead at the equator at noon.

Madrid and Manchester are roughly on the same line of longitude. In winter Manchester has shorter days than Madrid. But in summer Manchester has longer days and shorter nights than Madrid.

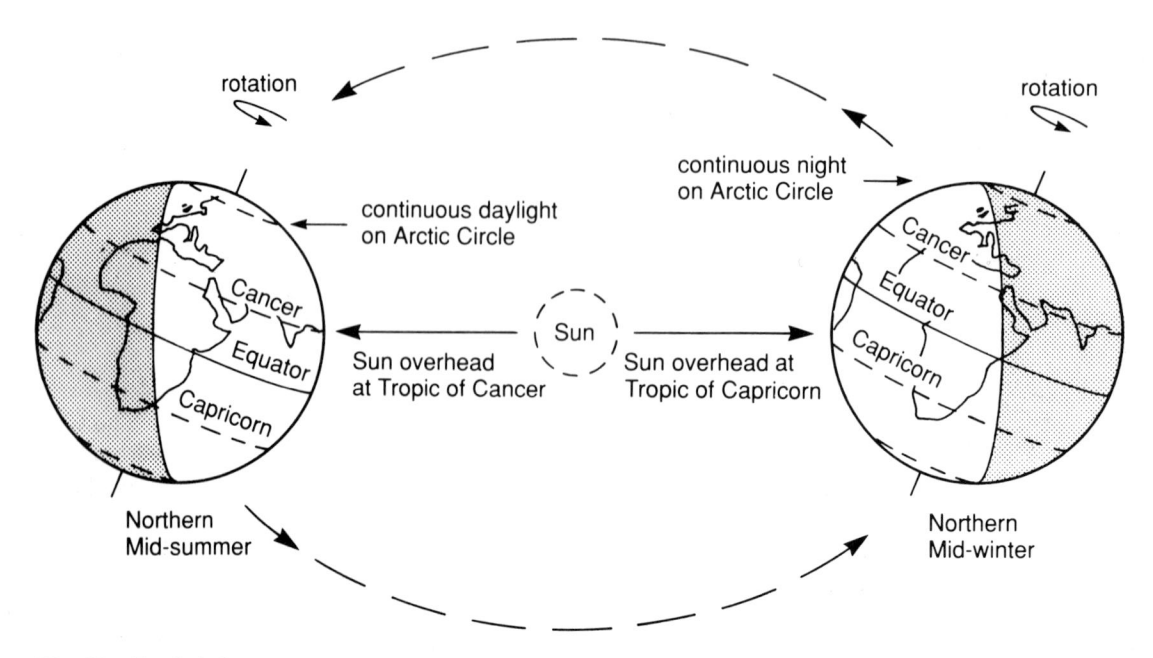

Fig. 89 *Earth circling the sun showing summer and winter*